Alberto De Franceschi | Reiner Schulze
Dirk Staudenmayer [eds.]

The Value of Consumer Data in the Digital Economy

Nomos

This Volume is funded under the National Recovery and Resilience Plan (NRRP), Mission 04 Component 2, Investment 1.5 – NextGenerationEU, Call for tender n. 3277 dated 30/12/2021, Award Number: 0001052 dated 23/06/2022, Dipartimento di Scienze dell'Ambiente e della Prevenzione - Università degli Studi di Ferrara, via Luigi Borsari 36, Ferrara, Italy.

The Deutsche Nationalbibliothek lists this publication in the Deutsche Nationalbibliografie; detailed bibliographic data are available on the Internet at http://dnb.d-nb.de

ISBN 978-3-7560-1934-2 (Print)
978-3-7489-4827-8 (ePDF)

Online Version
Inlibra

1st Edition 2026

Table of Contents

IV. The Determination of the Value of Data

The Value of Consumer Data in the Digital Economy – Introduction

Alberto De Franceschi / Reiner Schulze / Dirk Staudenmayer

I. Overview

This volume is the result of a conference held in Ferrara, attended by academics from several European countries, which examined the value of consumers' personal data in the digital economy from a legal perspective. It has been said that data is the blood in the veins of the digital economy[1], that in the 21st century data is set to replace land and materials as the most important factor of production,[2] and that there is an emerging dependency in the data economy between the 'data-haves' and the 'data-have-nots', resulting from the growing significance of data as factor of production[3].

However, while such statements are correct, it is not easy to determine the actual value of data in general or in a specific economic transaction. Nevertheless, determining the value is by no means irrelevant – neither for the data economy as a whole, nor for those involved in accessing, using and sharing data, nor for lawyers with regard to the legal issues of the digital economy. This applies to personal data as well as to non-personal data. It concerns personal data both when used in consumer-to-business (B2C) relationships and when used in trade or processed in the context of business-to-business (B2B) relationships.

As far as the economic relevance of consumer data in B2C and B2B relationships is concerned, both the enormous scale of its value in economic transactions and the methodological difficulties of determining its exact value can be seen in a number of investigations, such as the OECD

1 Lohsse/Schulze/Staudenmayer, Trading Data in the Digital Economy: Legal Concepts and Tools (eds), 2017, p. 15.

2 Yuval Noah Harari, 21 Lessons for the 21st Century, 2018, p. 97.

3 Lohsse/Schulze/Staudenmayer, The Data Act – a Cornerstone for the European Data Economy, in: Lohsse/Schulze/Staudenmayer, Private Law and the Data Act (eds), 2024, p. 11.

Digital Economic Papers on "*Exploring the Economics of Personal Data*"[4] or the study commissioned by the Expert Council for Consumer Affairs at the German Federal Ministry of Justice and Consumer Protection[5]. It may suffice here to referring to three figures with regard to the order of magnitude of the economic value of data and in particular of personal data that is already evident from such studies: The annual economic benefit of data in Europe has been estimated at approximately 330,000 million Euros in 2020. An average revenue per capita per year worth around €20 has been calculated for Facebook and around €40 for Google.[6] More than 90 % of the revenue of companies such as Facebook and Google has come from advertising based on the exploitation of personal data. According to the DMA "*The Value of Consumer Data Report 2025*", customer data-driven campaigns generate a 14 % higher return on investment, deliver 21 % more effects per campaign and see a 38 % increase in response effects for performance campaigns. When used in integrated multi-channel campaigns, customer data generates 23 % more effects.[7]

With this topic, the present volume addresses subjects that not only have recently attracted increasing attention in policy debate, jurisprudence and legal literature, but which will also need to be solved for the application and implementation of EU acquis.

The question of the value of consumer data is a cross-cutting issue that affects several areas of law. At the European level, the treatment of personal data constitutes, in a sense, an 'open flank' of legislation that has been growing dynamically right up to the recent Data Act[8], which is so far the last legislative building block of the data economy.

---

4 OECD, Exploring the Economics of Personal Data, available at <https://www.oecd.org/en/publications/exploring-the-economics-of-personal-data_5k486qtxldmq-en.html>, accessed 4 February 2026.

5 Irina Domurath/Irene Neubeck, Verbraucher-Scoring aus Sicht des Datenschutzrechts, available at <https://www.svr-verbraucherfragen.de/wp-content/uploads/2024/11/WP09_Verbraucher-Scoring_und_Datenschutzrecht.pdf>, accessed 4 February 2026.

6 Maximilian Heller, in Leupold/Wiebe/Glossner, IT-Recht, 2021, T. 6.4, n. 9, fn. 49, 47, 43.

7 DMA, The Value of Customer Data 2025, available at https://www.dma.org.uk/resources/report/the-value-of-customer-data-report-2025, accessed 4 February 2026.

8 Regulation (EU) 2023/2854 of the European Parliament and of the Council of 13 December 2023 on harmonised rules on fair access to and use of data and amending Regulation (EU) 2017/2394 and Directive (EU) 2020/1828.

In this process, the Digital Content Directive[9] of 2019[10] (DCD) has been a very important milestone. Art. 3 para. 1 sub-para. 2 DCD included personal data in its scope and thus recognised (implicitly) that personal data can be counter-performance in consumer contracts, just like the payment of money. While the inclusion of data in the Digital Content Directive scope was very controversial and had an impact on its drafting,[11] it was ultimately done because the other alternative, i.e. not to include consumer data in the scope, would have deprived consumers of their remedies in case they 'pay' digital content or services with personal data. Therefore, with its establishment of remedies in case of non-conformity of digital content or services independently whether the consumer pays a price or provides personal data, the Digital Content Directive did not only re-establish the equivalence in the contract of the performance of digital content or services with the counter-performance of payment of money, but also with the counter-performance of 'paying' with personal data. The Digital Content Directive is thus based on the assessment that the provision of personal data has a similar value as the payment of a price.

Following the adoption of the Digital Content Directive, the legislator has taken it for granted that personal data is used instead of money to pay for a contractual performance. In the area of European private law, one example is the recently adopted revised Product Liability Directive[12]. According to its Article 6 para. 1 (c), it includes damage to data as to be compensated in its scope, but only if such data is not used for professional purposes. In order to explain this, Recital 14 specifies that "where software is supplied in exchange for a price, or for personal data used other than exclusively for improving the security, compatibility or interoperability of the software, and is therefore supplied in the course of a commercial activity, this Directive should apply." Without much attention drawn to it,

9 Directive (EU) 2019/770 of the European Parliament and of the Council of 20 May 2019 on certain aspects concerning contracts for the supply of digital content and digital services. For details on the DCD see Schulze/Staudenmayer (eds), EU Digital Law, 2nd ed., 2025.

10 See for a Study on the Implementation of the DCD in all 27 EU Member States, De Franceschi/Schulze (eds), Harmonizing Digital Contract Law. The Impact of EU Directives 2019/770 and 2019/771 and the Regulation of Online Platforms, 2023.

11 See for details Dirk Staudenmayer, in Schulze/Staudenmayer (eds), EU Digital Law, 2nd ed., 2025, Art. 3 DCD, mn. 53 et seq.

12 Directive (EU) 2024/ 2853 of the European Parliament and of the Council of 23 October 2024 on liability for defective products and repealing Council Directive 85/374/EEC.

the EU legislator has reversed thereby the approach of the Digital Content Directive where it had taken particular care to delete references in the Commission proposal that "in exchange" for digital content or services the consumer provides personal data and to replace such drafting with more neutral wording.[13] Five years later, the legislator does not only explicitly state that "software is supplied in exchange (sic!) ... for personal data", but also concludes that such software "is therefore supplied in the course of a commercial activity". It thereby goes beyond the approach of Recital 24, sentence 2 DCD[14] towards acknowledging that personal data is a tradeable asset in a commercial context.

Although the DCD provision only applies to consumer contracts on digital content and digital services, its approach could also be substantially extended to many contracts of a different kind.[15]

In particular, the Data Act has extended the DCD approach of the inclusion of personal data into its scope to contracts on purchase or rent/leasing of connected devices and on related services.[16] In the contracts regulating the modalities of accessing, using and sharing of data between the user and the data holder, the user allows the data holder to access, use and share also personal data. In the contracts on the modalities of accessing, using and sharing of data between the user and the data recipient, the user allows the data recipient to request access to the personal data held by the data holder as well as to use and share it. Therefore the issue of calculating the value of personal data arises not only within the scope of the Digital Content Directive if the consumer provides the trader with personal data as part of the counter-performance in addition to or instead of monetary payment, but also for contracts on purchase or rent/leasing of connected devices and on related services under the Data Act where the user provides access and allows use and sharing of personal data to the data holder

13 Dirk Staudenmayer, in Schulze/Staudenmayer (eds), EU Digital Law, 2nd ed., 2025, Art. 3 DCD, mn. 54.

14 Where it still emphasised "that the protection of personal data is a fundamental right and that therefore personal data cannot be considered as a commodity".

15 Reiner Schulze, 'European Private Law in the Digital Age – Developments, Challenges and Prospects', in André Janssen et al. (eds.), *The Future of European Private Law*, II. 2. c) cc).

16 See as to the different contracts presumed and regulated by the Data Act Lohsse/Schulze/Staudenmayer, The Data Act – a Cornerstone for the European Data Economy, in: Lohsse/Schulze/Staudenmayer, Private Law and the Data Act (eds), 2024, p. 14 et seq.

or the data recipient. Thus, the Model Contract Terms[17] recommended by the Commission[18] according to Art. 41 Data Act, which also apply to contracts with consumers as users and personal data,[19] foresee a clause on compensation for the use and sharing of the data gained through the use of connected products or related services[20].

Finally it could appear for any other contracts where the consumer purchases other goods or receives other services and pays with data. Accordingly, the Model Contract Terms recommended by the Commission also foresee a clause[21] on compensation for the use and sharing of the data in contracts between the data user and the data recipient.

However, none of these legislative measures answer the related questions about the criteria and methods for determining the value of data. With regard to consumer data, this question initially (but not only) concerned consumer law. What is the value of the performance that consumers provide in the form of personal data in a contract? Consumers can only protect their interests in this respect, if they are aware that their provision of data has a value and have an idea of the size of this value. Obviously, in the framework of the digital economy, the model of the informed, responsible consumer requires consumers to be informed about the value of their data.

However, this does not only affect consumer law. Rather, the question of the value of consumer data also arises in B2B legal relationships, insofar as companies conclude contracts with each other about consumer data, in particular about their resale and processing (possibly in addition to corresponding contracts about company data or integrated into these). In this respect, the question of the value of consumer data is also a question with relevance for commercial law.

---

17 As to the role and significance of the Model Contract Clauses see already Lohsse/Schulze/Staudenmayer, The Data Act – a Cornerstone for the European Data Economy, in: Lohsse/Schulze/Staudenmayer, Private Law and the Data Act (eds), 2024, p. 23 et seq.; for more details see Lohsse/Schulze/Staudenmayer, Model Contract Clauses under the Data Act (eds), 2026 (to appear).

18 Communication to the Commission of 19. 11. 2025 Approval of the draft Commission Recommendation on non-binding model contractual terms on data access and use and non-binding standard contractual clauses for cloud computing contracts (with Annexes), C(2025) 7750 final, https://digital-strategy.ec.europa.eu/en/library/draft-recommendation-non-binding-model-contractual-terms-data-access-and-use-and-non-binding.

19 Annex I, point 1, Annex II, point 2, Annex III, point 2 of the Commission Recommendation.

20 Annex II, point 9 of the Commission Recommendation.

21 Annex III, point 5 of the Commission Recommendation.

Using the traditional categories of civil law, the question of the value of consumer data can affect various core areas of the law of obligations. This includes not only contract law (sales contracts and service contracts), but also the area of unjust enrichment, for example when a consumer (or a trader) demands reimbursement of the value of personal data provided by him and used by the other party in cases of failed contracts. In these cases, the question arises as to whether such data is an object of restitution or compensation under contract law or the law of unjust enrichment and, if so, how the value of the data is to be assessed.

Furthermore, the question of the value of consumer data has also arisen in tort law. The revised Product Liability Directive includes in its Article 6 para. 1 (c) as damage to be compensated also the destruction or corruption of data that are not used for professional purposes. In order to calculate respective damages, it would be necessary to quantify the value of the damage in form of the corrupted or destructed data. While the legislator saw this challenge, it shied away from solving it in the Directive. Instead, its Recital 23 leaves the task to calculate compensation to national laws. For implementing the revised Product Liability Directive, national legislators will have to face this challenge; it will be interesting to see how they are going to do this.

To conclude this journey through the legal landscape, it remains to mention procedural law. This legal field is of relevance for our topic because consumers are unlikely to assert the value of their data individually in court. Prices that are not calculated transparently with regard to the personal data provided, even data obtained by misleading the customer, etc. – all this might generally not be worth the effort of a lawsuit for the individual consumer from a rational economic point of view in face of the small amounts in dispute in each individual case. The procedural possibilities of collective judicial enforcement and the possibilities for associations to take legal action are therefore decisive for the realisation of the value of consumer data in the event of a dispute. In this context, it is worth considering the methods and procedural practices of calculating data on a collective basis (and, for example, discussing approaches such as the aforementioned calculation of the average revenue per user and per year of data processing companies).

Against the background of this broad spectrum of legal issues that need to be discussed with regard to the value of consumer data, this volume focuses on four main topics: firstly, the general framework of trade in data, and in particular the tension between data as an object of trade on the one hand and as a subject of personal rights on the other; secondly, the central issues of the "monetisation" of consumer data, including the protective instruments that become necessary due to this "monetisation"; thirdly, the most recent developments regarding this issue in and beyond the Data Act; fourthly, some approaches to determining the value of data, including the related economic aspects.

II. Challenges for research

1. Trading Consumer Data

a) The tension between the Data Act and the General Data Protection Regulation

The immense growth in the importance of data trading and the commercial use of data forms the backdrop and general framework for the discussion on the value of consumer data. At European level, two pieces of legislation with different scopes and objectives play a key role in relation to personal data as an object of trade: on the one hand, the Data Act (DA) which became applicable in September 2025 and, on the other, the General Data Protection Regulation (GDPR).

The scope of the Data Act covers personal and non-personal data (Art. 1 (3) DA). The legal act aims to remove obstacles that prevent the optimal distribution of data for the benefit of society and the proper functioning of the internal market for data.[22] Accordingly, it focuses on the multiple use or reuse of data for different purposes[23] and thus on the accessibility of data and data sharing. The General Data Protection Regulation, on the other hand, focuses on the protection of personal data. Its scope is therefore limited to personal data (Art. 2 (1) GDPR). This protection concern is embedded in the general framework of privacy protection and concretises the fundamental right that Art. 8 of the EU Charter of Fundamental Rights grants to every person with regard to data concerning them.

Both legal acts emphasise and recognise the relevance of the objectives to which the other legal act is dedicated. Thus, Art. 1(3) GDPR stipulates that the free movement of personal data within the Union shall not be restricted

22 See Recitals 2 and 4 Data Act.
23 See Recital 1 Data Act.

or prohibited for reasons of protecting natural persons with regard to the processing of personal data. The recitals mention – in line with the Data Act adopted later – that one of the concerns of this General Data Protection Regulation is to eliminate differences that could hinder the free movement of personal data in the internal market.[24] For its part, the Data Act refers explicitly to the General Data Protection Regulation in the first sentence of Art. 1(5), which states that this legal act "applies without prejudice to the protection of personal data, privacy and confidentiality of communications". The third sentence of Art. 1(5) DA also stipulates that in the event of a conflict between the Data Act on the one hand and Union or national law on the protection of personal data on the other, the provisions on the protection of personal data shall prevail. Both the Data Act and the General Data Protection Regulation thus take into account that Union law treats personal data (including that of consumers) both as an element of privacy and as an object of trade in the internal market.

When including personal data in its scope, the Data Act closes the abovementioned 'open flank', finding a pragmatic approach to treat personal data,[25] and thus solves the controversy raised at the time of adoption of the DCD. It distinguishes between personal and non-personal data and between the legal base and the modalities of the data use.[26] The Data Act upholds the principle that for processing personal data the legal base must be found in Art. 6 GDPR.[27] The Data Act adds however the contract law dimension, which designs the modalities of access to, use and sharing of personal data.[28] For non-personal data, the legal base for processing, access and sharing of non-personal data is the contract;[29] such contract regulates also the modalities of the use of non-personal data.[30]

Nevertheless, the Data Act's aim of enabling access to data and the General Data Protection Regulation's goal of protecting privacy may in practice be in conflict with each other in a way that is not easily resolved, as an

24 Recital 13 GDPR.
25 For more details see Lohsse/Schulze/Staudenmayer, The Data Act – a Cornerstone for the European Data Economy, in: Lohsse/Schulze/Staudenmayer, Private Law and the Data Act (eds), 2024, p. 20 et seq.
26 Rec. 4 sentence 1 Data Act.
27 Rec. 6 sentences 5 – 7; 34 sentences 2, 6, 7; 33 sentences 5, 6; Art. 4 (7); 5 (7) Data Act.
28 Rec. 25 sentence 8; 35 sentences 8 et seq.; 37 Data Act.
29 Art. 4 (13) 1; Rec. 25 sentences 2, 8, 10; 26; 33 sentences 5, 7 Data Act.
30 Cf. Art. 4 (14); Rec. 26 sentences 7 – 9; 31 sentence 4; 35 sentences 8, 9; 37 Data Act.

article in the first part of this volume shows in more detail.[31] This tension between the concerns of the two legal acts is already evident in the fact that the Data Act generally seeks to promote the accessibility of data, including, for example, accessibility by design (Art. 3 DA), while the General Data Protection Regulation establishes various limiting principles for the use and, in particular, the processing of data (such as purpose limitation, data minimisation and storage limitation; Art. 5 (1) lit. b, c and e GDPR) and establishes the principle of privacy by design in Art. 25.[32]

In view of the potential for conflict resulting from these differing objectives, legal doctrine and case law are faced with a number of questions and tasks in order to achieve a practical coordination of both legal acts. These include, for example, the precise determination of the relationship between Articles 4, 5 and 6 of the Data Act and the legal basis for data processing in the General Data Protection Regulation,[33] in particular the analysis of the requirements of the General Data Protection Regulation for valid consent with regard to the processing of personal data within the scope of Articles 4 and 5 DA. The article in this volume dealing with this topic draws particular attention to the complex consent cascades involved in data processing. Against this background, it seems convincing that the development of efficient and effective consent management systems is likely to be crucial for the successful synchronisation of the General Data Protection Regulation and the Data Act.[34] This approach makes it apparent that, following the adoption these two central pieces of legislation, the focus must now shift to ensuring the compatibility of data protection and data trading, as postulated by the legislature, in practice.

b) Contract law and data protection

However, the tension between the commercial use of data and data protection is not limited to the scope and objectives of the Data Act. Rather, it also extends to consumer law and general contract law. This has recently been discussed in particular with regard to the consequences of withdrawal

31 Andreas Sattler, Chapter I., in this volume.
32 See Andreas Sattler, Chapter I., in this volume.
33 Andreas Sattler, Chapter III., in this volume.
34 Andreas Sattler, Chapter IV. and V., in this volume.

under data protection law for contract law[35] in relation to the Digital Content Directive.

In particular, in way of the implementation of the DCD, some EU Member States explicitly regulated the contractual consequences of consumer's withdrawal of consent to the processing of personal data (Art. 16 DCD). E.g. the Estonian legislator clarified that withdrawal of consent by the consumer should not be considered a breach of contract and does not entitle the trader to exercise any remedies against the consumer. The same provision excludes the trader's claim for damages in case of withdrawal of consent.[36] Worth mentioning is the solution provided by the Greek legislator, according to which, in case of termination, the value of the data provided by the consumer should be calculated and reimbursed. The problem of calculation of the value of personal data will also arise when the recipient chooses to invoke the right to ask for a (proportionate) reduction of the price.[37] An attempt to regulate this issue was made – but in the end did not find concretisation in the implementing rules of the DCD – by the Lithuanian legislator: the later withdrawn proposal provided that if after the withdrawal of the consent the consumer still uses the digital content (or services) but no longer wants to remunerate the trader with personal data, he would have assumed the duty to pay in money.[38] In any case, the calculation of the amount of money may be cumbersome.

Such situations highlight the need to coordinate contract law and data protection law where data is the subject matter of contracts.

However, it should also be noted that the tension between the functions of contract law and data protection rules can lead to different perspectives when assessing legal issues. These different perspectives may become relevant, for example, when calculating damages: in order to calculate the amount of damage pursuant to Article 82 GDPR, the severity of the viola-

35 See, for example, Reiner Schulze, Datenschutz und Verträge über digitale Inhalte, in Kindl/Arroyo/Vendrell/Gsell (eds), Verträge über digitale Inhalte und digitale Dienstleistungen, 2018, p. 123, 130, 135 et seq.

36 See more details in Karin Sein, Estonia, in De Franceschi/Schulze (eds), Harmonizing Digital Contract Law. The Impact of EU Directives 2019/770 and 2019/771 and the Regulation of Online Platforms, 2023, p. 216 et seq.

37 See Zafeirios Tsolakidis, Greece, in De Franceschi/Schulze (eds), Harmonizing Digital Contract Law. The Impact of EU Directives 2019/770 and 2019/771 and the Regulation of Online Platforms, 2023, p. 314 et seq.

38 See Laurinas Didžiulis, Lithuania, in De Franceschi/Schulze (eds), Harmonizing Digital Contract Law. The Impact of EU Directives 2019/770 and 2019/771 and the Regulation of Online Platforms, 2023, p. 435 et seq.

tion of the data subject's privacy rights must be taken into account. However, this amount of damage may well differ from the transactional value or price of the personal data concerned, which is the focus of considerations regarding the 'monetisation' of personal data and which is regularly referred to in contractual relationships.[39] In view of this, the relationship between data protection law and contract law presents the task of coordinating the legal structures that follow from both perspectives and, at the same time, taking into account their different assessments for the assessment of claims.

c) The Common Law Perspective

Before examining the 'monetisation' of data in light of EU law and the civil law tradition in most of its member states against the backdrop of this tension, it may be instructive to approach the topic from a different perspective. One of the articles in the introductory section therefore highlights how common law treats the value of consumer data.[40] Consideration is given not only to the legal approaches to determining value, but also to the question of how consumers can be enabled to determine and establish the value of personal data. The rules of general contract law (including consideration and misrepresentation) and the principles of unjust enrichment and restitution serve as the main legal reference points for these considerations. However, according to the analysis in this article, they only form the 'baseline' and are likely to need to be supplemented by future legislation in order for the 'consumer data economy' to actually kick-start and for consumers to be able to realise the value of their data.[41] However, it remains an open question whether legislation on a scale comparable to that of the EU will be necessary under English common law and to what extent models from recent EU legislation can be used (also in view of the fact that this is 'largely untested and still must prove itself').[42]

---

39 See Hans Schulte-Nölke, Chapter IX.2, in this volume; Alexander Hellgardt, Liability for damages for data protection violations in the system of EU liability law, ZEuP 2022, p. 30 et seq.; for a different approach, however, Marc Strittmatter et al., Assessment of damages for data protection violations using the example of data leakage cases, Computer und Recht (CR) 2019, pp. 787 et seq.

40 Christian Twigg-Flesner, in this volume.

41 Christian Twigg-Flesner, Chapter. VII., in this volume.

42 Christian Twigg-Flesner, Chapter VII., in this volume.

2. The "Monetisation" of Consumer Data

a) Judicial price review

Looking at the development of civil law in the continental European tradition, the question of determining the value of data is one of a long series of discussions on a wide range of issues concerning whether and how the value of a performance provided by one party to another can be judicially reviewed. The historical review ranges from concepts such as '*laesio enormis*' and '*iustum pretium*' in late antiquity and the Middle Ages to new perspectives on judicial price control in the context of economic changes in modern times, some of which can be seen as a "*renaissance*" of '*laesio enormis*'[43] in a changed social and economic context.[44] The spectrum of such approaches to judicial price control in the 20th and 21st centuries ranges from case law and legislation on change of circumstances[45] to comprehensive theories on 'social private law'[46] and 'materialisation' of the law of obligations.[47]

According to the analysis presented in this volume, the main areas in which the concept of judicial price control has recently developed at European level include not only the control of price-determining clauses in accordance with the Unfair Contract Terms Directive (provided that such clauses are not formulated in 'plain intelligible language' according to Article 4(2) of this Directive),[48] and the judicial determination and review of the appropriateness of prices in intellectual property law (for which Art. 102 TFEU has already paved the way by citing, among other things, 'imposing unfair purchase or selling prices' as an abuse of a dominant

43 See Theo Mayer-Maly, Renaissance der laesio enormis?, in Festschrift für Karl Larenz zum 80. Geburtstag, 1983, p. 395 et seq.

44 Hans Schulte Nölke, in particular Chapter IV., in this volume.

45 See the overview in Ewoud Hondius/Hans Christoph Grigoleit (eds), Unexpected Circumstances in European Contract Law, 2011.

46 See, for example, with reference to European law, Thomas Wilhelmsson, Social Contract Law and European Integration, 1995.

47 Fundamental Rudolf Wiethölter, Materialization and Proceduralization in Moderen Law, in Gunther Teubner (ed), Dilemmas of Law in the Welfare State, 1986, pp. 221 et seq.; Claus-Wilhelm Canaris, Wandlungen des Schulvertragsrechts – Tendenzen zu seiner „Materialisierung", Archiv für die civilistische Praxis (AcP) 200 (2000), pp. 273 et seq.

48 Hans Schulte-Nölke, Chapter VII., in this volume, in critical discussion with the decision of the CJEU, 16 March 2023, Case C-269/19 – Banca B. SA/A. A.A.

position within the internal market).[49] Rather, this analysis – with specific reference to non-personal data generated by a connected product[50] – recognises the remuneration that the data holder may charge the data recipient under Art. 8 and 9 DA as a new and potentially far-reaching field in which judicial review of prices may unfold (for which the 'FRAND' criteria are also decisive according to Art. 8(1) DA.[51] This means that data is becoming a central subject of judicial price control in the latest developments in European law – albeit in a profoundly changed context and with different functions compared to the traditional '*laesio enormis*'.[52]

b) Consequences of 'monetisation'

The inclusion of both contracts relating to non-personal data and many types of contracts relating to the provision and use of personal data in several provisions in the newer EU legislation on the data economy takes account of the fact that the trade in and processing of personal data have become a significant factor in the digital economy. In this respect, it reflects the advanced commercialisation of personal data, which includes 'monetisation' in view of the value of this data.

The 'monetisation' of personal data is reflected in contractual practice and contract law, not only in the expansion of the subject matter of contracts, but also in corresponding new interests in the relationship between contracting parties and the resulting types of contractual relationships and contractual structures. As an important factor in the current and future development of European contract law, such consequences of 'monetisation' for contract types and contract structures deserve special attention. Insofar as personal consumer data is concerned, these new developments in contract law extend both to the contractual relationships between consumers and businesses that receive consumer data and to the 'secondary data market', where businesses conclude contracts with each other for the

---

49 Hans Schulte-Nölke, Chapter VIII., in this volume, with reference, among other things, to the case law of the European Court of Justice on the obligation of holders of standard essential patents to offer licences in accordance with the 'FRAND' criteria ('Fair, Reasonable And Non-Discriminatory').

50 Hans Schulte-Nölke, Chapter IX., in this volume.

51 In contrast to Art. 8(1) DA, however, Art. 9 (1) DA does not mention the criterion of 'fair', so that only 'RAND' criteria may apply within the framework of this provision; see Björn Steinrötter, Data Act Art. 9 Rn. 29 in: Specht/Hennnemann (ed.), HK-Datenrecht, 2nd ed., 2025.

52 For more details, see Hans Schulte Nölke, Chapter X., in this volume.

provision, processing and other use of consumer data. They therefore cover consumer contract law as well as B2B legal relationships.

The examination of these consequences of the 'monetisation' of consumer data in this volume[53] therefore covers a wide range of contractual relationships and obligations between the parties involved in the data markets. Against the backdrop of the General Data Protection Regulation and the Data Act, it starts from the basic situation of data custody and services provided in the name and interest of a data subject or the user of an IoT device as original right holders.[54] It focuses in particular on the position of the other market participants vis-à-vis these original right holders and highlights the services and custody obligations in the interest of persons with 'better rights' to the data within the contractual relationships between the various parties involved (taking into account more comprehensive contract structures that result from the fact that, in practice, the contractual design usually does not refer to pure data contracts, but rather ancillary obligations and mixed contracts are widespread).[55] It is precisely this focus on services and custody obligations in the context of legal responses to the 'monetisation' of data that could prove to be a remarkable starting point for understanding European contract law in view of the growing social and economic importance of data.

3. The Value of Consumer Data in and Beyond the Data Act

The investigations into the consequences of the 'monetisation' of consumer data indicate the wide range of data-related contracts and mixed contracts, including items such as use and storage, in which the question of the value of data may arise. Within the scope of the Data Act, the question of the price and thus the value of data arises particularly prominently in relation to the remuneration mentioned above,[56] which the data holder charges on the data recipient. However, this question may also be relevant in other legal relationships covered by the Data Act. This may apply, for example, even to obligations that are to be fulfilled free of charge if claims for damages due to non-compliance with these obligations are considered (e.g. with regard to the manufacturer's obligation under Art. 3 (1) DA that the

53 See Martin Schmidt-Kessel, in this volume.

54 Martin Schmidt-Kessel, Chapter II., in this volume.

55 Martin Schmidt-Kessel, Chapter IV. and V., in this volume.

56 See above III. 2.

product data and related service data must be easily accessible to the user of a connected product; or with regard to the data holder's obligation under Art. 4 DA to provide data to the user in the manner specified therein).

In many such situations, the value of data of different types and origins may be taken into account. In the case of consumer data, this does not necessarily have to involve contractual relationships directly between a consumer and a business (i.e. the traditional core area of consumer contract law). Rather, as mentioned above,[57] the value of consumer data can also be the subject of contracts (e.g. for the purchase or processing of such data) and related legal disputes in a variety of relationships between businesses, and in this respect the issue of the value of consumer data can also be assigned to the area of B2B legal relationships. In view of the spectrum of such situations, the aim of European legislation to facilitate data accessibility and data sharing extends to both consumer data and data from other sources and thus differs from specific consumer protection legislation.

Accordingly, a contribution in this volume addresses the Data Act from a perspective that goes 'beyond consumer protection.'[58] It considers consumers as one of the potentially involved parties in the ensemble of data sharing participants (alongside micro-enterprises, SMEs, and other enterprises) and refers to overarching aspects in the regulation of data accessibility and use.[59] With regard to the concept of 'fairness' in Art. 41 DA and in the Model Contract Terms provided for in the same article, which the European Commission had presented in November 2025, it may seem entirely consistent, given this overarching perspective in data law, that various models for these terms shall not be drafted separately to cover B-B and B-C situations and no special model terms shall be included to address consumer protection concerns.[60]

However, from a consumer protection perspective, it would also be consistent for these general rules on data sharing to be complemented by specific consumer protection measures where consumers are involved in the data sharing market.[61] This applies not least to the concern to ensure that consumers receive an appropriate share of the value of their data among those involved in data sharing. In this regard, 'beyond the Data Act',

57 See II.1.
58 Teresa Rodriguez de las Heras Ballell, in this volume
59 Teresa Rodriguez de las Heras Ballell, Chapter II., in this volume.
60 Teresa Rodriguez de las Heras Ballell, Chapter II., in this volume.
61 Teresa Rodriguez de las Heras Ballell, Chapter III., in this volume.

it remains to be considered whether the existing framework of rules on unfair contract terms and unfair commercial practices is sufficient.[62]

The analysis of specific market failure problems in B-C contexts in this volume argues in particular for the further development of consumer protection in view of the new circumstances in data sharing.[63] The negative effects highlighted therein with regard to consumer control and choice over their IoT data and with regard to the fair sharing of the value of consumer data suggest that it would be advisable to introduce at least a right for consumers to choose between IoT devices with and without the collection and use of non-necessary data, in line with the 'consent or pay' approach.

Beyond such a minimum standard of choice, this study presents a whole range of other measures worth considering that could give consumers more control and choice over their IoT data and devices (e.g. rights to terminate data use contracts in the event of continued use of IoT devices and rights regarding the change of data holder). In particular, it points to the need and opportunities to strengthen consumers' *de facto* control over their IoT data devices through regulations at the technological level (e.g. with regard to greater technological interoperability and standardisation, which could give consumers more control in this regard).[64] This provides a wealth of ideas for the discussion on further adapting consumer protection to the changes brought about by the growing importance of data trading and data sharing.

4. The Determination of the Value of Data

An essential task in adapting consumer protection to the realities of data trading is to make it easier for consumers to assess the value of their data or, in many cases, to enable them to do so at all. This concern raises the question of the appropriate methods for determining the value of data. However, the question of determining the value of data, including consumer data, arises not only from the perspective of consumer protection, but also in legal transactions between companies in a variety of situations, for example with regard to the performance of contractual agreements between

62 See Wolfgang Kerber/Karsten K. Zolna, in this volume.

63 Wolfgang Kerber/Karsten K. Zolna, in this volume, Chapter II., in this volume.

64 Wolfgang Kerber/Karsten K. Zolna, in this volume, Chapter III. and IV., in this volume.

companies on fee-based data sharing and in the case of judicial price control based on Articles 8 and 9 DA.[65]

The three articles in the concluding section of this volume offer a series of suggestions that may contribute to developing consistent criteria in this area. The study on 'Data as an asset and data trade'[66] combines analyses from economic and legal perspectives. Among other things, it deals in detail with the 'significant externalities' associated with the collection, processing, use and sharing of data, and on this basis describes the complexity of determining the value of data assets.[67] Among other things, it examines network effects in the use of the data in question, complementarity with artificial intelligence and the combination of data assets with other products or services as important factors in determining value. Taking into account such a multitude of dimensions of data as an asset, this analysis leads to a holistic, 'consequence-oriented' rather than 'right-oriented' approach with a focus 'on what data does'.[68] Both this methodological approach and the multitude of individual elements of value calculation discussed in the article are likely to be valuable for coping with the growing tasks of legal doctrine and jurisprudence in determining the value of data in numerous subject areas. A further analysis deals specifically with the value of those structured sets of data that, as databases, have become indispensable for the economy, science and many other areas of modern society.[69] The examination of methods and criteria for determining the value of such databases presupposes that they are tradeable assets at all if they contain (only or, among other data) personal data. In legal practice, the question of whether a database is tradable and what its value is can arise in many different situations, for example when it is disputed whether the proceeds from the sale of the database would cover a credit.[70] Art. 8 of the European Charter of Fundamental Rights and the data protection provisions based on it are in tension in this regard not only with the individual relevant legal acts for the data economy (such as the Data Act in particular), but

65 See above III. 2. a).

66 Fernando Gómez Pomar / Mireia Artigot Golobardes, in this volume.

67 Fernando Gómez Pomar / Mireia Artigot Golobardes, Chapters III. and IV., in this volume.

68 Fernando Gómez Pomar / Mireia Artigot Golobardes, Chapter V., in this volume.

69 Vincenzo Zeno-Zencovich, in this volume.

70 Vincenzo Zeno-Zencovich, Chapter I., in this volume with reference to Court of Justice of the European Union – Opinion of Advocate General Pikamäe delivered IN C-693/22 on 22 February 2024.

also with the right of property enshrined in Art. 17 of the European Charter of Fundamental Rights.[71] Ultimately, therefore, a balancing of fundamental rights is necessary, as a result of which databases are to be regarded as tradable provided that the purchases comply with the obligations set out by the GDPR, as the article explains in more detail (focusing on the sale of databases in insolvency proceedings).[72]

Finally, the latter contribution embeds the issues of data monetisation and determining its value in a set of pointed theses on the aims of the Data Act and conceivable alternatives to the market solutions in it (such as the model of establishing collecting societies and data trusts, which could then be tasked with valuing the data.[73] With regard to the fair share of the value of data in the relationship between the user of an IoT device and the data holder, particular attention is paid to the approach of co-generation of data by both of them, and the focus is on the concept of a 'partnership agreement' that enables the both to agree on how to monetise 'their' data.[74] The issues of determining the value of data and the fair share of its value thus lead back to fundamental questions about the structure of data trading and data sharing and underscore the need to review, after a certain period of time, how data markets are developing under the current system.[75]

III. Conclusion

Determining the value of data is increasingly relevant – for the national economy as a whole, for those involved in the economic activities concerned, and for lawyers with regard to the legal issues arising in the framework of the digital economy. This applies to personal data as well as to non-personal data; and it concerns personal data both when used in consumer-business relationships and when used in trade or processed in the context of legal relationships between businesses.

In economic terms, the availability of personal and non-personal data gives those who possess such information a decisive competitive advantage in the online advertising market, where the use of data is of vital impor-

71 Vincenzo Zeno-Zencovich, Chapter I., in this volume.
72 Vincenzo Zeno-Zencovich, Chapter III. and IV., in this volume.
73 Herbert Zech, Chapter IV., in this volume.
74 Herbert Zech, Chapter IV., in this volume.
75 See Herbert Zech, Chapter IV., in this volume, for more on this 'wait and see' approach.

tance in the offering of products/services – so-called 'primary use of data' –, while also allowing for the development and improvement of the products/services offered – so-called 'secondary use of data'. The high value of this information for creating specific consumer habit profiles drives online platforms to capture as much attention as possible, including through the promotion and offer of content that appeals to users. The data collected in this way is further monetised by selling it to third parties, in some cases in violation of data protection rules, in other cases by using personal data in a way that goes beyond the consent obtained from the user and violates individual rights and freedoms.

The transparency of data processing is a key factor that must be pursued in both the private and public sectors. However, this does not prejudice any assessment of the legitimacy, from the point of view of privacy protection legislation, of the collection and use of personal data, the 'necessity' and 'relevance' of which must be verified on a case-by-case basis in relation to the purpose for which the data was acquired and the service offered. Any 'excess' of data in relation to the purpose for which it was collected or used may also be relevant from an antitrust perspective to the extent that it is likely to lead to restrictions on competition in the markets concerned.

A different issue is whether and to what extent, even within the existing regulatory framework, the structure of interactions between users and businesses in relation to the collection and use of personal data can also be assessed in the light of the principle of fairness. For example, without prejudice to the principles of relevance and non-excessiveness provided for in the GDPR, the principle of fairness could be understood as the degree of sharing of the economic value generated by the use of personal data.

In this context, however, Big Data tends to change the terms of information asymmetry between consumers and businesses. Before the digital age, the use of personal data tended to reduce information asymmetries, whereas now its use seems rather to generate them, shifting them to consumers. The marketing of such products as 'free' without informing consumers about how data relating to their preferences, personal data and user-generated content will be used in certain circumstances may be considered, beyond any further violations of data protection rules, a misleading commercial practice.

Against the current challenges and legislative background, there is a clear call for more legal certainty in view of the new circumstances in data sharing and data trading. In particular, it is worth considering a range of new measures that could give consumers more control and choice over their IoT data and devices, ensuring a fairer balance between their rights and duties.

In this context, the High Level Forum on Justice for Growth[76] discussed among others different options on this topic. The discussion paper and the final report note imbalances in the distribution of data value when data is shared.[77] The final report recognises that balanced distribution of value to data providers for granting access to data is an area that deserves more attention and that there are issues relating to a lack of transparency, consumer empowerment and control, the complexity of assessing the concept of data value and the balanced distribution of data value, which are worth exploring further. It concludes that the topic merits further attention, discussion and research so that a proper assessment of the issues can be supported, when preparing the evaluation of the Data Act.

However, it was also clear from the discussion that it was not the right time to announce concrete initiatives or new legislation. Accordingly, the 2025 Data Union Strategy of the Commission, adopted soon after the conclusion of the High Level Forum on Justice for Growth, did not include any initiatives on this topic. At the same time, the High Level Forum on Justice for Growth concluded also that the focus should be on the results of the already mentioned monitoring of the uptake of the Model Contractual Terms. It will thus be interesting to see in the monitoring of the uptake of the Model Contract Terms by market players, announced in Data Union Strategy of the European Commission,[78] whether and to what extent contracts between the data holder and the data user will contain clauses on sharing the value of data.

---

76 High-Level Fora on Justice for Growth and on the Future of EU Criminal Justice – European Commission.

77 https://commission.europa.eu/document/download/fe6466d9-41b9-4125-aa70-67eb2bd207a6_en?filename=Discussion%20paper%20on%20automated%20contracting%20-final_0.pdf, p. 2 et seq.; https://commission.europa.eu/document/download/90a2f675-e963-4d05-a128-201e5bc693aa_en?filename=JUST_template_comingsoon_standard_15.pdf, point 64.

78 Data Union Strategy – Unlocking Data for AI, COM(2025) 835 final of 19. 11. 2025, p. 17.

I.
Trading Consumer Data: Background and General Framework

Personal Data as Object of Trade – The Regulatory Framework of the Data Act and the GDPR

Andreas Sattler[*]

At first, superficial glance, there appear to be clear guidelines for the relationship between the Data Act (DA) and the General Data Protection Regulation (GDPR). In fact, there remains a fundamental tension between enabling access to data and protecting privacy. If the objective pursued by the DA, i.e. the promotion of data markets, is also to be achieved for personal data, this requires a synchronisation of the rights to access, use and share data in accordance with Art. 4 and Art. 5 DA and the requirements for consent under data protection law. If the objectives pursued with the DA are to be achieved, it is therefore necessary to create the legal conditions for effective Personal Information Management Systems (PIMS).

I. Introduction

Starting with its data strategy in 2020, it is the *EU Commission's* goal to "to create a single European data space [...] where personal as well as non-personal data, including sensitive business data, are secure and businesses also have easy access to an almost infinite amount of high-quality industrial data [...]".[1] The *EU Commission* is convinced that "the value of data lies in its use and re-use", explicitly including "mixed data-sets" which contain personal and non-personal data.[2]

The *EU Commission* assumes that this data has not yet been sufficiently used in the Union and hopes that European data spaces will "foster an ecosystem (of companies, civil society and individuals) creating new products

---

* This contribution is based on a comprehensive analysis of the relationship between Data Act and GDPR which is available as open access publication: *Sattler/Zech* (eds.), EU Data Act: First Assessments, 2024, Chapter 7.

1 EU-Commission, A European strategy for data, 19.2.2020, COM(2020) 66 final, p. 6.

2 EU-Commission, A European strategy for data, 19.2.2020, COM(2020) 66 final, p. 7.

and services based on more accessible data".[3] At the same time, however, the *EU Commission* leaves no doubt that any European data strategy must ensure that "European rules and values, in particular personal data protection [...] are fully respected".[4]

This dual objective is also reflected in Art. 1 of the Data Act. Art. 1 (2) DA provides that the DA applies to both personal and non-personal data. However, Art. 1 (5) s. 1 DA clarifies that the DA applies "without prejudice" to the protection of personal data, privacy and confidentiality of communications as provided for in the GDPR,[5] Regulation (EU) 2018/1725[6] and the e-Privacy Directive.[7] Finally, it follows from Art. 1 (5) s. 3 DA that in the event of a conflict between the DA and the GDPR, the latter takes precedence.[8]

This priority in favour of the GDPR easily ignores the fact that the objectives pursued by the DA and the GDPR are in fundamental conflict with each other. While Art. 3 DA establishes *accessibility by design*, the GDPR establishes the principles of *data minimization* (Art. 5 (1) lit. b GDPR), of *purpose limitation* (Art. 5 (1) lit. c GDPR), of *storage limitation* (Art. 5 (1) lit. e GDPR) and the *principle of privacy by design* (Art. 25 GDPR).[9]

---

3 EU-Commission, A European strategy for data, 19.2.2020, COM(2020) 66 final, p. 6.

4 EU-Commission, A European strategy for data, 19.2.2020, COM(2020) 66 final, p. 6.

5 Regulation (EU) 2016/679 of 27.04.2016 on the protection of natural persons with regard to the processing of personal data and on the free movement of such data, and repealing Directive 95/46/EC (General Data Protection Regulation), OJ L 119, 4.5.2016, p. 1–88.

6 Regulation (EU) 2018/1725 of 23.10.2018 on the protection of natural persons with regard to the processing of personal data by the Union institutions, bodies, offices and agencies and on the free movement of such data, and repealing Regulation (EC) No 45/2001 and Decision No 1247/2002/EC, OJ L 295, 21.11.2018, p. 39–98.

7 Directive 2002/58/EC of 12.07.2002 concerning the processing of personal data and the protection of privacy in the electronic communications sector (Directive on privacy and electronic communications), OJ L 201, 31.7.2002, p. 37–47.

8 The rule in the event of conflict had been demanded by the European Data Protection Supervisor (EDPS) and the European Data Protection Board (EDPB): EDPB-EDPS Joint Opinion 02/2022 on the Proposal of the European Parliament and of the Council on harmonised rules on fair access and use of data, 04.05.2022, p. 7.

9 According to Rec. 8 S. 3 DA all parties to data sharing should use pseudonymisation, encryption and technology that permits algorithms to be brought to the data and allow valuable insights to be derived without the transmission of the analysed data.

After all, the European legislator refers to this tension between the DA and the GDPR in Rec. 20 s. 9 DA[10] and in Rec. 24 s. 6 DA.[11] Nevertheless, Art. 1 (5) s. 3 DA is not a meta-collision rule that allows to resolve the lack of consistency in European legislation.[12] Rather, it only decides that the GDPR takes precedence if there is a conflict within the scope of application of the DA.

In order to analyze the relationship between the DA and the GDPR, the following contribution first recalls that personal data had been an object of trade for many years and that such trade in personal data is – from a legal perspective – different to the trade of other immaterial goods (II.). Hereafter this contribution turns to the DA and explains that the DA is not a "gamechanger" for such trade in personal data as it neither establishes a legal basis for the processing of such data nor supplements the legal basis provided in Art. 6 GDPR (III.). This contribution emphasises that – due to the CJEU's case law – there are hardly any meaningful use cases for the other legal bases provided by Art. 6 GDPR in the context of the DA. Therefore, consent of the data subjects will be the central instrument for synchronising the DA and the GDPR (IV.). Following the wide scope of application of Art. 4 and Art. 5 DA, typically a large number of data subjects will be affected. Consequently, it remains a challenge to create effective and efficient consent mechanisms that comply with the requirements of the GDPR (V.). The article ends with a conclusion (VI.).

---

10 According to Rec. 20 s. 9 DA „the design obligations in this Regulation are also without prejudice to the data minimisation principle laid down in [Art. 5 (1) lit. c GDPR]" and Art. 3 DA "should not be understood as imposing an obligation to design connected products and related services in such a way that they store or otherwise process any personal data other than the personal data necessary in relation to the purposes for which they are processed".

11 According to Rec. 24 s. 6 DA the data holder „cannot be expected to store the data indefinitely in view of the needs of the user of the connected product, but should implement a reasonable data retention policy, where applicable, in line with storage limitation principle pursuant [Art. 5 (1) lit. e GDPR] that allows for the effective application of the data access rights provided for in this Regulation".

12 Despite (repeated) acceptance in Art. 1 (2) DA that personal data is both, an object of trade and a crucial source of data-based innovation, the European Data Protection Board, nevertheless, insists that personal data is "no commodity": *EDPB*, Opinion 08/2024 on Valid Consent in the Context of Consent or Pay Models Implemented by Large Online Platforms, 17.4.2024, p. 38/para. 180.

II. Personal Data: An object of trade – not of transfer

An economic good is characterised by the fact that it creates a subjective benefit for at least one (legal) person, that this person therefore demands the good and thus has a positive willingness to pay. However, as has already been pointed out many times, data – as an immaterial object – has some special characteristics that distinguish it from other, typically physical goods.[13]

Personal data is of particular economic value if its analysis either reveals an important pattern that helps to improve a product or a service or if it enables a controller to predict a future change in consumer behavior. For example, a change of one's employment combined with a change in income, a change of the matrimonial status or the birth of a child lead to fundamental shifts in consumption.[14] If personal data reveals such consumption-relevant changes, it is particularly valuable for marketers and thus the different forms of data traders. However, as access to relevant data from registry offices and tax offices is limited by law and data on the use of credit cards reveal obsolete demands which were satisfied, anyone wishing to detect significant changes in personal preferences before a relevant transaction takes place, needs to rely on the analysis of continuous real-time data streams – for example through technologies which track online behaviour.

For some years now, there has been a lively debate as to whether an intellectual property right should be established for data. The outcome of this discussion can have very important consequences for data trading because it leads to a change in the costs of trading data. The clear assignment of data to one specific person increases legal certainty, consequently increases the willingness to conclude contracts with data as object of performance and therefore reduces the costs of data transactions. In terms of legal policy, a "right to data" continues to be highly controversial, goes far beyond the scope of this contribution and is the subject of other parts in this volume.[15]

---

13 *Duch-Brown/Mayer/Langer*, The economics of ownership, access and trade in digital data, 2017. p. 12ss. (https://ec.europa.eu/jrc/sites/jrcsh/files/jrc104756.pdf).

14 For the – often cited – example that a woman's pregnancy can be inferred from her purchasing behavior: NYT Magazine, How Companies Learn Your Secrets, 16.2.2012 (http://www.nytimes.com/2012/02/19/magazine/shopping-habits.html?pagewanted=all&_r=0).

15 *Kerber/Zolna*, in this volume; *Zech*, Data Access Rights as Property Rights, in: Sattler/Zech (eds.), The Data Act: First Assessments, 2024, p. 67ss.

With regard to personal data, there are valid reasons against the recognition of exclusive rights.[16] As a result, data trading in the form of a permanent and complete transfer of an absolute, subjective right will very likely be excluded. Copyright and the general right of personality are examples of such restrictions. Irrespective of whether copyright law (German: *Urheberrecht*) is – as in German tradition – regarded as a monistic right or – as in French and Italian understanding – a dualistic distinction is made between property rights and personality rights, a complete separation of the protected work from the author is not possible in either case.[17] Moreover, the protection of privacy (Art. 7 EUCFR) and the protection of personal data (Art. 8 (1) EUCFR, Art. 16 (1) TFEU) ensure a permanent and indissoluble link between the data subject and the personal data.[18] For the time being, therefore, contract law and data protection law provide the legal framework for trade in personal data.

However, as has already become obvious, the requirement of a valid consent and especially the right to revoke consent at any time and without cause according to Art. 7 (3) S. 1 GDPR would jeopardize all contracts in which celebrities, but also unknown persons, commit themselves as a so-called brand or product ambassadors ("testimonial") and thereby also consent to the processing of personal data. Such consent as part of a B2B advertising agreements must be legally binding, so that in the event of poor performance or non-performance by the data subject acting as an entrepreneur, a claim for performance, or at least for damages, can be enforced. Because such agreements are neither covered by the opening clause of Art. 85 (1) GDPR nor by the authorization of data processing ancillary to a contract (Art. 6 (1) lit. b GDPR, controllers and data subjects acting in an entrepreneurial capacity are reliant on temporary irrevocable consent to continue their previously stable legal relationships.[19]

---

16 With an analysis of the (German) fundamentals of the protection of person data: *Sattler*, From Personality to Property?, in: Bakhoum et al. (eds.), Personal Data in Competition, Consumer Protection and Intellectual Property Law, 2018, p. 27–54.

17 *Metzger*, Rechtsgeschäfte über das droit moral, 2002, p. 161ss.

18 *Beverley-Smith/Ohly/Lucas-Schloetter*, Privacy, Property and Personality – Civil Law Perspectives on Commercial Appropriation, 2005, p. 147ss.; *Sattler*, in: Bakhoum et al. (eds), Personal Data in Competition, Consumer Protection and Intellectual Property Law, 2018, p. 27 (41ss.).

19 For more details: *Sattler*, Informationelle Privatautonomie, 2022, p. 334ss.

Although this contribution cannot analyze contractual typological delimitation issues in detail,[20] a trend can be observed: While the provisions on sales law might apply accordingly to the permanent transfer of personal data, the duty of performance and warranty claims under sales law are typically inappropriate for continuous data streams. Put short: Personal Data is tradable, but not transferable[21].

As far as personal data is the subject of performance, continuing obligations with detailed service descriptions such as Service-Level-Agreements (SLA) for the use of software and databases will play an increasingly important role model. Although the term "license" is notoriously ambiguous – it is used in the context of intellectual property law for very different grants of rights – it can, nevertheless, serve the purpose of merely illustrating the indispensable content of contracts for the access, use and sharing of data.

III. No legal basis in the Data Act

The wording of Art. 1 (5) DA leaves – at best – little scope for an interpretation according to which Art. 4 and Art. 5 DA constitute independent legal bases for the processing of personal data (1). Art. 6 (2) lit. b DA, which sets out special legal requirements for profiling, does not establish an independent legal basis outside the GDPR, too (2).

1. Can Art. 4 and 5 DA serve as a legal basis for processing?

In principle, it appears possible that access to and use of personal data could also be lawful on the basis of Art. 6 (1) lit. c or lit. e GDPR and – as far as sensitive personal data is concerned – pursuant to Art. 9 (2) lit. g GDPR.[22] According to Art. 6 (1) lit. c GDPR processing is lawful if it is necessary for compliance with a legal obligation to which the controller is subject. Pursuant to Art. 6 (1) lit. e GDPR, processing is lawful insofar

20 For such discussion: *Metzger*, Contracts under the Data Act: Review of standard terms and FRAND conditions, in: Sattler/Zech (eds.) The Data Act: First Assessments, 2024, p. 79ss.

21 *Sattler*, Autonomy or Heteronomy – Proposal for a two-tier interpretation of Art. 6 GDPR, in: Lohsse/Schulze/Staudenmayer (eds.), Data as counter-performance – contract law 2.0?, 2020, p. 225 (249).

22 The explicit referral to consent and contract in Rec. 34 S. 8 DA is only exemplary ("such as").

as it is necessary for the performance of a task carried out in the public interest. Art. 9 (2) lit. g GDPR permits the processing of sensitive personal data insofar as it is necessary for reasons of important public interest on the basis of Union law or the law of the Member States.

On the basis of the preparatory documents, the DA Proposal of the *EU Commission* and the *Council's* mandate for negotiations with the *European Parliament* ("Council Mandate"),[23] it has already been argued that Art. 6 (1) lit. c, lit. e GDPR and Art. 9 (2) lit. g GDPR could be applicable as opening clauses of the GDPR in conjunction with Art. 4 (1) and Art. 5 (1) DA.[24] Consequently, both norms could provide such legal obligations outside the GDPR or a (substantial) public interest which – in connection with the opening clauses in Art. 6 (1) lit. c, lit. e GDPR and Art. 9 (2) lit. g GDPR – would help to achieve the objective of the DA to improve data-driven downstream innovation. However, such an interpretation of Art. 4 (1) and Art. 5 (1) DA has become difficult in view of the final wording of Art. 4 (12) and Art. 5 (7) DA. Accordingly, personal data may only be made available to a user, who is not the data subject, by the data holder if there is a valid legal basis for processing "under Art. 6 GDPR".[25]

In addition, Rec. 7 s. 7 DA emphasizes that the DA itself "does not constitute a legal basis for the collection or generation of personal data by the data holder"[26] nor "does [it] create a legal basis for providing access to personal data" where the user is not the data subject.[27]

Merely the statement that Art. 4 and Art. 5 DA refer to the GDPR for personal data if the user is not the same person as the data subject whose personal data is requested is ambivalent. This wording suggests a reverse conclusion, according to which Art. 4 (12) and Art. 5 (7) DA could allow a data holder to make personal data available to a user who is the same

23 Council of the European Union, Interinstitutional File of 17.3.2023: 2022/0047(COD).

24 *Specht-Riemenschneider*, ZEuP 2023, 638 (665 ss.).

25 Of the same opinion: *Antoine*, CR 2024, 73 (74/para. 7); *Czychowski*, CR 2024, 80 (83/para. 17). With different opinion, however, referring to a proposal of a Rec. 24 by the Councils's Mandate that was not successful in the Trilogue: *Specht-Riemenschneider*, ZEuP 2023, 638 (667 s.). *Specht-Riemenschneider* limits the application of Art. 6 (1) lit. c. and Art. 6 (3) GDPR to cases where a user is identical to the data subject and demands access to personal data according to Art. 4 (1) DA. Contrastingly, where a user is not the data subject but requests access to or the sharing of personal, Art. 6 (1) lit. c GDPR shall not apply.

26 Rec. 7 s. 7 DA.

27 Rec. 7 s. 10 DA.

person as the data subject or to a third party, regardless of whether one of the legal bases of the GDPR applies.

Such an interpretation could be supported by the fact that recital 7 DA also distinguishes between constellations in which the user is identical with data subject and constellations in which the user and data subject are different persons. According to Rec. 7 s. 8 DA only as far as the former is concerned "*this Regulation imposes an obligation* on data holders to make personal data available to users or third parties of a user's choice upon that user's request".[28] This statement seems to imply that Art. 4 (1) and Art. 5 (1) DA constitute such a legal obligation, as required by Art. 6 (1) lit. c GDPR. However, any request by a user who *is* identical to the data subject already contains an implicit consent of this user for all data processing necessary to fulfill the claim under Art. 4 (1) and Art. 5 (1) DA. Therefore, Rec. 7 s. 8 DA and the obligation of the data holder mentioned therein – at least as far as personal data is concerned – is redundant and only refers to the obligations of the data holder under the DA. Although it is the aim of the DA to promote data-based innovation in Europe and such innovation is also beneficial from a general social perspective, it does not qualify the entrepreneurial pursuit of innovation as a (substantial) public interest in the data processing.

As a result, Art. 4 and Art. 5 DA do not provide a legal basis for the processing of personal data that is independent of the GDPR, nor do they constitute accessory permissions to the GDPR in the sense of a legal obligation (Art. 6 (1) lit. c) or an (important) public interest (Art. 6 (1) lit. e and Art. 9 (2) lit. g GDPR).

2. No legal basis in Art. 6 (2) lit. b DA

Art. 6 (2) lit. b DA is a particularly puzzling provision. First of all, Art. 6 (1) DA stipulates that third parties who have received data in accordance with Art. 5 DA may only process it for the purposes and under the conditions agreed with the user and, insofar as personal data is concerned, in compliance with the GDPR. According to Art. 6 (2) lit. b DA the third party shall not "notwithstanding [Art. 22 (2) lit. a and lit. c GDPR] use the data it

28 Emphasis added.

receives for profiling, unless it is necessary to provide the service requested by the *user*".[29]

At first glance, it is surprising that a user's request for a service should be sufficient to legitimise the processing of personal data for profiling purposes. The corresponding recital is not very enlightening, too. Rec. 39 s. 1 DA merely repeats that third parties should "refrain from using data falling within the scope of this Regulation to profile individuals unless such processing activities are *strictly necessary to provide the service* requested by the user".[30]

Since Art. 6 (1) lit. b GDPR permits the processing of personal data insofar as it is necessary for the performance of a contract, it stands to reason that Art. 6 (2) lit. b DA implicitly refers to Art. 6 (1) lit. b GDPR or Art. 22 (2) lit. a GDPR. However, both are only applicable in cases where the controller and the data subject have concluded a contract. Neither Art. 6 (1) lit. b nor Art. 22 (2) lit. a GDPR are applicable if the user has concluded or requested a contract with a third party within the meaning of the GDPR.[31] Furthermore, the reference in Art. 6 (2) lit. b DA to Art. 22 (2) lit. a GDPR ("without prejudice") – i.e. the provision that corresponds to Art. 6 (1) lit. b GDPR in the case of profiling – is meaningless if Art. 6 (2) lit. b DA itself is to have any scope of application independent of Art. 22 GDPR ("without prejudice").

Consequently, it is not convincing to interpret Art. 6 (2) lit. b DA as a legal basis for profiling outside of the GDPR.[32] Indeed, any event in which a mere request by the user towards a third party for particular services could legitimise the profiling of a data subject would amount to a contract which

29 Emphasis added.

30 Emphasis added.

31 Art. 6 DA seems to be applicable irrespectively of whether third party acts as controller (Art. 24 (1) GDPR) or merely as processor (Art. 28 (1) GDPR). However, if the third party undertakes the profiling in order to fulfil its own service obligations towards the user, the former will more likely be a controller or a joint controller (Art. 26 GDPR).

32 Likewise, EDPB-EDPS Joint Opinion 5/2021 on the proposal for a Regulation of the European Parliament and of the Council laying down harmonised rules on artificial intelligence, 18.6.2021, p. 16s. para. 57–58; *Specht-Riemenschneider*, ZEuP 2023, 638 (664); Arguing in favour such a legal basis outside of the GDPR, however based on the DA-Proposal: Position Paper of the German Bar Association on the Proposal for a Regulation on harmonised rules on fair access, July 2022, p. 17, available at https://anwaltverein.de/de/newsroom/sn-40-22-vorschlag-der-eu-kommission-fuer-ein-datengesetz (28.2.2024).

is detrimental to the data subject.[33] Such a contract would be void, both, according to Sec. 242 German Civil Code ("*BGB*") and according to the European principle of good faith.

As a result, two interpretations of Art. 6 (2) lit. b DA are possible: Either, it could be a drafting oversight that Art. 6 (2) lit. b DA refers to the user, regardless of whether the user is identical to the data subject. This is supported by the fact that the tension between the DA and the GDPR was only incompletely recognized during the legislative process. While this realisation was expressed in Art. 4 (12) DA and Art. 5 (7) DA, in that both regulations clearly differentiate between constellations in which the user is identical to the data subject or not, such a differentiation could have been overlooked in Art. 6 (2) lit. b DA.

Thus, the latter could be read as if it contained the words "user, who is the data subject" instead of "user". Such an understanding would allow for an application of Art. 6 (1) lit. b GDPR or – more convincingly – to interpret the request by the user, who is the data subject, for services based on a profiling to imply a consent (Art. 6 (1) lit. a GDPR) in such profiling.[34]

However, such an interpretation, which is contrary to the explicit wording, seems superfluous as Art. 6 (2) lit. b DA already refers to both options, the necessity for the performance of a contract (Art. 22 (2) lit. a GDPR) and the consent by the data subject (Art. 22 (2) lit. c GDPR).

In other words: Although Art. 6 (2) lit. b DA – unlike Art. 4 and Art. 5 DA – does not differentiate between scenarios in which the user is the same person as the data subject or not, in the event that there is no identity, it at least contains a reference to the need for a data protection basis for profiling in accordance with Art. 22 GDPR.

Consequently, a restrictive interpretation of Art. 6 (2) lit. b DA is convincing. According to this, Art. 6 (2) lit. b DA merely *restates* the requirements for profiling exclusively for the relationship between the third party and the user. This interpretation is supported by the title of Art. 6 DA ("Obligations of third parties receiving data at the request of the user") and the fact that Art. 6 (2) lit. b DA does not contain any significant statement

33 Similarly, it is doubtful that a contract between a user, who is not identical with the data subject, and a third party can – as such – constitute a legitimate interest in favour of the user according to Art. 6 (1) lit. f GDPR. However, supporting such a solution: Antoine, CR 2024, 73 (75/para. 10).

34 Likewise: *Hennemann/Steinrötter*, NJW 2024, 1 (4/para. 15); similar for any request by a user who is identical to the data subject: *Wiebe*, GRUR 2023, 1569 (1574); *Antoine*, CR 2024, 73 (74/para. 6).

on the protection of personal data. With this understanding, the provision merely clarifies that a third party may also use personal data for profiling in order to provide a service requested by the user. However, the lawfulness of such processing under data protection law would depend exclusively on whether a legal basis for such profiling is available to the user and thus to the third party[35] in accordance with Art. 22 (2) GDPR. According to this understanding, Art. 6 (2) lit. b DA only serves to (once again) safeguard the user-centric approach of the DA – this time in relation to third parties.[36]

Consequently, any profiling by third parties, who receive data mediated by a user, who is not identical to the data subject is prohibited, unless such profiling is lawful under the GDPR in relation to the data subject *and* necessary for the provision of the services requested by the user. Use cases for this rather abstract regulation are not immediately obvious. These are scenarios in which a third party provides the user with services that require the personalisation of products for a data subject that is not the user itself.

A potential example could be the offer by a service provider (third party) to the owner of a car (user) to display leisure or restaurant suggestions in the car's infotainment system that are geographically nearby and correspond to the sum of the preferences of the passengers (data subjects), for example the children who are already capable of giving consent themselves in accordance with Art. 8 (1) s. 1 GDPR. For this profiling, the service provider would have to access the passengers' smartphones, which are also connected to the car's infotainment system, in order to be able to analyse all passengers' preferences.

In the field of production, examples are conceivable in which a third party offers a user of rented,[37] connected production robots an optimisation of the operation and maintenance of these cyber-physical systems based on an analysis of the behaviour of certain employees (data subjects) who are permanently entrusted with the system's operation.

---

35 In this case the third party would most likely be a processor according to Art. 28 (1) GDPR, whilst the user remains the controller according to Art. 24 (1) GDPR.

36 See *Eckardt/Kerber*, in: Sattler/Zech (eds.) The Data Act: First Assessments, 2024, Chapter 1, Part. E; *Zech*, in: Sattler/Zech (eds.) The Data Act: First Assessments, 2024, Chapter 4, Part C; *Metzger*, in: Sattler/Zech (eds.) The Data Act: First Assessments, 2024, Chapter 5, Part C.

37 The use case of a lease agreement allows – at least potentially – to distinguish between the position of Data Holder (lessor) und User (lessee). However, depending on the contract the lessee van also be the Data Holder according to Art. 2 no. 13 DA.

Thus, Art. 6 (2) lit. b DA merely constitutes an additional requirement for the third party to always involve the user, who's relying on Art. 5 (1) DA has enabled the third party to process the respective personal data. Since the data subjects can and must continue to independently legitimise such profiling by third parties in accordance with Art. 22 (2) lit. a and lit. c GDPR, this obligation of the third party to additionally involve the user in the event of profiling does not affect the rights to which the data subject is entitled under the GDPR. As a result, Art. 6 (2) lit. b DA is compatible with the GDPR, as it does not cause a conflict between DA and GDPR within the meaning of Art. 1 (5) s. 3 DA.

Since neither Art. 4, Art. 5 nor Art. 6 (2) lit. b DA establish independent permissions for the processing of personal data, the interpretation and application of Art. 6 GDPR will determine whether the objectives of the DA are achievable or whether the rights to access, use and share personal data will fall over the cliff of data protection law.

IV. Consent as an instrument for synchronising DA and GDPR

Although all legal bases in Art. 6 (1) GDPR can enable the processing of personal data, the following analysis shows that neither Art. 6 (1) lit. b GDPR (1) nor Art. 6 (1) lit. f GDPR (2) provide a reliable basis for processing personal data within the scope of Art. 4 and Art. 5 DA. As a result, the success of the DA – as far as personal data is concerned – depends on the administration of complex consent cascades (3) and thus ultimately on the successful Union-wide implementation of efficient and effective Personal Information Management Systems (PIMS).[38]

1. Necessity for the fulfillment of the contract, Art. 6 (1) lit. b GDPR

According to Art. 6 (1) lit. b GDPR, the processing of personal data is lawful if it is "is necessary for the performance of a contract to which the data subject is party or in order to take steps at the request of the data subject prior to entering into a contract". At first glance, Art. 6 (1) lit. b GDPR

38 According to Rec. 33 s. 6 DA data intermediaries and PIMS are considered as useful tool when establishing commercial relations between users and third parties, especially for the purpose of aggregating access to data so that big data analyses or machine learning can be facilitated.

seems to be predestined to be applied in the context of the right to data access, because Art. 4 (13) s. 1 and Art. 4 (14) DA – even for non-personal data – presuppose a contract between the user and the data holder anyway.

However, the *Grand Chamber* of the *CJEU* recently emphasised that consent takes precedence and that Art. 6 (1) lit. b GDPR must therefore be "interpreted restrictively" as it allows a lawful processing of personal data in the absence of the data subject's consent.[39] Furthermore, the *CJEU* ruled that the processing of personal data is only necessary for the performance of a contract if is "objectively indispensable for a purpose that is integral to the contractual obligation intended for the data subject".[40] However, this should only be the case if the controller can prove that the processing is "essential for the proper performance of the contract concluded" because "there are no workable, less intrusive alternatives" available.[41]

In short: Art. 6 (1) lit. b GDPR should primarily be understood as an instrument that makes it possible to reduce the frequency of declarations of consent and the associated decision-making pressure on data subjects. If a controller and a data subject have concluded a contract or are planning to do so, it would be an unreasonable burden to always require the consent of the data subjects and thus exhaust their decision-making capacity (so-called consent fatigue), while this data processing is typically necessary in the context of such a contract – and thus foreseeable for the data subject.[42] This relief function of Art. 6 (1) lit. b GDPR and the requirement that such processing is indispensable for a purpose which is the main subject matter of the contract ("integral to the contractual obligation") limits the applicability of the standard to data such as bank details or postal addresses in the context of a distance contract.

The *CJEU's* restrictive interpretation means that Art. 6 (1) lit. b GDPR does not provide a legal basis if personal data is processed either for

---

39 CJEU (Grand Chamber), Judgement 4.7.2023, Meta/Bundeskartellamt, C-252/21, ECLI:EU:C:2023:537, para. 93; see also: CJEU, Judgment 24.2.2022, Valsts ieņēmumu dienests, C-175/20, EU:C:2022:124, para. 73.

40 CJEU (Grand Chamber), Judgement 4.7.2023, Meta/Bundeskartellamt, C-252/21, ECLI:EU:C:2023:537, para. 98.

41 CJEU (Grand Chamber), Judgement 4.7.2023, Meta/Bundeskartellamt, C-252/21, ECLI:EU:C:2023:537, para. 99.

42 *Sattler*, Autonomy or Heteronomy – Proposal for a Two-Tier Interpretation of Art. 6 I GDPR, in: Lohsse/Schulze/Staudenmayer (eds.), Data as Counter-Performance – Contract Law 2.0? Münster Colloquia on EU Law and the Digital Economy V, 2020, p. 223 (241 s); *Sattler*, Informationelle Privatautomomie, 2022, p. 287 ss.

personalised advertising or to offer individualised smart services or smart products to a data subject.[43] Therefore, Art. 6 (1) lit. b GDPR is also largely unsuitable to legitimise the processing of personal data in the context of Art. 4 and Art. 5 DA if the right to access, use and sharing of such data is asserted by a user. It is true that Rec. 34 s. 8 DA expressly provides that a user who requests access to personal data as a controller requires a legal basis for this processing "such as [...] the performance of a contract to which the data subject is a party". Despite this explicit reference to a contract between user and data subject, the significance of Art. 6 (1) lit. b GDPR is largely negligible as a result of its restrictive interpretation by the *CJEU*.

2. Processing as a legitimate interest, Art. 6 (1) lit. f GDPR

Art. 6 (1) lit. f GDPR permits data processing if it is necessary for the purposes of the legitimate interests pursued by the controller or by a third party, except where such interests are overridden by the interests or fundamental rights and freedoms of the data subject which require protection of personal data, in particular where the data subject is a child.

The objectives of the DA and, in particular, the claims pursuant to Art. 4 (1) and Art. 5 (1) DA are an expression of the legislator's will to improve access, use and sharing of personal data. This suggests that these objectives could be regarded as important legitimate interest within the meaning of Art. 6 (1) lit. f GDPR. Consequently, Art. 6 (1) lit. f GDPR could be an

43 CJEU (Grand Chamber), Judgement 4.7.2023, Meta/Bundeskartellamt, C-252/21, ECLI:EU:C:2023:537, para. 102. The CJEU concludes that although a personalisation of the services by Meta is useful to the user, as it enables the user to view content corresponding to a large extent to his or her interests, such personalisation does, nevertheless, not appear to be necessary in order to offer that user the services of the online social network. Contrastingly, such services may be provided to the user in the form of an equivalent alternative which does not involve such a personalisation. Arguably of a different opinion was the European Data Protection Board (EDPB), which stated in the context of the Digital-Content-Directive that "personalisation of content may (but does not always) constitute an expected element of certain online services, and therefore may be regarded as necessary for the performance of the contract with the service user in some cases". EDPB, Guidelines 2/2019 on the processing of personal data under Art. 6 (1) (b) GDPR in the context of the provision of online services to data subjects, 16.10.2019, para. 54.

important legal basis within the scope of application of the DA.[44] Such assumption is also supported by the fact that Art. 6 (1) lit. f GDPR is the only legal basis with the support of which a user, who is not identical to the data subject can assert the claims under Art. 4 and Art. 5 GDPR without having to rely on an active opt-in of all data subjects.[45] If users, who are not identical to the data subject, depended on consent (Art. 6 (1) lit. a GDPR) or on a contract with all data subjects (Art. 6 (1) lit. b GDPR), Art. 4 and Art. 5 GDPR would often be ineffective with regard to data with multiple personal references (so-called multi-relationality). The costs and effort involved in obtaining consent or concluding multiple contracts are typically prohibitive.[46]

Although Art. 6 (1) lit. f GDPR might – in general – provide a flexible tool to synchronise DA and GDPR, it would have been helpful if the EU legislator had clearly stated whether and to what extent Art. 6 (1) lit. f GDPR is available as a legal basis within the scope of application of the DA. The DA only insufficiently addresses the relationship between Art. 4, Art. 5 DA and Art. 6 GDPR in general and Art. 6 (1) lit. f GDPR in particular.[47] Furthermore, the legislative history of the DA and in particular the amendment resulting from the *Council's* Mandate[48] suggests that Art. 6 (1) lit. f GDPR was only assigned a subordinate role. According to Rec. 30 s. 8 of the *EU Commission's proposal*,[49] a user needed a legal basis for processing the data, "such as the consent of the data subject or *legitimate interest*".[50] However, as a result of the *Council's Mandate*, Rec. 30 s. 8 DA was amended. Therefore, the final wording of – finally – Rec. 34 s. 8 DA provides that a user who,

44 Similar: *Hennemann/Steinrötter*, NJW 2024, 1 (6); *Specht-Riemenschneider*, ZEuP 2023, 638 (667).

45 While Art. 6 (1) lit. a (consent) und lit. b GDPR (contract) require some form of opt-in by the data subject, contrastingly, Art. 6 (1) lit. f GDPR (balancing of interests) leaves such decision to the controller. Thus, the data subject has only the option to actively opt-out according to Art. 21 (1) GDPR.

46 On the crucial role of Art. 6 (1) lit. f GDPR when processing multi-relational data: *Sattler*, Informationelle Privatautonomie, 2022, p. 98 f.

47 See also: Position Paper of the German Bar Association on the Proposal for a Regulation on harmonised rules on fair access, July 2022, p. 5 s., available at https://anwaltverein.de/de/newsroom/sn-40-22-vorschlag-der-eu-kommission-fuer-ein-datengesetz (28.2.2024).

48 Council of the European Union, Interinstitutional File of 17.3.2023: 2022/0047(COD).

49 *EU Commission*, Proposal for a Regulation on harmonised rules on fair access to and use of data (Data Act), 22.3.2022, COM/2022/68 final.

50 Emphasis added.

as a controller, intends to request access to personal data generated during the use of a connected product or service requires a legal basis for the data processing, "such as the consent of the data subject or the *performance of a contract* to which the data subject is a party".[51] In short: The trilogue negotiations resulted in the reference to Art. 6 (1) lit. f GDPR being replaced by a reference to Art. 6 (1) lit. b GDPR.

Despite this change in wording in the course of the negotiations, Rec. 34 s. 8 DA should not be misinterpreted as an implicit exclusion of Art. 6 (1) lit. f GDPR within the scope of the DA. *Firstly*, recitals are merely ancillary guidelines for the interpretation of the statutory provisions and are therefore not legally binding. *Secondly*, although Rec. 34 s. 8 DA only mentions consent and contract expressly, this reference is only exemplary ("such as"). Therefore, the change in the wording of Rec. 34 DA rather suggests that the legislator lacked a thorough understanding of the interfaces between DA and GDPR. A careful attempt to synchronise these two European legal acts cannot be found in Rec. 34 DA nor elsewhere.

However, if one assumes – convincingly – that Art. 6 (1) lit. f GDPR can provide a legal basis in the context of Art. 4 (1) and Art. 5 (1) DA, then it becomes the "loose cannon" on the deck of the DA due to its potentially very broad scope of application. Turned positively: Art. 6 (1) lit. f GDPR allows for a careful balancing of the legitimate interests of the user or a third party on the one hand and the interests, rights and freedoms of the data subjects on the other. As a result, Art. 6 (1) lit. f GDPR can be described as a "pacemaker" as it provides a certain degree of flexibility within the otherwise rather static framework of the GDPR.[52] However, in order to prevent the requirements for valid consent from being undermined, Art. 6 (1) lit. f GDPR should also be interpreted restrictively in the opinion of the *Grand Chamber* of the *CJEU*.[53]

51 Emphasis added.

52 *Sattler*, Informationelle Privatautonomie, 2022, S. 139 ff.

53 ECJ (Grand Chamber), C-252/21, Judgement 4.7.2023, ECLI:EU:C:2023:537 -Meta/Bundeskartellamt, para. 93; see also: ECJ, C-175/20, Judgment 24.2.2022, EU:C:2022:124 – Valsts ieņēmumu dienests, para. 73. For a more comprehensive justification hereof: *Sattler*, Autonomy or Heteronomy – Proposal for a Two-Tier Interpretation of Art. 6 I GDPR, in: Lohsse/Schulze/Staudenmayer (eds.), Data as Counter-Performance – Contract Law 2.0? Münster Colloquia on EU Law and the Digital Economy V, 2020, p. 223 ss.; *Sattler*, Informationelle Privatautomomie, 2022, p. 278 ss.

At the same time, neither the EU legislator nor the *CJEU* have yet been able to develop reliable guidelines for the application of Art. 6 (1) lit. f GDPR. In its ruling on *Meta vs Bundeskartellamt*, the *CJEU* decided that the customers of a network such as *Facebook* cannot reasonably expect *Meta* to process their personal data for the purpose of personalised advertising without obtaining consent in advance. Consequently, the interests and fundamental rights of a *Facebook* customer outweighed *Meta's* interest in personalised advertising, with which it finances its business model.[54] Therefore, multi-sided platforms such as "social networks" cannot rely on Art. 6 (1) lit. f GDPR when processing personal data as a source for personalised advertising.

This interpretation by the *Grand Chamber* of the *CJEU* has implications for the DA, too. As a result, Art. 6 (1) lit. f GDPR can be considered as a legal basis if personal data is processed in order to fulfill the user's right to access, use and share data in accordance with Art. 4 (1) and Art. 5 (1) DA. However, according to the case law of the *CJEU*, this legal basis is only applicable if data subjects can *reasonably expect* such processing.[55] Unless the *CJEU* provides further specification of such reasonable expectation, it remains unclear whether Art. 6 (1) lit. f GDPR can be considered as a legal basis, for example, if the data is processed for the purpose of AI training or even just for the purpose of improving the connected product or connected services.

However, if a user is identical to the data subject anyway, the user's request for access, use or sharing can be interpreted as the user's implied consent to the data processing, insofar as is necessary to fulfill the claims under Art. 4 (1) and Art. 5 (1) DA.[56] In this case, Art. 6 (1) lit. f GDPR is only applicable if a user's claim includes data that also concerns other data subjects (multi-relationality).

Yet, the significance of the balancing of interests is severely limited because the processing of *sensitive* personal data is outside the scope of Art. 6 (1) lit. f GDPR.

---

54 CJEU (Grand Chamber), C-252/21, Judgement 4.7.2023, ECLI:EU:C:2023:537 – Meta/Bundeskartellamt, para. 117.

55 *Wiebe*, GRUR 2023, 1569 (1574); *Antoine*, CR 2024, 73 (74/para. 6).

56 *Wiebe*, GRUR 2023, 1569 (1574); *Antoine*, CR 2024, 73 (74/para. 6).

3. Consent to the processing, Art. 6 (1) lit. a / Art. 9 (2) lit. a GDPR

Although the scope of application of Art. 6 (1) lit. b and lit. f GDPR is already narrow due to their restrictive interpretation by the *CJEU*, their importance is further diminished by the fact that both legal bases do not apply to the processing of particularly *sensitive* personal data. Moreover, as a result of the *CJEU's* case law, it is hardly possible to reliably distinguish between personal data and particularly sensitive personal data within the meaning of Art. 9 (1) GDPR.

According to the *Grand Chamber* of the *CJEU* in its ruling on *Meta vs Bundeskartellamt*, Art. 9 (1) GDPR already applies if a data set contains both sensitive personal data and non-sensitive personal data and these data are "collected *en bloc* without it being possible to separate the data items from each other at the time of collection".[57] As a result, any processing of a data set is prohibited if it contains at least one sensitive data element and none of the exceptions in Art. 9 (2) GDPR apply.

Furthermore, according to the *CJEU*, data records do not only contain sensitive data elements if a user of an online network enters data, for example by registering as a customer or placing an online order. Rather, it is sufficient if the websites or apps that the user visits or uses relate to such a category of Art. 9 GDPR.[58] It is also sufficient for the operator of such a website or app to use integrated interfaces, cookies or similar tracking technologies to collect data about the user's website visit and the information entered there by the user that allows conclusions to be drawn about sexual or religious orientation or political opinion.[59] According to the *CJEU*, it is also irrelevant whether the information revealed by the processing is correct or not and whether the data holder is acting with the aim of obtaining such sensitive data.[60]

In addition, the data holder within the meaning of Art. 2 no. 13 DA typically has no influence on whether a user, who is also the data subject, uses a connected product and related service in such a way that (automatically)

57 CJEU (Grand Chamber), C-252/21, Judgement 4.7.2023, ECLI:EU:C:2023:537 – Meta/Bundeskartellamt, para. 89.

58 CJEU (Grand Chamber), Judgement 4.7.2023, Meta/Bundeskartellamt, C-252/21, ECLI:EU:C:2023:537, para. 73.

59 See also: CJEU, Judgement 1.8.2022, Vyriausioji tarnybinės etikos komisij, C-184/20, ECLI:EU:C:2022:601, para. 124–128.

60 CJEU (Grand Chamber), Judgement 4.7.2023, Meta/Bundeskartellamt, C-252/21, ECLI:EU:C:2023:537, para. 69.

generates data that falls under the category of sensitive data. Consequently, the linking of such data to a user's account and the use of such data constitutes processing of sensitive data. As soon as connected products or related services – such as fitness trackers or health apps – generate personal data about physical or physiological functions, the processing of such data is generally prohibited unless one or more of the exceptions provided for in Article 9 (2) GDPR apply. At least in the context of private law, such an exception or legal basis is typically the explicit consent of all data subjects concerned.[61]

As a result of this broad interpretation of particularly sensitive personal data, data holders are well advised to only grant access to data or use data if users can provide explicit consent in relation to the sensitive personal data.

Consequently, the combination of contract (Art. 4 (14) s. 1 DA or Art. 6 (1) s. 1 DA) and explicit consent (Art. 6 (1) lit. a, Art. 9 (2) lit. a GDPR) – in principle – meets the requirements of Art. 4 (1) and Art. 5 (1) DA in a manner that is permissible under data protection law. However, this combination must meet both the complex requirements of Art. 4 and Art. 5 DA and those of Art. 6 (1) lit. a, Art. 7 (3), (4) and Art. 9 (2) lit. a GDPR.

V. Complexity of consent management for multi-relational data

As mentioned above, the tension between Art. 4 and Art. 5 DA and the GDPR stems from the diametrically opposed objectives of the two European legal acts, the difficulty in distinguishing between personal and non-personal data and the difficulty in differentiating between personal and sensitive personal data.[62] Furthermore, and as a consequence of the user-centric approach of the DA, it is unlikely that third parties requiring access to personal data for data-based innovation will target users who are identical to the data subject. Such a small-scale and therefore time-consuming strategy usually leads to prohibitive costs, given the typically low economic value of individual data sets. The hoped-for benefits of data access typically do not justify the necessary effort. Instead, third parties will

61 CJEU (Grand Chamber), Judgement 4.7.2023, Meta/Bundeskartellamt, C-252/21, ECLI:EU:C:2023:537, para. 84. For Art. 9 (2) lit. e GDPR to be applicable, the data subject must have explicitly made the choice beforehand, for example on the basis of individual settings selected with full knowledge of the facts and by hereafter clicking or tapping on those "Like-Buttons" or "Share Buttons".

62 On such difficulties: *Matejek/Kremer*, CR 2023, 318 ss.

turn to professional users such as providers of IoT leasing or rental services (e.g. operators of car leasing pools or car rental companies), who as users – via their rights according to Art. 4 (1) and Art. 5 (1) DA – can grant access to such data sets generated by a large number of connected products and related services.

As such data sets potentially contain (sensitive) personal data of many data subjects, such professional users and their data recipients are usually dependent on the express consent of all data subjects involved. In the case of car leasing, for example, such data subjects can be the vehicle owner, the (main) driver and family members. In the case of a smart home, for example, the data may relate to the owner, the landlord, the (main) tenants, other residents and even guests of the residents.

Both, the obtaining of consents of a large number of data subjects and the subsequently administration of such data, require efficient and effective mechanisms such as data intermediaries and technical solutions. However, Rec. 33 s. 6 DA only contains a weak reference to the fact that "Business-to-business data intermediaries and personal information management systems (PIMS), [...] may support users or third parties in establishing commercial relations with an undetermined number of potential counterparties for any lawful purpose falling within the scope of this Regulation."

It is beyond the scope of this article to analyse all the challenges that such explicit consent and its administration entail. It must therefore suffice to highlight three key points.[63] Overcoming these challenges is a necessary but not sufficient condition for achieving the objectives pursued by the DA as far as personal data is concerned.

63 Additionally, it could be considered whether data subjects have the capacity to temporarily waive their right to withdraw a given consent at any time and without cause under Art. 7 (3) GDPR. Such a right would allow for more stable contractual relationships between data subjects and controllers in general and seems particularly crucial in order to facilitate the right to access and share personal data in real-time. Such an option to waive the right to withdraw consent seems imperative when data subjects act in exercise of their trade, business or profession. However, even data subjects who are consumers should – under additional safeguards – be able to temporarily waive their right to with-draw consent: *Sattler*, Autonomy or Heteronomy – Proposal for a Two-Tier Interpretation of Art. 6 I GDPR, in: Lohsse/Schulze/Staudenmayer (eds.), Data as Counter-Performance – Contract Law 2.0? Münster Colloquia on EU Law and the Digital Economy V, 2020, p. 225 (243 ss); *Sattler*, Informationelle Privatautonomie, 2022, p. 328–356.

1. Voluntariness of consent

It is important that Art. 4 (11) and Art. 7 (4) GDPR are not interpreted as a strict prohibition of linking a contract and a consent. According to the view expressed here and in line with the prevailing view in private law literature, the requirement of *voluntariness* pursuant to Art. 7 (4) GDPR ("freely given") does not establish a prohibition of bundling, but merely requires to take all circumstances of the individual case into account.[64] In other words, Art. 7 (4) GDPR warns the controller *ex ante* and the data protection authorities and courts *ex post* to exercise caution if a controller links the conclusion of a contract to giving a consent, although the performance of the contract does not necessarily require such consent.

This understanding can already be inferred from Rec. 43 S. 1 GDPR, which cites a situation in which there is a structural imbalance between the data subject and the controller ("a public authority") and in which it is therefore – according to the European legislator – unlikely that consent was freely given.

As a result, Art. 7 (4) GDPR requires controllers to separate the contract from the consent and – if these declarations are linked – to examine whether this combination of contract and consent may only be accepted by the data subject because he/she is in a structurally ("imbalance") or situationally ("all circumstances") inferior position *vis-à-vis* the controller. In this case, it may be right to no longer legally recognize the data subject's declaration of consent as a manifestation of autonomy.[65]

With regard to a structural imbalance, the *CJEU* has already stated that the requirements for effective consent "must be interpreted as meaning that the fact that the operator of an online network holds a dominant position on the market for online social networks does not, as such, preclude the users of such a network from being able to validly consent." Instead, even in cases where the operator of such a network has a dominant market position, this fact is only "an important factor in determining whether the consent was in fact validly and, in particular, freely given".[66]

---

64 *Sattler*, Informationelle Privatautonomie, 2022, p. 298–327 ss.

65 With examples for such structural or situational inferiority: *Sattler*, Informationelle Privatautonomie, 2022, p. 298 s.

66 *CJEU* (Grand Chamber), Judgement 4.7.2023, Meta/Bundeskartellamt, C-252/21, ECLI:EU:C:2023:537, para. 154. Contrastingly, suggesting a stricter interpretation of Art. 7 (4) GDPR as regards a consent *vis-à-vis* gatekeepers (Art. 3 DMA): *Sattler*, Informationelle Privatautonomie, 2022, p. 311–316.

While the specific obligations arising from Art. 7 (4) GDPR remain controversial, it is clear that the provision serves to substantiate the material self-determination of data subjects. Art. 7 (4) GDPR thus represents a central pillar for the informational autonomy of data subjects.

2. Informed consent

According to Art. 5 (1) lit. a GDPR data processing is only lawful if it is carried out in a transparent manner. Art. 4 no. 11 GDPR requires that consent must be an informed indication of the data subject's wishes by which the data subject signifies agreement. This is the case if the data subject know that the declaration constitutes consent to specific data processing. The information must enable data subjects to easily determine the consequences of the consent they have given and to assess the impact of their actions. It must be sufficiently detailed to enable data subjects to understand the technical functioning[67] and duration[68] of the data collection and processing.

The requirement for *informed* consent is not only a crucial objective of the GDPR, but moreover, the controller is obliged to provide the data subject with the necessary information before consent is given. However, "being informed" cannot mean that the data subject must be in a certain mental state at the time of consent. Instead, data subjects should be considered informed once they have had reasonable opportunities to inform themselves about the essential characteristics of the data processing and if they are able to intellectually grasp its significance before consenting. The requirement of being informed within the meaning of Art. 4 no. 11 GDPR should therefore be understood as a (only) potential status of an average data subject. However, a status that the data subject can actually achieve with reasonable effort.[69]

As a result, the lack of interest of a data subject in easily accessible and factually correct information is at the expense of the data subject. The controller does not have to bear the risk of explanatory negligence on the part of data subjects.

While data subjects are generally responsible for actually taking note of the accessible information, the controller bears the risk of ensuring that the

67 *CJEU* Judgement 1.10.2019, Planet 49, C-673/17, ECLI:EU:C:2019:801, para. 74.
68 *CJEU* Judgement 1.10.2019, Planet 49, C-673/17, ECLI:EU:C:2019:801, para. 78.
69 *Sattler*, Informationelle Privatautonomie, 2022, p. 219 ss.

content of the essential information is correct, transparent, complete and is made available in such a manner that the average data subject can easily perceive and comprehend it.[70]

As the GDPR takes a risk-based approach, the information duties depend on the risk associated with the particular processing.[71] This is important because the effect of information – as with medicine – depends on the dose (risk of information overload). There is a dilemma between the comprehensibility and completeness of the information. However, multi-tiered and modular consent forms can provide a solution.[72] While the first level enables the data subject to understand the main risks of such data processing, the granularity and complexity of the information is increased at the – easily accessible – higher levels. Such a tiered model will ensure that those data subjects who either have a high data protection preference or who are willing to deal with complex information are adequately informed.

3. Consent for specific purposes

It is obvious that the DA's goal of enabling downstream innovations based on personal data can easily fall over the data protection cliff of purpose limitation. According to Art. 6 (1) lit. a GDPR, the data subject must consent to a processing "for one or more specific purposes". Art. 5 (1) lit. b GDPR stipulates that personal data collected for specified, explicit and legitimate purposes may not be further processed in a way that is incompatible with those purposes (principle of 'purpose limitation'). However, Art. 5 (1) lit. b GDPR provides that further processing for scientific research purposes "shall not be considered to be incompatible with the original purposes".

70 In order to provide the controller with a certain degree of legal certainty, the most important information obligations are specified by the GDPR, although these are not exhaustive. This includes information on the identity of the controller, the purposes of the data processing (Recital 42), the category of data processed (Art. 9 (1) GDPR) and the types of processing, including their use for automated decision-making in accordance with Art. 22 (2) lit. c) GDPR or their transfer to third countries (Art. 49 (1) s. 1 lit. a GDPR). According to Art. 7 (3) s. 3 in conjunction with Art. 13 (2) lit. c GDPR, the controller must also inform the data subjects about the – regularly existing – right of withdrawal.

71 See Art. 35 GDPR.

72 Suggesting a combination of a unitary risk-based labelling similar to a nutrition label and a Privacy Control Cockpit: *Sattler*, Informationelle Privatautonomie, 2022, p. 363 ss./383 ss. (https://www.mohrsiebeck.com/en/book/informationelle-privatautonomie-9783161619069?no_cache=1).

On the basis of this exception, the *German Medical Informatics Initiative* has proposed a "Patient Consent Form Template", which includes information and consent forms for patients and the use of – usually pseudonymised – health data for research purposes.[73] According to Art. 1 (2) of this Template, patient data can be made available to companies conducting medical research for specified scientific research purpose. In addition, such use of health data requires prior review and approval by an independent ethics committee.

While it is not possible to comprehensively analyse and evaluate this proposal in the context of this publication, the Template acknowledges that innovation based on (sensitive) personal data must – by definition – be dynamic and open to the future. It is therefore necessary to find consent mechanisms that leave some leeway for an only subsequent specification of processing purposes. The recognition of broader processing purposes (so-called broad consent) combined with closer supervision can promote data processing for socially desirable purposes. As a result, not every small-scale change of purpose would require a new prior consent by all data subjects. However, even if such a renewal of consent is nevertheless considered necessary for certain specific purposes and to ensure the revocability of consent in accordance with Art. 7 (3) GDPR, this approach, nevertheless, depends on a future technical implementation in the form of PIMS, too.

VI. Conclusion

The fact that the DA also includes personal data in its scope of application in accordance with Art. 1 (2) DA has two decisive advantages.

Firstly, the DA thus proves to be a truly horizontal approach which bridges the difficult and often impossible distinction between personal and non-personal data. *Secondly*, the broad scope of application of the DA emphasises the – often neglected – second purpose of the GDPR, namely to enable the free movement of personal data within the Union (Art. 1 (3) GDPR).

However, the recognition of personal data and even sensitive personal data as a resource for data-based innovation requires a comprehensive

73 Medical Informatics Initiative, Consent Working Group, Patient Consent Form Template, version 1.6d (16.4.2020), English translation (10.11.2020) availble: https://www.medizininformatik-initiative.de/en/template-text-patient-consent-forms.

synchronisation of the DA and the GDPR. Otherwise, the user's rights to access, use and share data will be undermined. The EU legislator has not yet achieved such synchronisation, leaving this crucial task to the judiciary and thus eventually to the CJEU.

When natural persons use connected products and related services, personal data is typically generated. The (actual) behavior of data subjects also determine whether particularly sensitive personal data is generated. Consequently, the controller (data holder/user/data recipient) should always assume that the automatically generated data contains a "mixed set" of data typically including personal as well as particularly sensitive personal data. However, because the DA itself does not introduce any legal basis for the processing of such sensitive personal data, the interpretation and application of the GDPR's requirements for valid consent will ultimately determine the fate of the DA.

As the user's rights to access, use and share data under Art. 4 (1) and Art. 5 (1) DA are typically dependent on complex cascades of consents involving a large number of data subjects, a successful synchronisation of the GDPR and the DA will require efficient and effective consent management systems to be developed and implemented throughout the European Union.

The value of consumer data: a common law perspective

*Christian Twigg-Flesner**

I. Introduction

The task for this paper is to explore how the common law (in this case, the English common law) deals with both determining the value of consumer data and how a consumer can unlock the value of that data, or indeed establish the value of such data in a variety of different situations. For instance, consumers can agree to provide access to their data, personal or otherwise, to a business as a form of consideration or counter-performance for access to digital content. But there might be instances when a consumer provides data or agrees to provide data to a business and circumstances where the business's intentions were misrepresented to the consumer. In those circumstances, the contract itself might be open to challenge, but a consumer will struggle to assert the damages that could be recovered because of the misbehaviour by the business. It is also possible that a business may have obtained data from a consumer under a contract which subsequently fails.[1] This raises questions about the potential application of principles of unjust enrichment or restitution to the value which might have been extracted by the business from that data that was provided, until perhaps the legal basis for providing data was successfully challenged.

Why a "common law perspective"?

This paper takes a common law perspective, more precisely, an English common law perspective. Unlike other European common law jurisdictions, the United Kingdom, of which England is one constituent jurisdiction, has not been a member of the European Union since the end of

* Professor of Contract and Consumer Law, University of Warwick. Email: c.twigg-flesner@warwick.ac.uk.

1 Cf *Rotam Agrochemical Co Ltd v GAT Microencapsulation GmbH* [2018] EWHC 2765 (Comm) (unjust enrichment claim where data access agreement was not concluded).

January 2020. As a result, the UK's legal landscape of both consumer law and data law is already diverging considerably from that in the EU. This has mostly been the consequence of the political approach to the implementation of the UK's withdrawal from the EU, and the last Conservative government's ideological position regarding the EU.[2] As a result, there are increasing gaps emerging as far as the governance and regulation of the digital economy is concerned, and there have been limited efforts thus far to catch-up on developing a clear legal regime for the digital and data economy. The UK effectively stopped implementing EU consumer law directives as long ago as 2017,[3] as soon as notice of its intention to withdraw had been given, and that has created a number of gaps. For instance, the UK did not implement the provisions of the Digital Content Directive (2019/770/EU), nor does it apply the Digital Services Act (Regulation (EU) 2022/65), the Data Governance Act (Regulation (EU) 2022/868), let alone the new Data Act (Regulation (EU) 2023/2854). Immediately before Parliament was dissolved for the 2024 General Election, the Digital Markets, Competition and Consumers Act 2024 ("DMCC") was adopted, which includes some aspects of what the EU addressed in its Digital Markets Act (Regulation (EU) 2022/1925), although the DMCC is much more of a collection of a variety of digital, competition and consumer law aspects. Against this background, this paper seeks to offer an English law perspective on how "trading" in data, particularly consumers trading in "their" data, might work.

The economic value of data in a consumer context first became a key issue during the legislative process towards the DCD, with data initially treated as a non-monetary counter-performance.[4] Although this approach was toned-down during the legislative process, there is still recognition that the provision of data by consumers is an integral feature of many contracts for the supply of digital content or digital services, particularly in the absence of monetary consideration. The UK was ahead of the EU in adopting legislation on contracts for the supply of digital content when in introduced rules on conformity and remedies in chapter 3 of part 1 of the

---

2 One need not adduce evidence beyond pointing to the news archives from recent years, which reveal the past Conservative governments pro-Brexit and anti-EU position.

3 With the exception of measures that had to be implemented before the UK's withdrawal date.

4 C. Langhanke and M. Schmidt-Kessel, "Consumer Data as Consideration" (2015) 4 *Journal of European Consumer and Markets Law (EuCML)* 218.

Consumer Rights Act 2015 ("CRA").[5] However, the CRA explicitly restricted those rights to instances where a consumer has paid money for digital content[6] and therefore excluded contracts where the "consideration" is only the supply of data or permitting the collection of data. There is provision in the CRA to extend the scope of chapter 3 by secondary legislation, but this power has not yet been utilised.[7]

The UK's provisions on digital content very closely follow those that were already in place in respect of goods, and so the CRA is not particularly innovative, beyond the recognition that contracts involving the supply of digital content are distinct from contracts for the sale and supply of goods, or contracts for the supply of services. Notably, the CRA does not include any provisions concerning updates of digital content, nor does it recognise digital services in the way the DCD does.

Although the UK has been much slower than the EU in developing its digital law and is equally slow in recognising the potential of the data economy, particularly from a consumer perspective, both the Online Safety Act 2023 and the DMCC 2024 are key elements of the emerging UK Digital Law.

In the field of data law, developments have been slower. The previous government had promoted a Data Protection and Digital Information Bill ("DPDI"), which had made considerable progress through Parliament but was lost when the General Election was called at the end of May 2024. The incoming Labour government proposed a new Digital Information and Smart Data Bill in the King's Speech on 17 July 2024. Interestingly, the Labour Party's manifesto[8] did not contain any specific proposals on data-related measures. The Data (Use and Access) Bill was introduced into Parliament in October 2024, and the the Data (Use and Access) Act 2025 received Royal Assent on 19 June 2025.

---

5 Cf. C. Twigg-Flesner and R. Canavan, *Atiyah and Adams' Sale of Goods*, 14th ed. (Pearson, 2020), pp.492 – 497.

6 Section 33(1) CRA 2015.

7 Section 33(5) CRA 2015.

8 Labour Party, *Change* (2024). Available from https://labour.org.uk/change/ [accessed 12 July 2024].

II. The status of data in English Law

In the absence of specific legislation on access to data, let alone a data economy, it is necessary to consider how the common law has treated data so far, and also whether, and how, trading in both personal and non-personal data is possible in English law.

In essence, the general position at common law is that there cannot be property as such in information, and as data is a form of information, the assumption is that there cannot be property in data at common law. This conclusion has to be pieced together from cases dealing with specific doctrines that rely on a form of proprietary interest (either outright property (i.e., ownership) or possession). This is a distinct feature of the common law, where, in the absence of legislation, particular positions have to be deduced or extrapolated from decisions in individual cases.

Several cases display the unwillingness of the courts to recognise the increased significance of intangibles for the development of the law. One such instance was the the ruling by what was then the House of Lords (now the Supreme Court) in *OBG v Allan.*[9] This was an appeal dealing with three separate cases which raised similar issues, on of which concerned the so-called economic Torts and the question whether it is possible for the Tort of Conversion to apply to the conversion (i.e., misappropriation) of contractual rights. The salient facts were that a receiver had taken over the running of a company in financial difficulties and sought to modify or terminate some of the contracts entered into by that company. The question arose whether this constituted the conversion of the contractual rights and therefore a tort. The House of Lords, by a majority, concluded that it did not, mainly because the tort of conversion had developed historically in relation to chattels, i.e., tangible property, and therefore the tort of conversion could not be applied to so-called choses in action, i.e., intangible personal rights. In denying the extension of the tort of conversion to intangibles, the court seemed to set a general view that the changing significance of intangibles in a commercial context did not justify changes to the common law, with any developments in the law a matter for Parliament.[10]

9 [2007] UKHL 21

10 See e.g. Lord Walker at para 271: "This [conversion] is an area in which reform must come from Parliament...".

Related to the issue in *OBG v Allan*, the Court of Appeal in *Your Response Ltd v Datateam*,[11] rejected an argument that a lien could exist over a database. A lien is a right which a person in possession of another's asset has in order to secure the payment of money owed.[12] The asset has to be capable of (physical) possession, and the functionally equivalent notion of "control", which could be applied to intangible assets such as a database, was not regarded as sufficient. Floyd LJ observed that

> "[42] ... Although information may give rise to intellectual property rights ... the law has been reluctant to treat information itself as property. When information is created and recorded, there are sharp distinctions between the information itself, the physical medium on which the information is recorded and the rights to which that information gives rise. *Whilst the physical medium and the rights are treated as property*, the information itself has never been..."

From this, it is clear that there may be instances when information triggers intellectual property rights but beyond this, the common law has been reluctant to treat information itself as property. As data is a form of information, then, if information is not treated as property, data cannot be subject to property rights either. However, Floyd LJ *does* note, in passing, that information can give rise to other rights (referring, in particular, to intellectual property rights), and that those rights can be treated as a form of intangible property. Similarly, in *Oakley v Information Commissioner*, David Richards J noted that "Ownership of data may be a complex subject, but it cannot be doubted that intellectual property rights in respect of the relevant data were vested in the company ... Those property rights *and all rights to control the data* remained vested in the company".[13] So property rights in data can arise in two ways: directly as an intellectual property right, and indirectly through the rights to control the data, i.e., access to the data.

In *Computer Associates v Software Incubator*,[14] the distinction between tangibles and intangibles was applied in concluding that software did not constitute goods within the meaning of Regulation 2(1) the Commercial

11 [2014] EWCA Civ 281.

12 *Tappenden (t/a English & American Autos) v Artus* [1964] 2 Q.B. 185.

13 *Oakley Smith v Information Officer* [2013] EWHC 2485 (Ch), para [34], emphasis added.

14 [2018] EWCA Civ 518.

Agents (Council Directive) Regulations 1993,[15] although the Court of Appeal's reasoning in this case must now be treated as having been rejected by the Supreme Court, despite the lack of a substantive judgment.[16] This is slightly disappointing because the Court of Appeal had offered detailed reasoning on this point and the Supreme Court missed an opportunity to provide clarity about the treatment of intangibles such as digital content by the common law more generally. Although *Computer* Associates was, strictly speaking, a case concerned with statutory interpretation and was dealt with accordingly, the limited opportunity afforded to the common law courts to develop the law in line with new business practices, such as aligning the law with the changes in the digital environment does mean that not taking up an opportunity to offer at least *obiter dicta* on these issues creates a real block in the development of the common law. This also raises questions for the development of the law for related issues; for instance, the Law Commission recently proposed a very short draft Bill to facilitate the common law's ability to address legal issues associated with digital assets.[17] This was implemented, and any further development of the law will be for the common law courts (Property (Digital Assets etc) Act 2025).

The position at common law therefore is that there are no property rights in data as such;[18] however, data, as a form of digital information, does give rise to other rights which are regarded as property rights. Some of these are covered by intellectual property laws and constitute a distinct set of property rights,[19] but other rights cover the rights over data which can be described as *control rights.* In the case of personal data, these control

15 The Supreme Court subsequently referred a question on the interpretation of the Commercial Agents Directive (86/653/EEC) to the CJEU, which held that software *did* qualify as goods for the purposes of the Directive: Case C-410/19 *The Software Incubator Ltd v Computer Associates (UK) Ltd* ECLI:EU:C:2021:742.

16 The Supreme Court subsequently gave effect to the CJEU's ruling by a procedural order rather than a full reasoned judgment which effectively dismissed the earlier appeal to the Court of Appeal and reinstated the High Court's ruling that software did qualify as goods.

17 Law Commission, *Digital assets as personal property – short consultation on draft clauses* (February 2024). The proposed clause of the Bill states that "A thing (including a thing that is digital in nature) is capable of being an object of personal property rights even though it is neither— (a) a thing in possession, nor (b) a thing in action." This would seek to displace the common assumption that English personal property law only recognises two categories of personal property, neither of which would seem to cover digital assets.

18 See also *DRSP Holdings Ltd v O'Connor* [2021] EWHC 626 (Ch), para [229].

19 Cf. *Oakley Smith v Information Officer* [2013] EWHC 2485 (Ch), para [34].

rights *de facto* flow from the requirements for lawful data processing under UK-GDPR, often requiring consent to processing by the data subject. In the case of non-personal data, it can be the simple fact that a person has legal or practical controls over who can access data.

III. The Economic Value of Data: Contracts and Consideration

The control rights over data referred to above can be used for contracting, both as a distinct subject-matter of a contract (e.g., by assigning a right[20]) and as a form of value that can constitute a counter-performance, or consideration, for digital content etc provided in return.

English contract law does not require equivalence of value in the consideration provided by the parties to a contract, as long as what each party provides has some, even if very small, economic value.[21] Thus, even if the economic value attached to individual data is minute, it is value nonetheless and sufficient to constitute "good" consideration – not dissimilar to the infamous wrappers from consumed chocolate bars.[22] The real value is unlocked by having lots of data accumulated and processed, but that does not mean that there is no value in the data an individual consumer controls and grants access to. A consumer has the right to control access to data especially personal data, and each consumer can decide to whom to grant access and what is required in return. In short, consumers have the right to commercially exploit access to "their" data, whether that is data produced by or saved on devices they own, or personal data collected in other ways.

Interestingly, if the agreement between a consumer and a business for granting access to data contains limitations or restrictions on what can be collected or processed, and those restrictions are breached subsequently, then this raises the question whether a consumer would be entitled to compensation. The non-rivalrous nature of data might make it difficult to

---

20 For an effective *legal* assignment, the requirements of s.136 of the Law of Property Act 1925 must be satisfied (in writing, signed by assignor, and notice given to the other party (e.g., a contracting party))

21 *Thomas v Thomas* (1842) 2 QB 851 ("something of some value in the eyes of the law"); *Currie v Misa* (1875) LR 10 Exch 153("valuable consideration, in the sense of the law, may consist either in some right, interest, profit or benefit accruing to one party or some forbearance, detriment loss or responsibility, given, suffered or undertaken by the other", p.162).

22 *Chappell & Co Ltd v Nestle Co Ltd* [1960] AC 87.

establish that a consumer has suffered a loss as such, but even in the absence of loss, the common law recognises that in some instances, damages may be awarded as so-called "negotiation damages",[23] if it is accepted that the consumer's right in respect of the data is regarded as a "valuable asset" protected by the consumer's contractual rights.[24]

In short, it is possible for consumers to enter into contracts for data, but crucially, the subject-matter of such a contract is not the data itself but a right of access to the data.

IV. The Regulatory Context

Although the UK does not have the equivalent of the EU's data laws, there are some elements corresponding to EU law in place. Although the UK has left the EU, it has retained a version of the GDPR, supported by the Data Protection Act 2018. This "UK-GDPR"[25] is substantively the same substantively as the GDPR. At the moment of the UK's withdrawal from the EU, much of EU and EU-derived legislation and case-law were made part of UK domestic law under the European Union (Withdrawal) Act 2018. Initially categorised as different forms of "retained EU Law" under the 2018 Act, it is now referred to as "assimilated law", following the changes made by the Retained EU Law (Revocation and Reform) Act 2023. In domestic law, the UK-GDPR is one such instance of assimilated law. Whilst it has been amended by the UK Parliament, the UK-GDPR essentially does the same thing as EU's GDPR. Several changes were made to some of the UK-GDPR's requirements by part 5, chapter 1 of the Data (Use and Access) Act 2025.

Readers will be broadly familiar with the requirements and limitations of the GDPR[26] that permit the lawful processing of personal data. In particular, consent by the data subject remains key in many instances (although

23 *Morris-Garner v One Step (Support) Ltd* [2018] UKSC 20.

24 *Ibid.*, [95]).

25 Section 3(10) of the Data Protection Act 2018 defines this as "Regulation (EU) 2016/679 of the European Parliament and of the Council of 27 April 2016 on the protection of natural persons with regard to the processing of personal data and on the free movement of such data (United Kingdom General Data Protection Regulation), as it forms part of the law of England and Wales, Scotland and Northern Ireland by virtue of section 3 of the European Union (Withdrawal) Act 2018."

26 Article 6, GDPR/UK-GDPR.

some of the very large digital corporations increasingly argue that they have a legitimate interest in processing personal data, lack of consent notwithstanding), although is not always required, nor always sufficient.[27] These requirements seem to have the effect of granting the data subject some measure of control over who can access, collect and process personal data about them. Although not expressed in the UK-GDPR as "control rights" or similar,[28] one can treat the requirement of consent as such a right in all but name; consequently, a decision to exercise this right to get something in return is a means of unlocking, in a loose sense, the value inherent in that data. For instance, giving consent to the processing of personal data in return for the provision of digital content would be recognised as a sufficient form of consideration, and would consequently result in a legally binding contract.

In addition to the UK-GDPR, there are also the Privacy and Electronic Communications Regulations 2003,[29] which are the UK's implementation of the e-privacy Directive[30] (also known as the "cookie law"). In regulation 6(1), there is a requirement that a person – which could be a business, including a business active in the Internet of Things – must not gain access to information stored in the terminal equipment of a subscriber or user. "Terminal equipment" is equipment that is connected to an electronic communications network, such as the internet. The guidance published by the UK Information Commissioner makes it clear that this is "can also cover other types of technology, including apps on smartphones, tablets, smart TVs or other devices".[31] Therefore, an IOT device would be covered.

The Regulations impose a restriction on accessing information stored on such equipment. It is not expressed to be restricted to personal data, so must extend also to non-personal data (bearing in mind that the UK-GDPR's requirements in respect of personal data continue to apply in any case). Any information stored on the IOT device cannot be transmitted for

---

27 *Lloyd v Google LLC* [2021] UKSC 50, per Lord Leggatt JSC at [109].

28 Cf. Lord Leggatt JSC in *Lloyd v Google LLC* [2021] UKSC 50: "...none of the requirements of the [Data Protection Act 1998] is predicated on "control" over personal data by the data subject..." (at [109]).

29 S.I. 2003/2426.

30 Directive 2002/58/EC concerning the processing of personal data and the protection of privacy in the electronic communications sector (2002) OJ L201/37, as amended.

31 Information Commissioner, *Guide to Privacy and Electronic Communications Regulations* (no date). Available at https://ico.org.uk/for-organisations/direct-marketing-and-privacy-and-electronic-communications/guide-to-pecr/ [last accessed 12 July 2024].

processing unless the requirements of the Regulations have been complied with. This includes the provision of clear and comprehensive information about why access to the information is required. Furthermore, it is necessary for the customer the consumer to give consent; in the case of personal data, this must be given in the same manner as is required under Article 7 of the UK-GDPR, although Reg.6(3A) also states that consent can be given by setting or amending browser controls or settings in another application or programme which signify consent.

The key point is that any utilisation of data produced by IOT-connected devices requires consent provided by the user before this can be done. The right to require consent, or to refuse to give consent, is also the kind of right that is treated as a property right and can be exercised in return for valuable consideration.

V. The Data (Use and Access Act 2025)

The previous Conservative government, which lost the 2024 General Election, had put a Bill before Parliament, the Data Protection and Digital Information Bill, that would have made changes to the UK's data protection regime and would, additionally, have introduced new provisions regarding access to customer and business data (essentially personal and transactions data to replace shorter enabling provisions in ss.89 – 91 of the Enterprise and Regulatory Reform Act 2013.[32] Althoguh the Bill was lost due to the election, a revised Bill was introduced by the new Labour government and is now the Data (Use and Access) Act 2025. Part 1 of the Act implements earlier proposals concerning so-called "smart data schemes".[33] A typical example of such a smart data scheme is a digital service that would enable consumers to switch from their current suppliers of utilities or Telecom services or banking services to a different supplier through a simple automated process. The underlying desire was to make it easier for consumers to switch suppliers. Another type of smart data scheme as bank account management services where one digital banking application could manage all the accounts held by a consumer even if they're held by different banks. Section 2 of the Data (Use and Access) Act 2025 has introduced enabling powers for access to customer and business data, rather than doing so

32 No Regulations were adopted on the basis of these earlier powers.

33 Department for Business & Trade, *The Smart Data Roadmap* (April 2024).

through directly applicable provisions. The relevant Secretary of State has been empowered to develop secondary legislation to implement these smart data schemes. Nevertheless, Part 1 has set detailed constraints on the scope of the Secretary's powers, including matters that would have been required to be addressed in secondary legislation, with other matters being recommended.[34] It might be of interest to highlight some features that could be introduced. Thus, the legislation deals with access to "customer data". This is defined as information relating to a customer (which could be a consumer, but also some businesses) of a trader, including information about the goods, services or digital content supplied or provided by the trader to its customers (or to another person at customer's request); the prices or other terms on which these goods, services or digital content were supplied; how the goods, services or digital content are used by customer, and their performance or quality when used by customer.[35] At least some of this information will be of the kind that is collected and stored on devices, such as IoT devices; in particular, information about the performance or quality of goods or digital content when used by a customer is likely to be data supplied by the device or digital content to the trader.

The provision of customer data enabled by the Data (Use and Access) Act 2025 include providing access to customer data or ability to provide other persons with access to such data, i.e., the ability to collect and process such data.

A so-called "data holder", defined as a person who processes customer data,[36] will be subject to regulations that will require the data holder to provide the customer data to the customer themselves or to somebody the customer has authorised. The fact that such data could be provided to another person authorised by the customer allows for the sharing of such data. For example, a customer could instruct a data holder such as a bank to transfer account information to another bank. Furthermore, the Act allows an person, i.e., a person who holds data for another customer, to have taken whatever action the customer could themselves have taken.[37] For example, if a customer wanted to switch one of their suppliers, then another person who has been given information about the customer could then take the legal steps necessary to make this switch, i.e., that person

34 Sections 2-7, Data (Use and Access) Act 2025.
35 Section 1(2), Data (Use and Access) Act 2025.
36 *Ibid.*
37 Section 2(4), Data (Use and Access) Act 2025.

could take the steps to terminate the contract with the original supplier and then conclude a new contract with another supplier for the customer. The Act includes other provisions relevant to the supplier of customer data; however, all of this is subject to the overriding requirement that none of the data regulations adopted under Part 1 of the Act could have authorised or required the processing of personal data where this would contravene data protection legislation.[38]

Although it has only just come into force, it is nevertheless worth noting the Data (Use and Access) Act as one example of a UK measure with the objective, at least in part, to unlock the value of customer data by allowing customers to get better goods and services. Unlike the EU's Data Act, which is primarily concerned with unlocking the value of IoT-generated data and therefore the direct value inherent in such data, the UK's Data (Use and Access) Act focuses on the indirect value that would be unlocked by utilising customer data to get easier access to different suppliers, promote market competition and therefore competitive prices. Here, it is not the value of the data itself that is the primary focus, but rather the ability to use that data to get better value in the provision of goods, services and digital content. It is worth bearing in mind that earlier, less detailed, powers to make secondary legislation on customer data under the Enterprise and Regulatory Reform Act 2023 were never used. The powers in the Data (Use and Access) Act 2025 are more extensive. It will therefore be very interesting to see how the Act will be implemented through secondary legislation, and the practical effects this will have.

VI. The primacy of contracts

Beyond the UK-GDPR, the Data (Use and Access) Act 2025 and the supporting provisions of the Data Protection Act, the ability of consumers to unlock the value of their data will come down to individual contracts, i.e., agreements by consumers to use the control rights, i.e., their consent rights, as something they can exercise in favour of a business in return for appropriate payment.[39] Whilst in the case of personal data, such contracts will be subject to the relevant data protection legislation, there is hardly

38 Section 20, Data (Use and Access) Act 2025.

39 Cf. *Rotam Agrochemical Co Ltd v GAT Microencapsulation GmbH* [2018] EWHC 2765 (Comm).

any relevant legislation in place that deals with non-personal data, and therefore the terms of such contracts will govern the basis for granting access to data and therefore realising the value inherent in such data.

Unfair Terms and Consumer Data Access Agreements

From a consumer's perspective, this invariably leads to concerns over the use of standard terms in a contract with a supplier that would default to granting the supplier broad rights of access to non-personal data generated by goods or digital content. One might expect suppliers to grant themselves unlimited and exclusive rights to such data, and to preclude consumers from granting access to the data to a third-party. This would amount to the supplier securing the functional equivalent of ownership over such data. However, such terms would at the very least be open to challenge under Part 2 of the Consumer Rights Act 2015, which contains the UK's version of the unfair contract terms regime in the EU's Unfair Terms in Consumer Contracts Directive (93/13/EEC). Thus, any such term would fail the fairness test if "contrary to the requirement of good faith, it causes a significant imbalance in the parties' rights and obligations to the detriment of the consumer".[40] At present, the application of this test follows the same broad approach as developed by the CJEU,[41] i.e., a court would ask whether a consumer would have agreed to the relevant term in individual negotiations, and whether the term alters the default legal position of a consumer in a manner that overall results in a weaker position of the consumer under the contract. To answer the latter question, one might need to consider what the default position would be in the absence of any contractual terms regarding access to data. For example, assume a consumer has bought a smart product which is connected to the internet. The device collects various types of data, and access to any non-personal data is required to be granted fully and exclusively to the manufacturer of the product. The contract under which the consumer acquired the smart product is likely to be a contract of sale, which would mean that ownership of the product has transferred to the consumer. Anything which is subsequently done with the product, including any data collected, would, presumably, belong to

40 Section 62(4) CRA 2015.

41 C-415/11 *Aziz v Caixa d'Estalvis de Catalunya, Tarragona i Manresa* ECLI:EU:C:2013:164; see *ParkingEye v Beavis* [2015] UKSC 67, paras [105] and [204].

the consumer in the first instance. Although the analogy is not altogether neat, one might draw a parallel with raw materials used to make a finished product: where such raw materials are supplied under reservation of title clauses,[42] ownership in the raw material might stay with the supplier[43] but once the manufacturing process has started, the raw material ceases to be the supplier's and is presumed to belong to the buyer.[44] One might similarly argue that once data is generated and collected during the use of the smart product by the consumer, such data is presumed to be governed by the consumer's control rights, and the default position is that a consumer has the right to determine to whom to grant access. If that is the case, then a default term in a contract, such as the licence agreement for activating the smart features, might be regarded as creating a "significant imbalance to the detriment of a consumer". Furthermore, the question of whether a consumer would have agreed to such a term in contract negotiations is likely to be met with a negative answer. There is a strong argument that such a term would not be fair under s.62 CRA, and therefore not be binding on a consumer.

Contract Classification

A further difficulty is that the legal classification of a contract under which access to data is granted is unclear. If this were a business-to-consumer contract under which the business supplied data (i.e., digital content) to a consumer, then it would be a contract for the supply of digital content and thus be within the Consumer Rights Act 2015. However, the reverse situation is not covered by the Act, and both the respective obligations of the parties and the legal effects of such an arrangement would not be covered by existing statutory rules. Here, the common law would have to step in and develop relevant background, or default rules, by analogy as cases arise. The common law can recognise new, *sui generis*, contract types when the circumstance so require.[45] If it became necessary to do that for contracts for granting access to data, i.e., contracts involving a (partial)

42 *Aluminium Industrie Vaasen B.V. v Romalpa Aluminium Ltd.* [1976] 1 WLR 676.
43 *Clough Mill Ltd. v Geoffrey Martin* [1985] 1 WLR 111.
44 *Re Bond Worth Ltd.* [1979] 3 WLR 679; *Re Peachdart Ltd.* [1984] Ch 131.
45 E.g., *PST Energy 7 Shipping LLC v O W Bunker Malta Ltd* [2016] UKSC 23.

allocation of rights over data, to be classified in law, the common law could designate such contracts as a new *sui generis* category.[46]

It is important to recall that whilst the *contractual* aspects of such arrangements would have to await development at common law in the absence of action by Parliament to put in place relevant legislation to govern such contracts, such contracts would not operate in a legal vacuum. As well as the unfair terms controls under the Consumer Rights Act 2015, there would be the various rights in respect of personal data under the UK-GDPR and the Data Protection Act 2018, as well as the more specific rights under the Privacy and Electronic Communications Regulations 2013. Nevertheless, the overall legal framework in the UK with regard to data access and data sharing is rather more threadbare than EU Law, and this could ultimately work to the detriment of consumers seeking to unlock the full value of their personal data and the data produced by devices they own and digital content they are entitled to use.

Earlier, it was noted that a business which has accessed and processed consumer data in a way that exceeded any contractual agreement might be liable to compensate a consumer through negotiation damages. However, this remains untested at present. Similarly, a consumer's right to compensation in other contexts is, as yet, untested before the courts. For example, assume a consumer was persuaded to agree to grant access to data on the basis of misleading information given by a business. Under current law, this would likely constitute a misleading action under section 226 of the Digital Markets, Competition and Consumers Act 2024.[47] In those circumstances, a consumer would have a right to redress under Part 4A of the CPUTR if the contract was one for the sale or supply of goods by the trader, or a contract for the sale of goods to the trader. Obviously, a contract granting access to data is neither, so current consumer law would not help. Instead, a consumer would have to fall back to the common law, and the doctrine of misrepresentation in particular. The information given by the business would have to constitute a false statement of fact[48] that induced

46 E.g., a "data access contract" (cf *Rotam Agrochemical Co Ltd v GAT Microencapsulation GmbH* [2018] EWHC 2765 (Comm) concerning a data access agreement).

47 The DMCC 2024 replaced most of the provisions of the 2008 Regulations. However, the private right of redress is subject to further implementation requiring secondary legislation.

48 *Esso Petroleum v Mardon* [1976] QB 801; *Spice Girls Ltd v Aprilia World Service BV* [2002] EWCA Civ 15

the consumer to enter into the contract.[49] The consumer could rescind the contract, which would require the trader either to return what was provided by the consumer under the contract, or to pay the corresponding value instead.[50] However, this would require a court to assess the value of any data provided, but that is the challenge that remains to be addressed – how does one value data? Alternatively, a consumer could seek damages, but that would require quantifying the losses suffered as a result of the misrepresentation – which raises similar challenges. Until a court has to grapple with the question of how it should approach the valuation of data, or rather the rights to which data gives rise, this question will remain unresolved.

Little assistance is available in the context of rights to compensation for material or non-material damage suffered as a result of a breach of any of the provisions of the UK-GDPR.[51] In the same way that a common law claim for damages requires establishing and quantifying the losses suffered, a claimant under the UK-GDPR would have to establish and quantify the damage suffered (except where the claim is limited to one for non-material damage, i.e., distress).[52] Often, this will be an almost impossible task, with an exception being an instance of misappropriation of data, whether personal or non-personal, directly leading to clearly identifiable and measurable losses. In other instances, the recurring and seemingly intractable question will be how one values consumer data.

VII. Conclusion

This paper has provided a sketch of the UK's legal rules on the data economy, to the extent that they exist. It is clear that, unlike in the EU, there is no detailed data law in place. However, that of itself need not be seen as problematic; rather, what matters is whether the law can already provide solutions to common obstacles for consumers seeking to get the most value out of "their data", and, to the extent that it does not, whether it has the ability to develop such rules. In the absence of legislation, it

49 *Museprime Properties Ltd v Adhill Properties Ltd* (1991) 61 P & C R 111; *BV Nederlandse Industrie van Eirprodukten v Rembrandt Enterprises Inc.* [2019] EWCA Civ 596.

50 *Salt v Stratstone Specialist Ltd* [2015] EWCA Civ 745.

51 Article 82. See *William Stadler v Currys Group Ltd* [2022] EWHC 160 (QB).

52 Cf. *Lloyd v Google LLC* [2021] UKSC 50.

will fall to the common law to step up and provide those solutions. At the moment, there is relatively little to go on beyond the rules and principles of general contract law, supplemented by consumer legislation. Whilst this provides a baseline, it might not be enough to kickstart the consumer data economy and allow for the value of consumer data to be realised. Ultimately, Parliament might have to act, but whether it would need to do so on a scale comparable to what has already happened at EU level remains to be seen – although recently EU legislation appears comprehensive, it is largely untested and still must prove itself.

II.
The “Monetisation” of Consumer Data

Judicial Price Reviews and Fixing of Fair Prices by Judges: From *Iustum Pretium* to Modern Regulation of Data

Hans Schulte-Nölke

It is one of the fundamental beliefs of a market economy that prices are formed by supply and demand, and often also by individual negotiations between contracting parties. One consequence of this principle is that courts normally enforce contracts that have been validly concluded without checking the fairness of the price or even correcting it by a price that the court considers more appropriate. However, this principle has exceptions in which the appropriateness or at least the level of the price does play a role in the judicial enforcement of contractual claims.

The purpose of the following lines is to take a closer look at some examples from legal history and current law that deal with the judicial review or modification of prices. In particular, it will be about how such exceptional cases of price reviews are justified and by what means courts attempt to solve the seemingly impossible task of determining an appropriate or fair price, or at least of assessing whether a price is unfair. It will be seen that, due to certain developments in EU law, there has been an increase in cases in which courts have been given the task of reviewing or even setting prices. This is due, in particular, to new requirements for contracts that have only recently been developed in areas of law such as competition and data law, which are described by the abbreviation FRAND (standing for: 'Fair, Reasonable And Non-Discriminatory').

By looking at these examples, this paper sketches the historical evolution of judicial price reviews and examines their legal foundations, the emergence and decline of specific doctrines, and the countervailing forces that have shaped contemporary price regulation. It particularly focuses on the transition from traditional concepts like '*laesio enormis*' and '*iustum pretium*' to modern interpretations of judicial price review in the context of broad economic changes.

At the end of this article, an attempt will be made to formulate tentative overarching findings on judicial price review and thus shed some light on the relationship between market and state, with a particular focus on the role of civil courts.

I. From late antique price reviews to natural law codifications

The history of judicial price reviews is primarily the history of the so-called '*laesio enormis*'. It has been the subject of rather extensive research[1] and can be summarised quite succinctly for the purposes of this article.

The most important sources on *laesio enormis* date from late antiquity. These are two passages from the *Codex Iustinianus* (C. 4, 44, 2 and C. 4, 44, 8), which probably go back to two rescripts of the Roman Emperor Diocletian from 285 and 293.[2] The purpose of these rescripts was probably to protect small farmers who had fallen into hardship due to high taxes and inflation and were forced to sell their land for too low a price to land buyers who were exploiting their plight.[3] According to these rescripts, a seller of land who had not even received half the value of his property could have annulled the purchase contract on the grounds of excessive exploitation or, alternatively, demand the difference between the purchase price and the usual price (*iustum pretium*).[4]

---

1 See only Boudewijn Sirks, Laesio enormis again, Revue Internationale des droits de l'Antiquité 54 (2007), pp. 461 et seq.; Andreas Wacke, Circumscribere, gerechter Preis und die Arten der List, Zeitschrift der Savigny-Stiftung für Rechtsgeschichte, Romanistische Abteilung 94 (1977), pp. 184 et seq.; Reinhard Zimmermann, The Law of Obligations, 1996, pp. 255 et seq.; Herbert Kalb, Laesio enormis im gelehrten Recht, 1992; Hein Kötz, Europäisches Vertragsrecht, Vol. I, 1996, pp. 198 et seq.; Christoph Becker, Abweichen vom Marktpreis, Zeitschrift für Europäisches Privatrecht 1997, pp. 475 et seq.; Martin Pennitz, Zur Anfechtung wegen laesio enormis im römischen Recht, in: Festschrift für Theo Mayer-Maly, 2002, pp. 575 et seq.; Doris Regine Göttlicher, Die Suche nach dem gerechten Preis, 2004.

2 Jan Dirk Harke, Iuris prudentia Diocletiana, Kaiserliche Rechtsprechung am Ende des 3. Jahrhunderts, 2019, pp. 179–186; Martin Pennitz, Zur Anfechtung wegen laesio enormis im römischen Recht, in Martin Schermaier (ed.), Iurisprudentia universalis, Festschrift für Theo Mayer-Maly zum 70. Geburtstag, 2002, pp. 575–589; Wolfgang Kaiser, Der Index des Thalelaios zu C. 4,44,15 und die laesio enormis, Zeitschrift der Savigny-Stiftung für Rechtsgeschichte (Romanistische Abteilung). 141 (2024), pp. 349–429; Otto Gradenwitz, Interpolazioni e interpretationi, Bulletino dell'instituto di diritto romano 2 (1889), pp. 3–15 (assumes a possible interpolation of the sources).

3 Henry Monnier, Études de droit byzantin: XIV La lésion de plus de moitié dans la vente, Nouvelle revue historique de droit français et étranger 24 (1900), pp. 181–182; Karl Hackl, Zu den Wurzeln der Anfechtung wegen laesio enormis, Zeitschrift der Savigny-Stiftung für Rechtsgeschichte, Romanistische Abteilung 98 (1981), pp. 147–161 (pp. 160–161); Wim Decock, Theologians and Contrat Law. The moral Transformation of the Ius commune (ca. 1500–1650), 2013.

4 Boudewijn Sirks, La laesio enormis en droit romain et byzanzin, Tijdschrift voor Rechtsgeschiedenis / Legal History Review 53 (1985), pp. 291–307 (294); Emilio Albertario, Iustum pretium e iusta aestimatio, Bulletino dell'instituto di diritto romano 31

In the Middle Ages, these passages were further developed into the doctrine of *iustum pretium*, particularly by canon lawyers under the influence of a Christian-Aristotelian conception of justice, and were intended to benefit both sellers and buyers who had been exploited.[5] The theologians and jurists of the School of Salamanca developed this into a doctrine of exchange justice in contractual relationships and regarded any violation of the concept of fair price in general as 'enormous damage' (i.e. the literal translation of '*laesio enormis*') which, as a legal consequence, resulted in a right to annul the contract.[6] In the period of natural law, this remained the basic principle, but there was much debate about numerous details, in particular the exact value limit and whether the buyer had to pay the full value of the purchased item or only the *iustum pretium*.[7] The statement by Christian Thomasius, who described the *laesio enormis* as a hydra that gives birth to a new head for every head cut off, has remained in memory.[8]

The principle was then incorporated into the natural law codifications of Prussia, France and Austria, albeit with considerable differences.

According to the Prussian General Land Law of 1794 (Part I, 11, §§ 58 et seq.), a disproportionate difference between the purchase price and the value of the item gave rise to a presumption of error and a right to annul the contract.[9] The Prussian General Land Law, however, only allowed annulment on grounds of *laesio enormis* in favour of the buyer if the latter had

(1921), pp. 1–19 (4–5); Henry Monnier, Études de droit byzantin: XIV La lésion de plus de moitié dans la vente, Nouvelle revue historique de droit français et étranger 24 (1900), pp. 181–182.

5 John W. Baldwin, Medieval theories of the Just Price: Romanists, Canonists, and Theologians in the Twelth and Thirtheenth Centuries, Transactions of the American Philosophical Society 49.4 (1959), pp. 1–92 (22–23, 44 et seq.); on the Glossators' work, see James Gordley, Equality in exchange, California Law Review 69 (1981), pp. 1587–1656 (1638 et seq.).

6 Wim Decock, Theologians and Contrat Law. The moral Transformation of the Ius commune (ca. 1500–1650), 2013, pp. 536–589 and 602.

7 James Gordley, Equality in exchange, California Law Review 69 (1981), pp. 1587–1656 (1603 et seq.); Wolfgang Georg Schulze, Die laesio enormis in der deutschen Privatrechtsgeschichte, 1973, pp. 35 et seq.

8 Thomas Finkenauer, 'Laesio Enormis' in Jürgen Basedow, Klaus Jürgen Hopt, Reinhard Zimmermann, Andreas Stier (eds.), The Max Planck Encyclopedia of European Private Law, 2012, pp. 1029–1032.

9 Martin Josef Schermaier, Die Bestimmung des wesentlichen Irrtums von den Glossatoren bis zum BGB, in: Forschungen zur neueren Privatrechtsgeschichte (29) 2000, pp. 377–378.

paid more than double the value.[10] The drafters of the General Land Law were aware of the problem of determining value and addressed it in several sections (Part I, 11 §§ 61 et. seq.). Among other things, they stipulated that the value of the purchased item could only be determined by sworn experts.

The French Code Civil of 1804 contained and contains until today – allegedly at the insistence of Napoleon – in Article 1674 a provision protecting sellers of real estate only if the purchase price was less than 5/12 of the value of the property.[11] French law also regulated the problem of determining the value by the court. According to Article 1678, the deviation from the value had to be proven by three experts in a joint report. As a legal consequence of the existence of a *laesio enormis*, the buyer was entitled under Article 1681(1) to choose between annulment of the purchase contract (i.e. return of the item and refund of the purchase price) or maintenance of the purchase contract (i.e. retention of the property and payment of the difference reduced by 10 %).[12] This tradition also underlies the prohibition to impose obligations on the other party to the contract that are 'significantly disproportionate' to the counter-performance owed ('*déséquilibre significatif*'), applicable to producers, traders, manufacturers or persons registered in the trade register as was laid down in the former Article L.442 – 6 I No. 2 of the French Commercial Code.[13]

The Austrian General Civil Code of 1811 protected both the seller and the buyer in the event of a 'reduction by more than half' in Section 934. The reduction by more than half enabled the party who had been disadvantaged to annul the contract if, at the time of conclusion of the contract, the value

10 Wolfgang Georg Schulze, Die laesio enormis in der deutschen Privatrechtsgeschichte, 1973, pp. 83 et seq.

11 Wolfgang Georg Schulze, Die laesio enormis in der deutschen Privatrechtsgeschichte, 1973, pp. 91 et seq.; Yvaine Buffelan-Lanore, Virgine Larribau-Terneyre, Droit civil – Les obligations, 16th ed. 2018, pp. 470 et seq.

12 Philippe Malaurie, Laurent Aynés, Pierre-Yves Gautier, Droit des contrats spéciaux, 8th ed. 2016, pp. 174–175; Yvaine Buffelan-Lanore, Virgine Larribau-Terneyre, Droit civil – Les obligations, 16th ed. 2018, p. 473.

13 See, e.g., the ground-breaking decision of the French Court of Cassation's chamber of commerce of 25 January 2017; Case No. 15–23.547; the regulation was repealed with effect of 26 April 2019; it read: 'Engage la responsabilité de son auteur et l'oblige à réparer le préjudice causé le fait, par tout producteur, commerçant, industriel ou personne immatriculée au répertoire des métiers ... 2° De soumettre ou de tenter de soumettre un partenaire commercial à des obligations créant un déséquilibre significatif dans les droits et obligations des parties'; for the current (modernised) French law, see Article 1171 Code civil which also uses the term 'déséquilibre significatif', but is applicable also to B2B contracts.

of its performance was more than twice the value of the counter-performance.[14] However, the annulment of the contract could be averted by the contractual partner of the party who had been disadvantaged by paying the difference between the performances (right of substitution or *facultas alternativa*).[15] The list of exceptions regulated in Article 935 (including, for example, cases of a judicial auction or of a contract that mixes a sale and a donation) also contains a reference to the obvious problem of determining the value.[16] If the value of the subject matter of the contract cannot be determined, *laesio enormis* was excluded.

II. Economic liberalism and Adam Smith's market ideology of 'natural prices'

The late 18th and the 19th centuries marked significant shifts in the paradigm of judicial price review. In particular, the most notable doctrine, '*laesio enormis*', began to wane. The turning point towards free market ideology was marked by Adam Smith. Adam Smith introduced the concept of the 'Wealth of Nations', advocating minimal state intervention in markets.[17] This shift towards a *laissez-faire* ideology contrasted sharply with earlier traditions, leading to the diminishment of judicial price reviews in the course of the 19th century.

The theory that the famous invisible hand directs the opposing and conflicting interests and effects prices at their 'natural' level, with production costs being the decisive factor, appeared to be particularly convincing.[18] In light of such market ideology, judicial intervention in the contract concluded by the parties appeared not only unnecessary but even harmful. Many

14 Wolfgang Georg Schulze, Die laesio enormis in der deutschen Privatrechtsgeschichte, 1973, pp. 99 et seq.

15 Martin Winner, Wert und Preis im Zivilrecht, 2008, pp. 46–47; Peter Bydlinski, Die Stellung der laesio enormis im Vertragsrecht, Juristische Blätter 1983, pp. 410–420, 418–420.

16 Austrian Supreme Court of Justice, Juristische Blätter 2006, pp. 39–40, Martin Winner, Wert und Preis im Zivilrecht, 2008, pp. 47 et seq.; Rudolf Reinschauer, in: Peter Rummel, Meinhard Lukas (eds.) Kommentar zum Allgemeinen bürgerlichen Gesetzbuch, § 934 Nos. 28 et seq.

17 Adam Smith, An Inquiry into the Nature and the Causes of the Wealth of Nations (1776); Robert Heilbroner, The Essential Adam Smith, 1986, p. 151.

18 Robert Heilbroner, The Essential Adam Smith, 1986, p. 151.

codifications from the second half of the 19th century decisively rejected the legal doctrine of *laesio enormis*.[19]

III. Replacement of the laesio enormis *by usury in 19th century*

As a countervailing trend to the early liberalism, the so-called 'social question' became particularly apparent and began to dominate public debate in the second half of the 19th century. The German Reich responded, besides introducing social insurance against unemployment, illness and old age,[20] with legislation against usury, starting with the Usury Act of 1880.[21] The German Civil Code, adopted in 1896, incorporated this legislation in particular in Section 138(2). The provision reads (until today):

> 'A legal transaction is void by which a person, by exploiting the predicament, inexperience, lack of sound judgment or considerable weakness of will of another, causes a promise to be made to them or to a third party, in exchange for an act of performance, for pecuniary advantages that are clearly disproportionate to the performance, or causes such pecuniary advantages to be granted.'

---

19 Examples of such a departure from the doctrine of laesio enormis include, among others, the General German Commercial Code of 1861, the Saxon Civil Code (1863), the Swiss Code of Obligations (1881). For a particularly evident example, see Section 286 General German Commercial Code, which stated: "Commercial transactions cannot be contested on the grounds of excessive injury, in particular not due to injuries exceeding one-half." See also Hans-Peter Benöhr, Der Dresdner Entwurf von 1866 und das Schweizerische Obligationenrecht von 1881 in: Hans Peter, Emil Wilhelm Starck, Pierre Tercier (eds.), Hundert Jahre Obligationenrecht – Le Centenaire du Code des Obligations, 1982, p. 61, Heinrich Honsell, 100 Jahre Schweizer Obligationenrecht, Zeitschrift für Schweizerisches Recht 2011, p. 24.

20 For the shift to social policy interventionism within the German Empire during the drafting of the Civil Code (BGB) from 1880 onwards, see Hans Schulte-Nölke, Das Reichsjustizamt und die Entstehung des Bürgerlichen Gesetzbuchs, 1995, pp. 312 et seq.

21 Gesetz, betreffend den Wucher vom 24. Mai 1880. Reichsgesetzblatt (German Imperial Law Journal) 1880, No 10, pp. 109–110; on the legal and economic debates going along with this legislation, in particular in Germany and in the Austrian Empire, see Mischa Suter, Usury and the problem of exchange under capitalism: a late-nineteenth-century debate on economic rationality, Social History 2017, 42(4), pp. 501–523; https://doi.org/10.1080/03071022.2017.1368232.

When the German Civil Code was drafted, the incorporation of *laesio enormis* was expressly rejected.[22] As a result, *laesio enormis* has never formed part of the German Civil Code. The provision on usury in Section 138(2) of the German Civil Code differs from *laesio enormis* in that not only was a disproportion between performance and price a prerequisite, but also that the usurious party to the contract had to fulfil a subjective element of immorality, namely exploitation of weaknesses (such as predicament, inexperience, lack of sound judgment or considerable weakness of will) of the party who was taken advantage of. With the replacement of *laesio enormis* by usury, the blame shifted considerably. It was no longer sufficient for the protection of the disadvantaged party that there was an objective imbalance between the value of the subject matter of the contract and the price.[23] Protection against usury also required that one of the weaknesses specified in the law was present in the person who was the victim of usury, that the usurer exploited this weakness and that this was the cause for the conclusion of the contract. The Swiss Law of Obligations in the version of 1911 took the same road in Article 21,[24] whereas the old Swiss Law of Obligations of 1881 did not contain any such provision.

This legislation on usury is seen as a product of Immanuel Kant's ethics of freedom and the economic liberalism in the version of the late 19th century. The cited provisions of the German Civil Code and the Swiss Law of Obligations have not been applied frequently to date.[25] Similarly, other provisions allowing courts to set prices appear to be rarely applied. An example from German law is Section 315 of the German Civil Code, according to which, in a case where one party is allowed to determine the price at its reasonable discretion, this discretion is reviewable in court and, if it was not exercised properly, the court may set the price.

---

22 Franz Wieacker, Privatrechtsgeschichte der Neuzeit 1967, p. 482.

23 Christoph Becker, Die Lehre von der laesio enormis in der Sicht der heutigen Wucherproblematik, 1993, p. 174.

24 The provision reads: '(1) Wird ein offenbares Missverhältnis zwischen der Leistung und der Gegenleistung durch einen Vertrag begründet, dessen Abschluss von dem einen Teil durch Ausbeutung der Notlage, der Unerfahrenheit oder des Leichtsinns des andern herbeigeführt worden ist, so kann der Verletzte innerhalb Jahresfrist erklären, dass er den Vertrag nicht halte, und das schon Geleistete zurückverlangen.'

25 Reference could be made, however, to a landmark ruling of the Swiss Federal Supreme Court of 26 June 1997 (BGE 123 III 292).

IV. A 'renaissance' of laesio enormis in the 20th century

For the 20th century, in particular for Germany, again a counter-trend is described that is characterised by catchphrases such as the 'materialisation of private law' or 'renaissance of *laesio enormis*'.[26] This refers to a certain departure from the formal ethics of freedom, particularly in contract law, which focused centrally on the freedom of will of individuals, towards a more material ethics of justice that also asks whether the content of a contract is just or at least not obviously unjust.

In particular in periods of economic instability, courts began to reexamine their role in price regulation. The doctrine of 'change of circumstances' emerged as a judicial remedy to address unforeseen economic hardships. This legal innovation allowed courts to adapt contracts when extraordinary changes impacted the feasibility of fulfilling price obligations.[27]

A particularly prominent example is the so-called revaluation case law (*Aufwertungsrechtsprechung*) of the German Reich Court after the First World War. The new doctrine developed by this jurisprudence is based on a series of decisions made by the German Reich Court during the period of inflation. The hyperinflation, particularly in 1922 and 1923, led to a significant reduction in the purchasing power of the Mark. This made it necessary to adjust debts dating from before the inflation, as otherwise debtors would have been able to repay their old liabilities with actually worthless money, thereby depriving the creditors of these debts of the original value of their claims.[28] The Reich Court held in such a case, where payment in worthless paper money would have been manifestly unjust, that: '... it is relevant whether the basis of the transaction, understood as the assumption at the time of the conclusion of the transaction by the parties, of the existence of certain determining circumstances, has ceased to exist. This may also happen if the balance of values is disturbed, provided that

26 Theo Mayer-Maly, Renaissance der laesio enormis?, in: Festschrift für Karl Larenz zum 80. Geburtstag, 1983, pp. 395 et seq.; Thomas Finkenauer, Zur Renaissance der laesio enormis beim Kaufvertrag, in: Festschrift für Harm Peter Westermann, 2008, pp. 183 et seq.

27 Hannes Rösler, Change of Circumstances, in: Jürgen Basedow, Klaus Jürgen Hopt, Reinhard Zimmermann (eds.), The Max Planck Encyclopedia of European Private Law, 2012, pp. 163–167.

28 Heck, Das Urteil des Reichsgerichts vom 28. November 1923 über die Aufwertung Hypotheken und Grenzen von Richtermacht, Archiv für die civilistische Praxis (AcP) 122 (1924), pp. 216 et seq.

the continued equivalence of performance and counter-performance was assumed.'[29]

This ruling was characteristic in that, contrary to the wording of Section 138 (2) *BGB*, the Reich Court did not look for a subjective element of fault, i.e. exploitation of a weakness on the part of the contractual partner. Instead, it intervened in the contract solely because of the completely distorted balance between the value of the performance and the counter-performance. Admittedly, the difference in value in these cases was significantly more drastic than the mere reduction by half, which would have been sufficient for a *laesio enormis*. This was nevertheless historically remarkable, as the positivist view of law at the time assumed that legal development was a matter for the legislature, not the courts.[30]

In another hard case, in which a creditor as plaintiff demanded that his debtor as defendant settle a mortgage for a property in gold marks instead of paper marks, the Reich Court stated: 'The legislature did not envisage a significant devaluation of paper money, especially not to such an extent as has become increasingly apparent since the unfortunate outcome of the World War and the upheaval that followed, when it enacted the provision.'[31] From this, the Reich Court derived the authority to adjust the numerical amount of a debt to the changed monetary value, i.e. to 'revalue' it, even without a corresponding term in the contract or a specific provision in the law. In the absence of other options, the Reich Court chose Section 242 (good faith) of the German Civil Code as the point of reference for this case. This case law developed then into the doctrine of change of circumstances which became a common element of many European legal systems.[32]

29 Judgement of 3 February 1922, Decisions of the Imperial Court of Justice in civil matters (RGZ) 103, 328, see Translated German Cases and Materials Under the direction of Peter Schlechtriem, Basil Markesinis and Stephan Lorenz, translated by Irene Snook, available at https://law.utexas.edu/transnational/foreign-law-translations/german/case.php?id=954.

30 On this, see only Christiane Chlosta. Nur dem Gesetz unterworfen?, 2005, p. 67.

31 Judgement of 28 November 1923, Decisions of the Imperial Court of Justice in civil matters (RGZ) 107, 78

32 On this, see Ewoud Hondius and Hans Christoph Grigoleit, Change of Circumstances in European Contract Law – Convergencies, Distinctions and the Unsolved Mystery of Equitable Adjustment, in: Unexpected Circumstances in European Contract Law, E. Hondius & H. Grigoleit, Cambridge University Press, 2011, Available at SSRN: https://ssrn.com/abstract=2065874.

This case law is also seen as part of a broader development towards a 'materialisation of private law',[33] whereby private law, particularly through the legislature, has been supplemented with corrective and welfarist measures to ensure fairness, especially for the protection of weaker contracting parties. Prominent examples include laws protecting employees and tenants, which began to emerge after the First World War, but also case law on the protection of guarantors, for example.[34]

Particularly close to *laesio enormis* was a ruling by the German Federal Court of Justice on the immorality of interest, which in particular gave rise to the impression of a 'renaissance of *laesio enormis*' invoked in legal literature. The Federal Court of Justice established case law that a transaction is contrary to good morals and therefore void under Section 138(1) of the German Civil Code if there is a significant imbalance between the value of the performance and the counter-performance. The German Federal Court of Justice ruled that '... a significant disproportion is given if the contractual interest rate is more than twice as high as the standard market effective interest rate.'[35] The Federal Court of Justice therefore assumes, as in the classic case of *laesio enormis*, that such an imbalance exists when the difference in value is 100 % or more. In addition to the objective imbalance, however, the Federal Court of Justice also required subjective factors on the part of the party benefiting from the transaction. As a rule, their wrongful intent must also be established. According to the Federal Court of Justice, in cases of a particularly gross imbalance between price and counter-performance, there is a factual presumption of wrongful intent on the part of the favored party, which can only be refuted by special circumstances. According to this jurisdiction, the consequence of a difference in value of 100 % or more is not simply that the borrower can cancel the contract or demand an adjustment. However, an agreed interest rate that is more than double the market interest rate gives rise to a presumption that the lender acted with wrongful intent in a manner contrary to good morals, with the result that the interest rate agreement is void and the borrower receives the

33 Rudolf Wiethölter, Materialization and Proceduralization in Modern Law, in: Gunther Teubner (ed.), Dilemmas of Law in the Welfare State, 1986, pp. 221–249; Claus-Wilhelm Canaris, Wandlungen des Schuldvertragsrechts – Tendenzen zu seiner »Materialisierung«, AcP 200 (2000), pp. 273–364.

34 Claus-Wilhelm Canaris, Wandlungen des Schuldvertragsrechts – Tendenzen zu seiner »Materialisierung«, AcP 200 (2000), pp. 273 et seq.

35 German Federal Court of Justice, 13 March 1990, Case No. XI ZR 252/89.

loan at the market interest rate (or according to the – highly controversial – case law of the Federal Court of Justice, even without interest).

Thomas Wilhelmsson demonstrated particularly impressively in his ground-breaking work 'Social Contract Law and European Integration' (1995) that the development of contract law in many European countries increasingly integrated social and welfare elements and that the EEC (as it was then) has not only brought about harmonisation in terms of international trade and market integration, but has also strengthened the welfarist tendencies of national legal systems.

The legal systems of Member States, however, still differ significantly in terms of whether courts can adjust a contractually agreed price in favour of potentially disadvantaged parties, in particular consumers. This is not the case in many countries. In countries where *laesio enormis* is regulated by law, however, and even more so in countries where, as in Article 36 of the Nordic Contract Act, a general fairness review by the courts is possible, judicial review may also intervene in the contract in the event of an excessive price, i.e. grant a right to annul the contract or reduce the price.

Apart from details and interim adjustments, the legal systems of continental Europe follow either the older Diocletian model of objective price review or the late 19th century model preferred by the German Civil Code of protecting a party from immoral exploitation of its individual weaknesses under the doctrine of usury. In the latter case, a significant imbalance between performance and counter-performance additionally requires a reprehensible, immoral behaviour on the part of the beneficiary; the legal consequence of usury in this sense is usually the nullity of the transaction (and, as a rule, not a right to adapt the price).

It appears that the history of *laesio enormis* is one of pendulum swings. At certain times, there is a tendency towards protective legislation and greater price review, while at other times there is more reluctance to interfere in the market and more trust in the market forces and self-determination of market participants.

V. Criticism from the economic analysis of law

Only a brief reference can be made to the fundamental criticism of *laesio enormis* and similar legal institutions. Economists reject *laesio enormis*, among other things, because of the potential impairment of investment incentives. It is common understanding that in competitive market economies prices, in principle, need not be controlled, since in such markets the supply side cannot charge more than their cost of supply.[36]

In particular, *laesio enormis* can weaken incentives to invest in the production of information, such as searching for oil,[37] undiscovered valuable works of art, etc., if this information cannot be exploited due to a possible *laesio enormis.* The classic example is the purchase of a work of art by a well-known painter whose 'true value' is € 10,000, but which the seller estimates to be worth € 100.[38] *Laesio enormis* would force the purchaser to offer at least € 5,001. The purchaser would therefore be required to disclose to the owner the highly valuable information that his painting is worth much more than he believes. The purchaser would even have to provide this information to the owner free of charge and without any reassurance that the owner sells it to him. In doing so, the law would prevent the reimbursement of information costs, with the result that such costs would not be incurred. Valuable goods would thus not be found or their true value would not be recognised. The valuable goods that remain undiscovered (e.g. works of art, oil fields) would be lost to the general public and ultimately to the general welfare. It is widely accepted that intervention in the formation of prices and the resulting equilibrium by introducing price margins or price caps in a functioning market would likely reduce social welfare and hurt consumers.[39] This is probably true even if one assumes – in the light of the findings of behavioural economics – that humans often take decisions that differ from the predictions of standard economics because they are only boundedly rational, guided by systematic

36 Robert Cooter, Thomas Ulen, Law & Economics, 6th ed., 2016, pp. 28–37; Christopher DeMuth, The Case Against Credit Card Interest Rate Regulation (1985–1986), 12/3 Yale Journal on Regulation, pp. 201, 216.

37 For the legal and economic disadvantages of duties to disclose information about the value of the object of sale that is unknown to the seller (using the example of treasure found in a field), see only Hans-Bernd Schäfer, Ökonomische Analyse von Aufklärungspflichten, in: Ökonomische Probleme des Zivilrechts (1991), pp. 133, 135; for further details on information deficits and information costs when concluding contracts, see Hans-Bernd Schäfer, Claus Ott, The Economic Analysis of Civil Law, 2nd ed. 2022, pp. 453 et. seq.

38 Kristoffel R. Grechenig, Die laesio enormis als enorme Laesion der sozialen Wohlfahrt?, Journal für Rechtspolitik, Nr. 1, 2006.

39 See only Oren Bar-Gill, Price Caps in Multiprice Markets, (2015) 44 J Legal Stud, pp. 453–454.

biases in their predictions of future events and thereby often harm their own interests.[40]

VI. Need to differentiate from administrative price controls

A further brief differentiation is necessary, as state price setting or control is predominantly not carried out by the courts, but rather through administrative or legislative measures.[41] It may be worth mentioning that state price regulation played a special role in times of war. Examples of price regulation in peacetime include fee regulations through statutory instrument in sectors such as legal services, medical services, transport, water supply or other essential services, and in some cases also energy, telecommunications or basic financial services. In such sectors, prices are often simply set by public authorities, so that the problem of judicial price review, which in individual cases has to review the reasonable nature of a price agreed by the parties or developed by the market and thereby determine the 'fair' price, does not arise. This group of cases also includes sectors such as the residential rental market or the brokerage of rental and purchase properties by estate agents, in which official price indices or regulations guide the courts in their price review. For the purposes of administrative price setting or control, the determination of the appropriate price is not a question of fact or judicial assessment, but a question of political decision-making, which is subject to judicial review only to a very limited extent. The following discussion will focus 'only' on the question in which cases and by what means civil law courts may or can determine the appropriate price and intervene into contracts on that basis.

VII. Prices set by standard terms and judicial price review

A particularly striking example of a provision prohibiting judicial review of prices and its exceptions can be found in the law governing general terms

40 On the behavioural economics of consumer contracts, see only Anne-Lise Sibony, Geneviève Helleringer, EU Consumer Protection and Behavioural Sciences: Revolution or Reform? in: Alberto Alemanno, Anne-Lise Sibony (eds), Nudge and the Law – A European Perspective, 2015, pp. 209 et seq.

41 Meanwhile classic is John Kenneth Galbraith, A theory of price control, 1952.

and conditions. For example, Article 4(2) of the Unfair Contract Terms Directive 93/13/EEC (UCTD) states:

> 'Assessment of the unfair nature of the terms shall relate neither to the definition of the main subject matter of the contract nor to the adequacy of the price and remuneration, on the one hand, as against the services or goods supplies in exchange, on the other, in so far as these terms are in plain intelligible language.'

A rather similar provision can be found in Article 13(8) of the Data Act:

> 'This Article does not apply to contractual terms defining the main subject matter of the contract or to the adequacy of the price, as against the data supplied in exchange.'

The purpose of these exceptions from judicial review of general terms and conditions or contract terms pre-formulated by one party to the contract is typically stated as being that the courts should not review the appropriateness of prices (agreed in general terms and conditions) or the price-value ratio of performance and counter-performance.[42]

On the one hand, this is of course a legal policy decision that pricing should be left to the market, in which judges should not intervene as a matter of principle. Since the UCTD is a minimum harmonisation Directive, Member States may retain a more extensive power of the court to review prices, for example, a *laesio enormis* where this is regulated, but also a general fairness review including the appropriateness of the price, for example, under Section 36 of the Nordic Contract Act. The majority of Member States has followed the UCTD insofar that price review under consumer law in standard terms is excluded.[43] Examples are Section 307 (2) German Civil Code or Article L.212 – 1 French Consumer Code. According

42 Michael Schillig, Directive 93/13 and the 'Price Term Exemption': A Comparative Analysis in the Light of the 'Market for Lemons' Rationale, (2011) 60 ICLQ, pp. 933–936; Benedikt Karsten, in: Moritz Hennemann, Gordian Konstantin Ebner, Benedikt Karsten, Gregor Lienemann, Marie Wienroeder (eds.), Data Act – an Introduction, 2024, pp. 144 et seq.; Tobias Lettl, Rechtsfolgen der Missbräuchlichkeit einer Vertragsklausel nach Art. 6 Abs. 1 RL 93/13/EWG (Klausel-RL) und Art. 13 Abs. 1, 7 VO (EU) 2023/2854 (Datenverordnung oder Data-Act), Wertpapiermitteilungen 2024, pp. 185–186.

43 For an overview of the transposition in the EU Member States, see Andreas Piekenbrock, Die richterliche Preiskontrolle im Bankbereich aus europäischer Sicht, GPR 2014, pp. 26, 28; critical on judicial price review in consumer contracts Yesim M. Atamer, Why Judicial Control of Price Terms in Consumer Contracts Might Not

to the case law of the French Court of Cassation, price review under the Consumer Code may be excluded for reasons that do not necessarily apply equally to contracts between merchants.[44] The Court of Cassation does not elaborate on these possible reasons. However, it could be assumed that consumer contracts are generally specific contracts for consumption purposes, for which the consumer himself can sufficiently assess the price-performance ratio and freely decide whether to conclude the contract or not.

The extent to which the Data Act allows for (price) review under Member State law is controversial. In countries such as France and Germany, which provide for review of general terms and conditions for contracts between businesses, there is also a fundamental exception to review for terms that regulate the price or the price-value ratio.[45]

However, the prohibition on reviewing the appropriateness of the price (as stipulated in general terms and conditions) is itself subject to numerous exceptions. German doctrine distinguishes, for example, between price agreements and ancillary price agreements, in which it is not the total price but only additional charges that are stipulated. Only the former are exempt from review; ancillary price agreements regulated in general terms and conditions are subject to judicial review. Particularly prominent is the exception in Article 4(2) UCTD, which states that only price-determining clauses that are formulated 'in plain intelligible language' are exempt from review. This is a clarification of the transparency requirement, i.e. only those price terms and conditions that are easily accessible to the consumer (and which he or she can be expected to actually take note of) are exempt from judicial review.[46] Regarding Article 13(8) of the Data Act, which does

Always Be the Right Answer – Insights from Behavioural Law and Economics, The Modern Law Review (2017) 80(4), pp. 624–660.

44 Chamber of Commerce of the Court of Cassation, 25 January 2017 (Case No 15–23.547).

45 See for French law, the new Art. 1171 Code Civil 2nd sentence: 'L'appréciation du déséquilibre significatif ne porte ni sur l'objet principal du contrat ni sur l'adéquation du prix à la prestation.' For an overview on several EU Member States, see Francesco Paolo Patti, Unfair Terms Control in Business-to-Business Contracts, The Italian Law Journal 2019, p. 583.

46 See, e.g., CJEU, 21 March 2013, Case C- 92/11 – RWE Vertrieb AG v Verbraucherzentrale Nordrhein-Westfalen e.V., ECLI:EU:C:2013:180, para. 55, which requires that 'the contract sets out in a transparent fashion the reason for and method of the variation of those charges, so that the consumer can foresee, on the basis of clear, intelligible criteria, the alterations that may be made to those charges"; on the ration-

not regulate this exception, it is again controversial whether Member States may subject non-transparent price clauses to judicial review.

Insofar as judicial review of price-determining general terms and conditions may or must take place, the problem of judicial price determination is particularly acute and has not yet been convincingly resolved. It is also completely unclear whether and by what means a non-transparent or unfair price clause should be replaced or whether it should simply be omitted (and, as the most extreme solution imaginable, the contractual partner would receive the service free of charge).[47] In any case, it is not typically provided for that the judge simply replaces the unfair price with a fair one. Particularly unhelpful, almost bizarre, is the idea that appears in the ECJ's case law on the UCTD that in such a case the consumer and the business should renegotiate the price and then – as this case law seems to suggest – the court should review whether the new price is reasonable and, if necessary, send the parties back for further negotiations.[48] Much remains to be clarified here. The correct solution is likely to be that – at least in the case of ancillary price agreements – the price surcharge is waived without replacement and, if this is not possible, the party opposing the term has the right, in addition to the option of terminating the contract, to continue the contract at a particularly favourable price that is not completely unreasonable for the user of the term. *Laesio enormis* sends its regards.

VIII. Prices of SEPs: FRAND Requirements

There is a new field for judicial determination and review of the appropriateness of prices that has emerged in intellectual property law, particularly in patent law, which may have been somewhat overlooked by general civil law doctrine. This judicial and administrative activity is already laid down in principle in Article 102 TFEU, which deals with the abuse of a dominant

ale of Art. 4(2) UCTD in general, see Paolisa Nebbia, Unfair Contract Terms in European Law – A Study in Comparative and EC Law, 2007, pp. 124–125.

47 For more on this, see Hans Schulte-Nölke, Filling gaps in consumer contracts in the case of unfair terms. Is the CJEU's case law on Directive 93/13/EEC to the detriment of consumers?, Tijdschrift voor Consumentenrecht en Handelspraktijken 2023, pp. 239–245; idem, The objectives of Directive 93/13/EEC on Unfair Contract Terms. An overview after 30 years of case law, European Review of Private Law 2024, pp. 315–334.

48 CJEU, 16 March 2023, Case C-269/19 – Banca B. SA/A.A.A, ECLI:EU:C:2020:954, paras 41 et seq.

position within the internal market. As the first example of such abuse is mentioned in Article 102 TFEU(a) 'imposing unfair purchase or selling prices'. For the purposes of this paper, only one particularly interesting development arising from the case law on this provision will be touched upon here, namely standard essential patents (SEPs).

SEPs are patents that protect technologies that are essential for implementing a specific technical standard. These standards are necessary, e.g., for the interoperability and compatibility of various products and services, particularly in areas such as telecommunications or the automotive industry. It is estimated that several 10.000 SEPs exist which have an immense practical importance. According to the case law of the European Court of Justice on Article 102 TFEU, SEP holders are obliged to offer licences on 'fair, reasonable and non-discriminatory terms' (FRAND) in order to prevent abuse of monopoly power and ensure access to the technologies.[49]

The question of whether a licence offer is FRAND must sometimes be finally decided by the national courts, including the question of whether the price offered is reasonable. In certain situations, the courts may even be asked to fix a FRAND compliant price.[50] Interesting controversies have arisen between national courts, in particular the German courts (which have heard the vast majority of FRAND cases until now), the European Court of Justice and the European Commission.[51] The European Commission has even attempted, by means of a proposed EU regulation, to regulate a competence of the European Union Intellectual Property Office (EUIPO) to administer the FRAND determination for SEPs.[52] However, this proposed regulation is regarded as having little chance of success, so that the role of the courts, meanwhile in particular of the Uniform Patent Court,[53] in this task is likely to remain unchanged for the time being.

---

49 CJEU, 16 July 2015, Case C-170/13 – Huawei ./. ZTE, ECLI:EU:C:2015:477.

50 For comprehensive information on this see Mary-Rose McGuire, Wer bestimmt was FRAND ist? Über Rahmenbedingungen, Maßstab und Zuständigkeit für die Beurteilung der FRAND-Konformität, Mitteilungen der deutschen Patentanwälte (MdP) 2018, pp. 297–308.

51 See the amicus curiae brief of the European Commission of 15 April 2024 in the proceedings HMD Global Oy ('HMD') v. VoiceAge EVS GmbH & Co. KG ('VoiceAge') before the Munich Higher Regional Court, Case No. 6 U 5066/22 Kart.

52 COM(2023)232 – Proposal for a regulation of the European Parliament and of the Council on standard essential patents and amending Regulation (EU) 2017/1001.

53 The Agreement on a Unified Patent Court (UPCA) has entered into force on 1 June 2023.

In addition to these disputes there are differences in approach between the English and German courts, for example, when deciding whether a FRAND rate, i.e., a price for a license, is reasonable or not. The contrast between the German and English courts is of particular interest for the purposes of this paper. Whereas English courts, sometimes even with a claim to worldwide effect, try to fix fair and reasonable rates for SEPs down to the last cent (or penny),[54] the German courts tend to limit themselves to checking the contractual terms and prices proposed by the parties to determine whether or not they are fair and reasonable, but without themselves fixing a fair and reasonable price.[55] Insofar, the case law of German courts on FRAND in relation to SEPs assumes that FRAND, in relation to price, is not a specific amount, but a range. This appears to follow the tradition of *laesio enormis*, whereby courts should not set prices down to the last cent but rather limit themselves to examining whether prices fall outside a margin of appropriateness, i.e. whether they are not just slightly off an appropriate (market) price, but significantly so.

IX. Price and Value of Data

Against the backdrop of the examples of judicial price review and determination cited above, several examples from the area of data pricing, which is of particular interest here, will now be briefly outlined. It is important to note that although the subject matter, i.e. data, is relatively new, the issue of judicial price review is not. It is therefore to be expected that the same questions will arise as with other subject matters, namely whether judges should be entitled to review and correct prices at all and, if so, with what

54 UK Patents Court [2017] EWHC 711 (Pat) Nos. 98 et seq. – Unwired Planet/Huawei (the court, however, also indicated that, although it has set a price, it nevertheless considers a deviation from this to be legally compliant, see para. 275); for justification of the approach of the English courts' jurisdiction on FRAND, see, e.g., Igor Nikolic, The Approach of English Courts in SEP Disputes: No Standalone Actions for Determination of Global FRAND Rates (24 July 2023). Available at: https://ssrn.com/abstract=4519405.

55 See, e.g., Higher Regional Court of Düsseldorf, 17 November 2016, I-15 U 66/15 – Mobile communication system; Higher Regional Court of Karlsruhe, 8 September 2016, 6 U 58/16 – Decoding device; on this, see also Mary-Rose McGuire, Wer bestimmt was FRAND ist? Über Rahmenbedingungen, Maßstab und Zuständigkeit für die Beurteilung der FRAND-Konformität, Mitteilungen der deutschen Patentanwälte (MdP) 2018, pp. 297–308, 302.

intensity and by what means they should determine the appropriateness of a price.

1. Value of data in the early digital age

An early example of a case in which courts had to deal, at least indirectly, with the value of data is provided by the German Federal Court of Justice's ruling on the D-Info-CD. In 1996, a 'D-Info-CD' was launched on the market, for which 532 Chinese data typists copied all the printed telephone directory entries of the then German telephone monopolist Deutsche Telekom. Deutsche Telekom filed a lawsuit against this, i.a. for copyright infringement – and finally won.[56] However, the main reason was not copyright infringement, as the entries were not personal intellectual creations but merely contained information and were therefore not subject to copyright protection. Rather, Deutsche Telekom was fortunate that the special protection for databases granted by the EU came into force on 1 January 1998.[57] According to this, the producer of a database is granted a special right of protection which includes the exclusive right to reproduce, distribute or publicly reproduce the database or substantial parts thereof.[58] According to the Federal Court of Justice, this protection is not limited to electronic data collections. Rather, it also applies to conventional telephone directories. Data as such was therefore not assigned to specific rights holders and therefore did not have a value or price based on a protective or monopoly right. Only insofar as the data embodied a special intellectual property right was it protected and thus a suitable object for a market and therefore subject to price formation.

2. Personal data

Whether personal data has a price and how this price can be determined is one of the big questions not only in law, but also in economics, data science

56 Bundesgerichtshof (German Federal Court of Justice), 6 May 1999, Case No I ZR 199/96, 5/97, 210/96 and 211/96.

57 Art. 16(1) Database Directive (96/9/EC).

58 Sections 87a and 87b of the German Copyright Act (UrhG) based on the Database Directive (96/9/EC).

and many other disciplines.[59] It is certainly a commonplace that users of seemingly free online services such as search engines, navigation systems and messenger services 'pay' for these undoubtedly valuable services with their personal data. The question of the value of this payment therefore may also arise before civil judges, for example if the service provided in exchange for data is defective and users ask whether they can demand a defect-free service or whether they have other legal remedies due to the defects. The Directive on digital content and services has found an almost ingenious solution to this problem of determining value.[60] Article 3(1) states, among other things:

> 'This Directive shall also apply where the trader supplies or undertakes to supply digital content or a digital service to the consumer, and the consumer provides or undertakes to provide personal data to the trader, except where the personal data provided by the consumer are exclusively processed by the trader for the purpose of supplying the digital content or digital service in accordance with this Directive or for allowing the trader to comply with legal requirements to which the trader is subject, and the trader does not process those data for any other purpose.'

In other words, this means that the court only has to establish that the consumer provides or undertakes to provide any personal data which is not required for the service or for legal obligations. The value of this data, in particular whether and how this value could be expressed in monetary terms, is irrelevant.[61]

The problem of determining value or price does not therefore arise for the judge in these cases. The consumer's rights in relation to the contractual conformity of the digital service are – with very few exceptions – com-

59 See, e.g., Julia Busch-Casler, Marija Radic, Personal Data Markets: A Narrative Review on Influence Factors of the Price of Personal Data (14 May 2022). Available at: https://publica-rest.fraunhofer.de/server/api/core/bitstreams/65985129-79b7-4edd-b10d-c51dab788c22/content; Alessandro Acquisti et al., The Economics of Privacy (7 February 2020), available at https://papers.ssrn.com/sol3/papers.cfm?abstract_id=2580411; Marc van Lieshout, The Value of Personal Data (May 2015), available at: https://www.researchgate.net/publication/283668023_The_Value_of_Personal_Data.

60 The same wording (with the exception that supply on a tangible medium is not covered) also appears in Art. 3(1a) of the Consumer Rights Directive (2011/83), which was inserted by Art. 4(2)(b) of the Omnibus Directive (2019/2161).

61 Dirk Staudenmayer, Art. 3 DCD, in: Reiner Schulze and Dirk Staudenmayer, EU Digital Law, No. 72.

pletely independent of whether the consumer pays with money or 'only' provides personal data. For the purposes of this Directive, personal data therefore have a value that need not be expressed in monetary terms, but ultimately consists of the consumer obtaining the remedies that he would have had if he had paid with money.

The much-debated question of how damages are to be calculated under Article 82 GDPR can be left aside here, because it only appears to be related to the price and value of data. This is because the amount of damage concerns the severity of the violation of the data subject's privacy rights, which may be entirely independent of the transactional value or price of the personal data in relation to which the data subject's rights have been violated.[62]

3. Product-generated non-personal data: FRAND again

The Data Act, which applies from 12 September 2025, has opened up a completely new and potentially very extensive field in which judicial review of the fairness of prices will be necessary. According to Article 8 of the Data Act, data holders must make data that they are required to make available accessible on fair, reasonable and non-discriminatory terms and conditions.

Article 9 of the Data Act sets out further requirements for the amount of remuneration that the data holder may charge the data recipient. Article 9(1)-(3) of the Data Act read as follows:

'1. Any compensation agreed upon between a data holder and a data recipient for making data available in business-to-business relations shall be non-discriminatory and reasonable and may include a margin.
2. When agreeing on any compensation, the data holder and the data recipient shall take into account in particular:
   (a) costs incurred in making the data available, including, in particular, the costs necessary for the formatting of data, dissemination via electronic means and storage;

62 See only, with further references, Alexander Hellgardt, Die Schadensersatzhaftung für Datenschutzverstöße im System des unionalen Haftungsrechts, ZEuP 2022, pp. 30 et seq.; for an opposite opinion and, at least for cases of data leakage, a licence analogy based on economic value, see Marc Strittmatter et al., Schadensbemessung bei Datenschutzrechtsverstößen am Beispiel von data leakage-Fällen, Computer und Recht (CR) 2019, pp. 787–797.

(b) investments in the collection and production of data, where applicable, taking into account whether other parties contributed to obtaining, generating or collecting the data in question.

3. The compensation referred to in paragraph 1 may also depend on the volume, format and nature of the data.'

These provisions apply in particular to non-personal data generated by a connected product within the meaning of the Data Act. However, its content is strikingly similar to the FRAND criteria developed by case law for the licensing of SEPs.[63] It is also becoming increasingly clear that simply adopting existing negotiation models and approaches to determining FRAND in the field of SEPs will not suffice and that, for the purposes of the Data Act, a substantive specification of the FRAND criteria will be necessary.[64] Furthermore, the criteria for determining the price are likely to be different from those for SEP licences. This is because Article 9(2) of the Data Act states that the main factors to be taken into account (as is presumably to be understood) are the costs of making the data available and the investment made in collecting and producing the data, to which a profit margin may be added in accordance with Article 9(1) Data Act. However, the value of the data or the value of the intended use of the data for the data recipient (i.e. criteria that may be particularly important for SEP licences) are not mentioned. It therefore remains to be seen whether the courts will – possibly hastily and somewhat inappropriately – transfer the criteria for determining FRAND rates for SEPs to data under the Data Act or – which would probably be preferable – develop their own criteria for a FRAND-compliant compensation for product-generated data.

63 For further information, see, e.g., Peter Georg Picht, Caught in the Acts: Framing Mandatory Data Access Transactions under the Data Act, Further EU Digital Regulation Acts, and Competition Law, Journal of European Competition Law & Practice, 14(2) 2023, pp. 67–82, 74 et seq., available at: https://doi.org/10.1093/jeclap/lpac059; Benedikt Karsten, Gregor Lienemann, in: Moritz Hennemann, Gordian Konstantin Ebner, Benedikt Karsten, Gregor Lienemann, Marie Wienroeder (eds.), Data Act – an Introduction, 2024, pp. 114 et seq.

64 Marco Botta, Shall we share? – The principle of FRAND in B2B data sharing, European University Institute, Robert Schuman Centre for Advanced Studies Working Paper RSC 2023/30, available at: https://cadmus.eui.eu/server/api/core/bitstreams/5046049e-45ee-5849-ada7-f6e990b636a5/content; Jonas Coenen, FRAND-Bedingungen im Data Act — Eine Analyse der Art. 5, 8 und 9 DA unter Berücksichtigung einer möglichen Konkretisierung von FRAND, Computer und Recht (CR) 2025, pp. 353–361.

X. Overall findings and outlook for judicial price review

The many stages of judicial price reviews, from legal history to the present day, which have been touched upon here, make it possible to formulate some tentative conclusions on judicial price review in general, at least in the form of theses.

The historical development of judicial price review reflects a dynamic interplay between legal principles and economic realities. While the decline of traditional price review mechanisms in the 18th and 19th centuries marked a shift towards market economy ideologies, the opposite trend in the present days highlights increasing judicial review of prices with the aim of market regulation and market building.

The problem that judges, due to their educational background and socialisation, but also because of their role in the process and the procedural rules governing them, are not well suited to assess the appropriateness of prices or even to set prices has accompanied the historical development and is exacerbated by the expansion of judicial price review through the EU's regulatory private law.

Legal systems appear to require safeguards to ensure that judges do not normally have to decide on prices or review their appropriateness, but only in exceptional cases, not only because they are not well suited to doing so, but also because this could have negative effects on the market.

The basic principle may be that two restrictions apply to judicial price reviews. The first of these restrictions concerns the question of whether reviews should be imposed. State controls on prices agreed on the market are only imposed in exceptional cases and only for an overriding regulatory objective – an objective that (at least outside times of war) is a welfarist one. This applies even more for judicial price reviews. The other restriction concerns the question of how reviews are exercised. Usually, courts or authorities only intervene if prices or the price-value ratio deviate to an extreme or at least very significant extent from a 'fair' price, i.e. if a price is evidently unfair. In other words: If judicial price review does occur in exceptional cases, it is not usually done by determining or setting the price, but by determining a 'margin of appropriateness', i.e. ultimately by asking at what threshold a price is obviously and certainly inappropriate (obviousness test).

Administrative price control or statutory price fixing, on the other hand, is less a legal problem, but a field of political decision-making. Of course, this activity by the public authorities is also subject to judicial review, whereby the principle of non-reviewability of discretionary decisions within the permissible scope of discretion is a similar restriction on judicial power as the margin of appropriateness, which can be observed in civil law jurisdiction.

What is particularly striking, however, is a clear change in the purpose of judicial price review. *Laesio enormis* and usury aim to protect weaker individuals, especially when they are exploited due to market failure or individual weakness. The renaissance of *laesio enormis* was essentially a softening of the subjective element of the prerequisites for usury and thus a convergence of the practical results of case law between legal systems whose statutory provisions did not recognise *laesio enormis*, but only the initially much narrower concept of usury. The common feature of these types of judicial price control is that they are based on a welfarist purpose, whereby the nature of welfarism varies between safeguarding the interests and rights or the freedom of the individual.[65]

Judicial review of non-transparent price terms in general terms and conditions and, even more so, the FRAND requirements for licences for standard essential patents (SEPs) and data falling under the Data Act differ from this primarily in their purpose. The aim is not so much to correct market failures in individual contracts, but rather to improve or even to build markets through standardisation and making valuable innovations or data accessible – with the overarching goal of increasing market efficiency and thus general welfare.

By allowing price terms in general terms and conditions only if they are easily understandable and exempting them from judicial review in that case, the legal system facilitates the standardisation of business models, which reduces costs for both sides, particularly also search costs for customers, and improves transparency and thus market efficiency.

The obligation to make licences and data available under FRAND-compliant terms also enables or facilitates the standardisation of technical developments that can be based on licences for SEPs. The requirement that product-generated data must also be made available under FRAND-compliant terms not only creates a market for valuable data and thus enables data-driven developments. The FRAND requirements for product-

65 On the different welfarist directions in modern contract law, see Thomas Wilhelmsson, Varieties of Welfarism in European Contract Law, European Law Journal 10(6) 2004, 712–733.

generated data, supported by model terms and conditions,[66] also contribute to standardisation in the sense that uniform data access and data usage contracts are developed, which facilitate the distribution of data based on chains of contracts.

The most interesting finding of the considerations presented in this paper is that the latest legislative developments are giving civil courts a new task in the context of price review, namely to establish a functioning data market and data space by specifying the FRAND requirements of the Data Act.

---

66 For such model contract terms, see 'Final Report of the Expert Group on B2B data sharing and Cloud computing contracts', 2 April 2025, available at: https://ec.europa.eu/transparency/expert-groups-register/core/api/front/document/116180/download; or 'Musterbedingungen für den Bereich Vernetzte Landmaschinen' 21 October 2024, of the German Federal Ministry of Agriculture, Food and Regional Identity (BMLEH), available at: https://www.bmleh.de/SharedDocs/Downloads/DE/_Digitalisierung/musterbedingungen-digital-landmaschinen.html.

Consequences of the monetisation of consumer data for contract type and contract structure*

Martin Schmidt-Kessel[1]

One decisive factor in determining the value of consumer data traded on the data market is the specific way in which the rights and obligations – which are usually only obligatory and not effective *in rem* – are organised in the respective contracts. These contracts may be contracts directly with the consumer but may also be contracts concluded in the course of business – usually on a secondary data market with market participants who are data controllers (see Art. 4 No. 7 GDPR), data holders (see Art. 2 No. 13 DA) or both. In this sense, this paper does not address pricing or 'paying with data', but rather the consequences of the rights to deal with – hold or use – data as part of a contract and the structure of that contract. In doing so, I will concentrate on the content of contracts for the use of personal data (within the meaning of Art. 4 No. 1 GDPR) and IoT data (within the meaning of Art. 2 No. 15, 16 DA). I will discuss the resulting contract structures in three steps:

The first step (I.) is to separate the GDPR and the GDPR rules from those of the contract, and the key message of this part will be – and I will explain this later – that data protection law as a whole and the GDPR in particular, doesn't or only rarely effects the contractual level. Rather, the effects of the GDPR on contracts will primarily be indirect. By contrast, the DA for IoT-Data merely deals with the contractual level.

In the second step, I will present and discuss two types of contracts or contractual relationships, that deal with data. First, I will begin by outlining the basic situation of data custody and services provided in the name and interest of the data subject or the user of the IoT device (II.). This refers to the position of the controller in data protection law on the one hand and of the data holder in the Data Act on the other. The second part of this second step will concern the use of data as the subject matter of the

* LS-Schmidt-Kessel@uni-bayreuth.de.

1 The following is based on a lecture I gave in Ferrara on 18 April 2024. The lecture form has been retained. The references are kept to a minimum.

contract (III.). Here, too, custody and service obligations in the interest of the person who has better rights to the data (the data subject or user) are involved. However, the data processing is not carried out primarily in the interest of the data subject or user, but in the interest of another party, which may be the controller or data holder, or another market participant, such as the data recipient (cf. Art. 2 No. 14 DA).

In order to assess the behaviour of participants in data markets, it must first be clarified what position they hold vis-à-vis the original rights holders, i.e. the data subject and the user of the IoT device. As a core message of both, the GDPR and the Data Act, I will explain with regard to the content of contracts, that controllers and data holders are primarily obliged to act in the interest of the data subject or user, and that the use of data for their own purposes – including the passing-on of the data – requires special authorisation from the data subject or user. Therefore, the fundamental question for a data holder or data controller entering the secondary market is: on the basis of what kind of contract with the original rights holder they are acting. And the same question must be asked in the relationship between the person in the better position, i.e. the data subject or user, and the data recipient in the case of secondary market transactions.

In the third and final step, these contracts and obligations for custody and for acting in the interest of the person in the better position on the one hand, and contracts for and rights to use the data on the other, must be integrated into a more comprehensive contract structure. The contractual design is, in fact, very largely not limited to pure data contracts. Therefore, it is necessary to consider ancillary duties, rights and obligations (IV.) as well as mixed contracts, that include the storage and use of data (V.).

I. Separating the levels

When it comes to contract structures and contract types on data markets, it is important, at least for the argument, to distinguish between two levels: On the one hand, we have the data protection and privacy level, which is primarily determined by the GDPR and the e-Privacy Directive of 2002. At the obligation level, on the other hand, we find rights and obligations in contracts or based on other sources of obligations.

The separation of these two levels in the regulatory structure does not mean that there is no interaction between them. However, when structuring legal relationships on data markets, it is crucial to distinguish between the allocation of rights *in rem* by data protection law on the one hand and the determination of rights and obligations at the obligations level, mainly by contracts, on the other. This principle of separation has been part of EU law at least since the introduction of the GDPR.[2]

1. GDPR separates privacy from contract (Separation Principle)

There are many arguments to be found in the GDPR, and to some extent, also in the ePrivacy Directive 2002, that the data protection law itself does not govern contracts but is restricted to a kind of level, we could with all due care and caution, call proprietary, though it is at least a privacy law level:

The probably most important hint to that is to be found mainly in Art. 6(1)(b) GDPR (the great contract privilege) but also in Art. 9(h) and Art. 22 GDPR, which all aim to enable contracting and contract performance, without being impeded by data protection law. All three of these contractual privileges demonstrate that the GDPR considers contracts as belonging to a different category than privacy rules and the justification of data-processing.[3]

The second important argument demonstrating the separation of the two levels are the set of rules on consent in Art. 7, 6(1)(a), 4 No. 11 GDPR, which result in the separation of consent – and the particular privacy law rules governing it – from the contract. The probably most clear reference to this separation with regard to consent is to be found in Art. 7(2) GDPR, where

2 On this principle, see *Langhanke/Schmidt-Kessel*, EuCML 2015, 218, 219 f.; *Schmidt-Kessel/Erler/Grimm/Kramme*, GPR 2016, 54, 59, 70; *Metzger*, AcP 216 (2016) 817, 831–833; *Specht*, JZ 2017, 763, 765; *De Franceschi*, La circolazione dei dati personali tra *privacy* e contratto, Naples 2017, 12 et seq.; *Langhanke*, Daten als Leistung, 2018, 148–151, 168 f. (anders für die Schweiz 174–176); *Schmidt-Kessel*, in: de Franceschi/Schulze (Ed.), Digital Revolution – New Challenges for Law, München/Baden-Baden 2019, 75, 77 f.; *Schmidt-Kessel*, in: Lohsse/Schulze/Staudenmayer (ed.), Data as Counter-Performance – Contract Law 2.0?, Baden-Baden 2020, 129, 131; *Riehm*, in Pertot (ed.), Rechte an Daten 2020, 174, 186 f.; *De Cristofaro*, in Pertot (ed.), Rechte an Daten 2020, 151, 169 et seq. Critical of this view *Sattler*, Informationelle Privatautonomie 2022, 261–276 (based on the possibility of private restrictions on the revocation of consent under data protection law.).

3 *Schmidt-Kessel*, in: Lohsse/Schulze/Staudenmayer (Ed.), Data as Counter-Performance – Contract Law 2.0?, Baden-Baden 2020, 129, 131.

the contract parties, and in particular the future controller, are obligated to keep the consent declaration separate from other conditions of the relationship between the parties.[4]

A final and particularly strong argument in favour of the legal organisation of data markets through a principle of separation between data protection level and the obligation and contractual level in the structure of data protection law, ultimately arises from the fact that, under data protection law, the contractual level alone is not sufficient to establish another person's right to use data for their own purposes. In this respect, the contract for the use of data is structured differently from the vast majority of national experiences with rental contracts for tangible property: While the classic rental rules usually contain the mutual obligations and the authorisation of use in one agreement, this is not the case with personal data; additional justification is required for the contractually permitted use of data. The situation is presumably different for non-personal data under the Data Act; however, this has not yet been clarified.

2. Recent EU legislation confirming the Separation Principle

While there has been some debate as to whether the GDPR and data protection law really establish the need to normatively separate the levels of data protection and obligations, including contractual obligations,[5] European Union law has since confirmed the aforementioned principle of separation through subsequent legislative acts:

Probably the most important piece of legislation in this regard is the Data Act of 2024, in which the GDPR is mentioned primarily as a legal impediment to the fulfilment of contractual, and perhaps also extra-contractual, obligations to establish a right to use personal data; however, the requirements of the GDPR are not considered part of the contract and of contract law there. This applies in particular to the restrictions on access obligations and to Artt. 4(12), 5(7), (8), (13) and 6(2)(b) DA.[6]

---

4 *Schmidt-Kessel*, in: Lohsse/Schulze/Staudenmayer (Ed.), Data as Counter-Performance – Contract Law 2.0?, Baden-Baden 2020, 129, 131.

5 *De Cristofaro*, in Pertot (ed.), Rechte an Daten 2020, 151, 169 et seq.; *Sattler*, Informationelle Privatautonomie 2022, 261–276.

6 See *Schmidt-Kessel* in Bomhard/Schmidt-Kessel, Data Act, Art. 4 No. 136 ff., Art. 5 No. 98 ff., Art. 6 No. 12 f.

In addition, EU Directive 2019/770 on digital content and digital services – which will mainly become a directive on digital services, as it has more important tasks to fulfil there – also points in the same direction: The GDPR is in fact largely relevant to the application of this directive, but is ignored by significant parts of the regulatory context, particularly with regard to the introduction of the (in part fictitious) 'paying with data' in Art. 3(1) Directive 2019/770. Furthermore, the somewhat enigmatic reference to data protection remedies for data subjects in the event of termination of the contract for the supply of digital content and digital services in Art. 16(2) Directive 2019/770 – as well as for the consumer right of withdrawal in Art. 13(4) Consumer Rights Directive 2011/83/EU – must be interpreted as a clarification of the applicability of data protection law to such a situation[7] and not as the introduction of a general system of restitution or vindication by data protection law in place of the law of obligations and contract law.

In response to recital 40 Directive 2019/770, the German legislator has also autonomously regulated the contractual consequences of the withdrawal of consent under data protection law at the national level when implementing the Directive – and, going beyond the suggestion by the Recital, has extended this regulation to cover the objection under Art. 21 GDPR and the exercise of other data subject rights, without – as far as can be seen – any other Member State having followed its example: § 327q BGB clarifies in para. (1) that the exercise of such rights does not affect the validity of the associated contract and in para. (3) also excludes compensation for the business for doing so. In addition, para. (2) only allows the business to terminate long-term contracts and even this is only possible under strict conditions. All of this assumes the separation of contract and data protection law, which is supplemented here by a – national – principle of abstraction.[8]

3. First Consequences

Due to this well-founded principle of separation, structural conflicts between the GDPR and contract law are very limited: the special rules and justifications of data protection law for data processing rarely collide with contract law. This does not mean that data protection law has become

7 Cf. Recital 39 of Directive 2019/770.

8 On § 327q *BGB* see further infra III. 3. A.

completely irrelevant to the drafting of contracts. Rather, contract law aims to reflect the restrictions on data processing when organising contractual obligations. However, this is done at the obligations level and cloaks the stricter data protection rules by adapting the contract to the realities of data protection law.

Insofar as conflicts between contract law and the GDPR do arise, they cannot generally be resolved by the GDPR simply taking precedence (at least not anymore). This is because, in the hierarchy of EU law, many contract rules are now, as EU law, on the same hierarchical level as the GDPR; this probably is also a strong general argument for the GDPR not taking precedence over contract law as such in the event of a conflict. However, there are some special rules that give the GDPR precedence over other, mainly contract law-related, EU legal acts. For these particular cases, solutions must be found by contractually accepting the primacy of data protection.

Apart from these special rules, one of the rare cases in which the GDPR would override contract law rules is in the event that certain contract clauses are invalid. The most important examples of this are clauses that waive the data subject's right to revoke consent (Art. 7(3) GDPR) and their right to object to data processing in the interest of the controller (Art. 21 GDPR). In both cases, however, data protection law has more of a public law effect in that it prohibits certain parts and clauses of certain contracts. It is therefore in this respect not really part of private law and, in particular, not a part of contract law structure.

The development of the legal system for data contracts and data markets will integrate this principle of separation and the resulting consequences into the multi-level system of EU private law and must find a solution in the event of a conflict. In this respect, the principle of separation is also of great importance for the autonomy and contract law of the Member States, insofar as the latter is not regulated by the Union legislator. So far, however, European Union law has merely repeated the contractual pointillism (comparable to that of the 80s and 90s of the last century) and is only gradually revealing elements of a contract law system. This contract law system is no longer limited to consumer protection situations, but also covers, and increasingly so, commercial business transactions.

II. Controlling data and data holding as services in the interest and on behalf of another actor

What is the contractual situation of data processing, i.e. the control of personal data, and how about data holding? Both regulations – the GDPR and the Data Act – paint a picture that is shaped by various elements. This part of the article will now examine this picture from the perspective of a possible type of contract.

1. Controlling personal data

As already explained, the rights and duties of the parties under the GDPR have no direct influence on the content and type of contract. They are not to be qualified as contractual rights and duties and only influence the validity and content of the contract in limited cases. However, the totality of the provisions of the GDPR that deal with the rights and duties of the controller and the data subject, paints a picture of the relationship between the two parties, which will now be examined from a contractual perspective.

From a contractual point of view, the GDPR first of all makes the controller responsible for the personal data of the data subject with regard to the protection of the data. This arises primarily from Art. 32 GDPR, which obligates the controller to adequately protect the data subject's data by means of technical and organisational measures. This protection is in the interest of the data subject and applies independently to any justification by the controller for the processing of the data.

The GDPR also stipulates that the data controller must provide the data subject with their personal data and delete the data still under their control after their relationship has ended. This combination of Artt. 15, 20 GDPR on the one hand, and Art. 17 GDPR on the other, can be interpreted as a kind of digital obligation to 'surrender' the data subject's data.

This significant obligation goes hand in hand with a comprehensive accountability of the controller, which follows from the general principle in Art. 5(2) GDPR and which is calibrated by information duties towards the data subject as per Artt. 13–15 GDPR.[9] This includes, at least according

9 For further provisions of the GDPR that can be classified as manifestations of the principle, see *Malgieri* in D'Orazio/Finocchiaro/Pollicino/Resta (ed), Art. 5 No 10.

to some voices, the accountability for profits made from the use of the data. The accountability of the controller clarifies that the entire legal relationship is imposed on the controller, who acts in the interest of the data subject and, where applicable, on behalf of the data subject.

This finding is even strengthened by the principle of purpose limitation, which underlies the GDPR: According to this principle, which is formulated in Art. 5(1)(b) GDPR, data processing is not only limited to certain specified purposes, but their specification also lies within the competence of the data subject, without significant exceptions. Art. 6 I lit. a and f, 21 GDPR link every autonomous purpose to the autonomy of the data subject. By contrast, there is no relevant autonomous purpose by the controller, who must always take into account the interests of the data subject. The specific legal justifications in favour of the controller concern obligations imposed on the controller by the legal system in the public interest or in the interest of the data subject, but usually not in the interest of the controller. The controller is in no way free to use the data for their own purposes. Autonomy is therefore only granted in the event that the data subject acts and decides.

The controller's responsibility and obligation to 'surrender' the data, combined with accountability on the one hand, and the principle of purpose limitation and the absence of free use for one's own purposes on the other, paint the picture of a service provided exclusively for the benefit, in the interest and on behalf of the data subject.[10] This may come as a surprise to many of the parties involved, who primarily ask about the justification for data processing, but it is a pure consequence of the rights and obligations provided for in the GDPR. The data controller is the data subject's agent.

2. Data holding

When examining the pictures drawn by the new Data Act, the situation is somewhat different. The reason for this deviation is that the Data Act contains elements of two different situations and therefore two different pictures: the general picture drawn by Artt. 8–13 DA on the one hand, which applies to all kinds of data access rights, which are established by EU

10 See *Schmidt-Kessel* in Bomhard/Schmidt-Kessel (eds), Data Act, Art. 2 No. 33, Intro to Art. 3 No. 35 et seq., Art. 4 No. 98; *Schmidt-Kessel*, MMR 2024, 75, 81.

law or Member States law on or after the decisive point in time[11]. On the other hand, for the data produced by IoT devices and connected services, Artt. 3–7 and 13 DA provide elements of a somewhat different and more specific picture for access rights to data generated by IoT devices or related services in the sense of Art. 2 No. 5, 6 DA.

a. General rules on data access obligations (Artt. 8–13 DA)

The general picture painted by Artt. 8–13 DA is rather vague. Art. 8 DA mainly provides for the applicability of FRAND conditions to all parties using the data and therefore requires the data controller to include fair, reasonable and non-discriminatory contractual clauses for the organisation of any right of access to data. This rule in Art. 8 DA is accompanied by Art. 9 DA, which stipulates an obligation of data holders to ensure fair pricing.

Similar to some elements established by the GDPR, Art. 11 DA also deals with technical protection measures, but does not require the data holder to establish such measures, and merely grants the data holder the right to take such technical protection measures in their own interest vis-à-vis persons who have a better legal position with regard to the data. This distinguishes the right to establish protective measures under Art. 11 DA from the obligation under Art. 32 of the GDPR.

On the other hand – and completely in line with the general principles of the GDPR including Art. 5(1)(b) GDPR –, the Data Act also contains the principal of purpose limitation, which restricts the right to use data to the purposes underlying the access right. An explicit element of this purpose limitation rule can be found in Art. 11(3)(b) DA.[12] It is accompanied by restrictions to dissemination of the data (Art. 8(4) DA). The data controller is therefore not permitted to do whatever they want with the data.

Apart from these last points of purpose limitation and restrictions on dissemination, Artt. 8–13 DA do not provide a clear picture of the nature and type of the relationship between data holder and persons in a better legal position. The situation is different when it comes to the particular picture for the IoT device data regulated in Artt. 3–7 DA.

11 Which is 12 September 2025, cf. Art. 50(4) DA.

12 For IoT data, the principle is much clearer established, see Artt. 3(3)(c), 4(13) and (14), 5(9), 6(1) DA and infra sub II. 2. b., II. 3. and III. 2. In addition, see Artt. 4(5), 5(4), 6(2)(e) DA.

b. Holding IoT device data (Artt. 3–7, 13 DA)

The specific picture for IoT device data that emerges from the special provisions in Artt. 3–7, 13 DA is much more concrete:

This first concerns terminology. The definition of the data holder in Art. 2 No. 13 DA describes the data holder as a person, who has the right or obligation to use and make available data. The main case covered by this definition is that of the data holder as a data debtor, who is obligated to make certain data available. The definition presupposes a certain kind of control over the data, for which access is owed. However, this control is not part of the definition, but results from the respective provisions on the data holder's obligations to make the data available. For the IoT device data, for example, the relevant control is limited to readily available data within the meaning of Art. 2 No. 17 DA. Therefore, the position of the data holder is primarily that of a debtor to make available or 'surrender" the data covered by the respective obligation.

This terminological approach is reflected in the descriptions of the legal position of the data holder in relation to IoT device data within the meaning of Art. 2(15) and (16) DA, which is mainly derived from Artt. 4(13), (14), 8(4) DA and the provisions on third-party data access in accordance with Artt. 5, 6 DA:

In addition to the special position of the data holder as the debtor, these provisions first clarify the legal data sovereignty of the user of the IoT device or related services. This data sovereignty means that all rights to the IoT device data are concentrated in the hands of this user. The data holder is therefore prohibited by law from autonomously using the data, which they factually control. This prohibition arises from Art. 4(13) DA.[13] The second sentence of this article lays down specific prohibitions on the use of the data for fishing expeditions to determine the economic situation of the user and to undermine their economic position. The general prohibition contained in the first sentence of Art. 4(13) DA prevents the data holder from using the data in their own interest without being contractually justified by the user.

The legal data sovereignty of the user of the IoT device thus encompasses not only the general monopoly of licensing rights to use, but also, necessarily, the determination of the purpose of the use as part of the respective

13 On this provision see *Schmidt-Kessel* in Bomhard/Schmidt-Kessel (eds.), Data Act, Art. 4 No. 166–170.

contractual agreement. This is not dealt with directly in the Data Act, however, Art. 6(1) DA – in conjunction with all the references to the purpose of use, see Artt. 3(3)(c), 4(13) and (14), 5(9), 6(1) DA[14] – demonstrates, that purpose limitation applies as a general principle also under the Data Act and thereby for EU data contract law. It is worth noting, that the agreed upon purposes do not necessarily have to correspond with the purposes relevant for justified data processing under the GDPR. While both pieces of legislation and both spheres – data protection law and data contract law – follow a purpose limitation principle this does not preclude both layers from determining the purposes differently.

In addition to the lack of any autonomous right of the data holder to use the data, the data holder is also prohibited by Artt. 4(14), 8(4) DA from disseminating the data without the user's agreement.[15] The only exception to this prohibition is the fulfilment of a contract between the data holder and the user, who in this case also profits from their legal data sovereignty. Therefore, any passing-on of data requires a contractual basis between the data holder and the user in order to be lawful.

However, the position of the data holder is not solely a negative position without autonomous rights to use and to disseminate: additionally, the data holder has the positive obligation pursuant to Art. 5 DA to dispose of the data according to the user's instructions. Art. 6 DA clarifies that the instructions by the user do not only cover the disposal in favour of a third party, the data recipient, as such, which is to be determined by the user, but also include the determination of the purpose for which the data may be used by the third-party data recipient. This purpose determination is also obligatory for the data holder when – in fulfilment of a contract – it passes on the IoT device data to a third-party data recipient.

The provisions of the Data Act for IoT device data thus paint a very clear picture of the data holder's position: the data holder is regarded as a kind of subsidiary or vicarious agent to the user of the IoT device, who must follow the user's instructions. Although the scope of the user's discretion with regard to these instructions still needs to be clarified in detail (for example the Data Act does not determine exactly the obligations concerning storage of the data by the data holder), the data holder's dependence on the user's instructions and specifications shows that the data holder is not merely a subsidiary but also must act in the user's interests.

14 In addition, see Artt. 4(5), 5(4), 6(2)(e) and 11(3)(b) DA.

15 See *Schmidt-Kessel* in Bomhard/Schmidt-Kessel (eds.), Data Act, Art. 4 No. 171–178.

Overall, the position of the data holder is therefore very similar to that of the data controller vis-à-vis the data subject: The data holder is defined as the debtor with respect to the provision of data and does not profit from any autonomous rights to use or to disseminate the data. Moreover, they must largely comply with user's instructions and are therefore to be classified as a service provider acting in the interest of the user. The data holder under the Data Act is therefore the user's agent.

3. The position of the third-party data recipient

The Data Act presents more details concerning third parties receiving data from the data holder upon the request of the user under Art. 5 DA. In some cases, this third party and data recipient will also be a further data holder,[16] which raises further questions. Apart from these special cases, Art. 6 DA paints its own and in part even more restrictive picture on the position of the data recipient as a third party:[17]

For these third parties, Art. 6(1) DA formulates an explicit purpose limitation principle, which ties the right to use the data granted to the third party to the purposes and conditions agreed upon with the user. This purpose limitation principle binding the third party is so strong, that under Art. 6(1) 2nd sentence DA, the third party is even asked to erase the data when it is no longer necessary for the agreed on purpose. Unlike the erasure rule for data protection law in Art. 17 GDPR, the only justification for not deleting the data, which is only available in the case of non-personal data, is a deviating agreement with the user. In the case of personal data, however, the consequences of achieving the purpose are open according to the wording of the Data Act. It is very likely that the legislator intended this gap to be closed by applying Art. 17 GDPR. However, closing the gap this way would be highly questionable, as Art. 17 GDPR not only applies to the level of the legal rights attribution layer and not to the layer of contractual rights and obligations, but also focuses on the protection of integrity rather than on the balancing of contractual interests.

The various provisions of Art. 6(2) DA also restrict the passing-on of the data by the data recipient to further third parties and exclude gatekeepers

16 *Schmidt-Kessel* in Bomhard/Schmidt-Kessel, Data Act, Art. 2(16) No. 55 et seq.

17 For more details see *Schmidt-Kessel* in Bomhard/Schmidt-Kessel, Data Act, Art. 6 No. 3, 4, 6–17.

(in the sense of Art. 3 DMA) from becoming such further third parties (lit. c, d). In addition, the provision prohibits the third party from attempting to monopolise the data if the user is a consumer (lit. h); the consumer is therefore free to grant other third parties access to the data (or have them granted access). Furthermore, several prohibitions and restrictions on use are expressly regulated (lit. b, e-g). The generally non-mandatory nature of these provisions also requires the protection of user autonomy from so-called dark patterns (lit. a).

Of course, the contract between the user and the third-party data recipient also contains some elements of agency, which are reflected, among other things, in the specific prohibitions on use. On the other hand, there is no restriction on the third party to act solely in the interest of the user. In particular – apart from the case of overlap of a third party being a new data holder – the user has no general right to issue instructions. This would characterise the entire relationship as an agency and making the third-party recipient an agent solely acting in the interest of the user. Rather, the much more open wording of Art. 6(1) DA also covers third parties who are entitled to use the IoT data in their own interest on the basis of a contract with the user.

Therefore, Art. 6 DA describes the establishment of a contract for use (see III. below) rather than a relationship of agency. This does not release the third party from its obligation to also act in the interest of the user, which is demonstrated in particular by the prohibitions of dark patterns, Art. 6(2)(a) DA, and the responsibility for the security of the networked product, Art. 6(2)(f) DA – these demonstrate a general duty of care on the part of the third party in favour of the user[18]. However, the third party is, as a rule, not restricted to acting exclusively in the interests of the user. This is reflected in the fact that Art. 6(1) DA contains typical elements of contracts for use, including a time limit, and an element of custody with regard to the data and duties to 'surrender" the data used after the end of the use relationship (see again sub III.).

18 This is reinforced for personal data not in the least by Art. 32 GDPR. The third party also has duties of care towards the data holder, as set out in Art. 6(2)(e) and (g) of the GDPR, but these are not really relevant for figuring out the type of contract with the user of the IoT device.

4. Implications for data use by the data holder

Beyond regulating the position of the third party, Art. 6 DA also provides a model for legal relationships, where the data holder is permitted to use the data to some extent in their own interests in accordance with Art. 4(13) DA.

This special situation is – with regard to the content of the contract of use – not explicitly regulated in Artt. 4–7 DA. However, when controlling terms in the contract governing the relationship between the user and the data holder, the provisions on unfair contract terms in Art. 13 DA and the Unfair Contract Terms Directive 93/13/EC are to also be applied using the model provided in Art. 6 DA as a yardstick. Art. 6 DA will therefore become the legal model for data use contracts in general.

The mixture of elements of agency and elements of a contract for use, that will characterise such relationships, provides intricate challenges not only for the interpretation of the explicit rules of the Data Act, but also for the development of EU data contract law in general, which cannot be answered in detail here. However, a such contract, which organises an agency relationship and a contract for use, is a special hybrid contract, that will become a typical contract in the data economy and the European contract law for the digital world.

5. Consequences

EU law is in the process of establishing contract law categories of market participants, who exercise control over personal and non-personal data. These provisions apply in particular to situations where another person – the user or the data subject – has a better right to the data. This development of the EU legal system is largely supported by the rules on the position of the data controller under the GDPR and – insofar as data from IoT devices is concerned – also by the special provisions on the position of data holders established by the Data Act. The general provisions for data holders in Art. 8–12 DA do not preclude this and at least allow for a rough basis for the classification of contracts to be provided and the drafting of legal rules for them.

In developing these categories, the European Union tends to define market participants in control of data as acting in the best interests and on behalf of the person in the better position, i.e. the data subject or the user. Moreover, based on the special provisions of Art. 6 DA, those third parties, who become data recipients following a passing-on decision by the user, are seen by Art. 6 DA in particular as profiting from a contract to use data (see again infra sub III.). This contract model for the use of data laid down in Art. 6 DA, could in the future clarify the treatment of additional rights to use granted to a data holder under Art. 4(13) DA. It could also serve, at minimum, as a model for the control of unfair contract terms under the Unfair Terms Directive 93/13/EC and in the application of Art. 13 DA.

Both types of contracts and contractual situations – agency relationships in which the agent acts exclusively in the interest of the user or the data subject as the party in the better position, and contracts on the use of data – focus on the rights of use without abandoning all elements of agency and are dominated by a purpose limitation principle. This purpose limitation principle not only dominates data protection law, as established in Art. 5(1)(b) GDPR, but is also a guiding principle for position of market participants, who control data under the Data Act. One might even argue that this purpose limitation principle represents a new general principle of private law for the data economy and the digital world.

III. Use of data as object of a contract

Neither the GDPR and data protection law nor the data contract law established by the Data Act are limited to agency situations. Rather, both legislative acts contain essential guidance on how contractual relationships for the use of data should be structured.[19] Moreover, the Directive 2019/770 on digital content and digital services includes several structural decisions concerning data that is the subject matter of a contract of use. In this respect, the Directive is not limited to so called 'paying with data" situations but also applies to contracts for use of data by consumers. This second regulatory aspect of the Directive, which may come as a surprise to some

19 In this article, the term 'data use contract' is preferred. The frequently used term 'data licence contract' has the often misleading connotation that the licensor is the holder of an absolute right *in rem* or even data ownership. In fact, the position of the data holder is generally merely a contractual right, which, according to the legal basis of the Data Act, is solely vested in the user at the beginning, see Artt. 4(13), (14), 8(4) DA and *Schwamberger*, in Bomhard/Schmidt-Kessel (eds.), Data Act, Art. 13 No. 114–117.

readers,[20] allows more EU legal concepts, structuring the rules on contracts for the use of data, to be identified.

1. Indications by GDPR

The GDPR does not contain any specific provisions for contracts concerning the right to use personal data. In particular, Art. 6(1)(b) GDPR does not accept most contracts for use of the data as a justification for data processing by the user.[21] With this decision the GDPR deviates significantly from common experience with agreements for hire, rent or lease, which, at least in continental European legal systems, usually do not require justification for the use separate from the contract for use. In contrast, the European separation principle for data contract law and the data economy (see supra sub I.) presupposes not only the contractual justification of the user (to avoid unjustified enrichment by use) but also stipulates a separate legal basis for the data processing necessary to legally use the data.

This finding might not be generally avoided by referring to Art. 6(1)(f) GDPR, which to some extent could justify data processing on the basis of a contract for use. However, such a justification by the legitimate interest of the user would not preclude the data subject from objecting the use pursuant to Art. 21 GDPR and thus possibly frustrating the contract for use. On the other hand, the legal basis of Art. 6(1)(f) GDPR could be sufficient in the not uncommon case, that the use of the data only constitutes a part of the contract fulfilment. In this case as well, the GDPR provides little guidance on the content of the contract for use. Moreover, Art. 6(1)(f) GDPR rarely provides a legal basis for data processing beyond the contractual basis aside from the agreed upon or implied use, and the agreed upon or implied purpose.

Due to the wide-ranging non-applicability of Art. 6(1)(b) GDPR and the weak and accessory justification provided by Art. 6(1)(f) GDPR, the data subject's consent often remains the only reasonable way to organise the

20 Cf. *Bomhard* in Bomhard/Schmidt-Kessel (eds.), Data Act, Art. 1 No. 67; *Schmidt-Kessel* in Bomhard/Schmidt-Kessel (edss.), Data Act, Intro to Art. 3 No. 71; *Veil*, in BeckOK Datenschutzrecht Art. 1 DA No. 354.

21 Cf. ECJ, 4.7.2023, C-252/21 (Meta Platforms Inc. V. Bundeskartellamt), No. 97–126; *Bachelet*, Il consenso oltre il consenso, 2023, 43–46; *Poletti* in D'Orazio/Finocchiaro/Pollicino/Resta (eds.), Art. 6 No 4.

lawful performance of a contract for the use of data.[22] In this respect, the GDPR provides the parties with several additional and supplementary or ancillary rights and obligations, including the rights and remedies of the data subject under the aforementioned Regulation.

The latter also include the various elements of the relationship of custody associated with a data use contract, insofar as the authorised data recipient gains control over the data. This custodial relationship is governed primarily by the principle of accountability under Art. 5(2) GDPR in its various forms, in particular in the information obligations under Artt. 13 and 14 GDPR and the data subject's rights to information and access under Artt. 15 and 20 GDPR. In addition, the data controller has a particular responsibility for the security of their own data processing pursuant to Art. 32 GDPR and for the activities of their own processors (Art. 28 GDPR) and for persons acting under their authority pursuant to Art. 29 GDPR. Unlike the core of the contract on data use, the core content of any associated relationship of custody is thus clearly defined.

In summary, it can be said that the GDPR and the rights to use the data granted under data protection law do not provide special indications for the content of contracts for the use of such data, but rather are to be regarded as purely accessory to such contracts. Therefore, guidance from the GDPR as to the content of the contract is limited to the need to determine a lawful legal basis separate from the contract, and to a few limited ancillary duties and obligations of both parties. In particular, structures for a relationship of custody that may arise become visible under data protection law.

2. Indications by the Data Act

As explained above[23], Chapter II of the Data Act, mainly Art. 6 DA, contains a comprehensive framework of rules and provisions for contracts for the use of data. Some additional elements of a data use contract can also be found in Chapter III of the Data Act. It can also be argued, that these provisions set the tone for other kinds of contracts for use of data; this was demonstrated above in the relationship between the user of the IoT device and the data holder in the event of an additional agreement between these

22 *Bachelet*, Il consenso oltre il consenso, 2023, 46.
23 See II.3.

parties granting an exceptional right of use of the data to the data holder for their own purposes under Art. 4(13) DA[24].

For contracts regarding the use of IoT data by a third-party recipient, the Data Act begins with elements of a start-up phase, mainly dealt with in Art. 5 DA, which contains the general obligation of the data holder to establish a direct relationship between the data holder and the third-party recipient. Art. 5 DA also provides some further rules for this first start-up part of the contractual relationship, which at the same time determine the content of the relationship between user of the IoT device and the third-party recipient of the data.[25]

Art. 6(1) DA then defines the core content of the contract for use of the data, by establishing the purpose limitation principle as a general principle on the obligatory layer of the relationship between the parties of the contract for use.[26] This contractual (and not in rem, cf. Art. 5 II lit. b GDPR) principle of purpose limitation means that the contract on the use of the data is a temporary undertaking: it is in any case limited to the period during which the data are necessary for the purpose agreed upon between the user of the IoT device and the data recipient, see Art. 6(1) 2nd sentence DA. Unlike under Art. 5(1)(b) GDPR, the determination at the time of data generation is not decisive. Rather, the user is free to specify other purposes in the contract with the third party in accordance with their data sovereignty. Moreover, the purpose may also be changed by subsequent amendment of the contract.[27] Upon expiry of the period necessary for the agreed purpose, the relationship of use ends, which is emphasised in the Data Act in the expressly formulated obligation to delete data under Art. 6(1) 2nd sentence DA.

For the core part of the contract fulfilment Art. 6(2) DA lists a number of specific obligations of the data recipient, which includes the responsibility for the integrity and the security of data subjects in the case of personal data, see e.g. Art. 6(2)(f) DA[28]. This responsibility represents a general contractual duty of the parties involved, including the data recipient, and this obligation also includes a prohibition on the use of the data for profiling purposes, Art. 6(2)(b) DA. The responsibility for integrity and security also

24 On this point see above II.4.

25 *Schmidt-Kessel* in Bomhard/Schmidt-Kessel (eds.), Data Act, Art. 6 No. 7.

26 *Schmidt-Kessel* in Bomhard/Schmidt-Kessel (eds.), Data Act, Art. 6 No. 11. See again II.3.

27 *Schmidt-Kessel* in Bomhard/Schmidt-Kessel (eds.), Data Act, Art. 6 No. 11.

28 See again *supra* II.3.

includes the security and the integrity of the IoT device and the connected service, for which the contracting parties are responsible within the framework of the Data Act's network of contracts, Art. 6(2)(f) DA.

The extent to which the position of the third-party recipient is restricted within the framework of such contracts for the use of data, is particularly evident in two key prohibitions: Whereas the third-party recipient is allowed to use the data for their own purposes (in accordance with the agreement with the user of the IoT device), they are prohibited from unconsented dissemination under Art. 6(2)(c) DA. This prohibition cannot even be overcome by agreement between the parties in case of a gatekeeper pursuant to Art. 3 DMA, Art. 6(2)(d) DA. Moreover, consumers as users of the IoT device of the connected service remain free to disseminate their own data elsewhere due to the prohibition on data recipients monopolising these data for their own purposes, Art. 6(2)(h) DA.

Compared to the usual regulatory density of national codifications for classical contracts for hire, rent or lease, the Data Act contains a high number of detailed provisions, that establish a differentiated internal structure for the data use contract. This differentiated regulatory system is primarily aimed at balancing the interests within the relationships involved, without neglecting the pure service provision and agency position of the data holder.

3. Indications by the Directive 2019/770

Additional indications on the general structure of the contract for the use of data may be drawn from the Digital Content and Digital Service Directive 2019/770.[29] The Directive addresses aspects of use of data from two different perspectives: On the one hand, the rules on 'paying with data" must be taken into account; on the other hand, the Directive also applies to cases, in which the consumer is the creditor of a right to use data granted by the trader; and in the latter case, the rules of the Directive are not even limited to personal data.

29 Directive (EU) 2019/770 of the European Parliament and of the Council of 20 May 2019 on certain aspects concerning contracts for the supply of digital content and digital services, OJ No L136 of 22 May 2019, p. 1.

a. Transfer of data as kind of payment by the consumer

The provisions of Directive 2019/770 on the scope of application indicate that it applies not only to the provision of digital content or digital services for money, but also to contracts, where 'the consumer provides personal data to the trader or undertakes to do so,' Art. 3(1) subsection 2 Directive 2019/770. This extension of the scope of application of the Directive, which finds a parallel in Art. 3(1a) Consumer Rights Directive 2011/83/UE, treats the actual or promised provision of personal data by the consumer as a substitute for a monetary payment for the purposes of determining the scope of application of the Directive.

This extension of the scope of both Directives does not apply to cases where the personal data provided by the consumer are processed solely for the purpose of providing the digital content or the digital services. Furthermore, arrangements where the data processing serves only to enable the trader to comply with their legal obligations, are not covered by the Directive. However, if the trader processes the data provided or to be provided for purposes other than the two excluded purposes – fulfilment of the obligation to supply or compliance with legal requirements – the two Directives apply to the contract with only a few modifications (including the exclusion of price reductions) as if it were for monetary consideration.

The two Directives hardly regulate the further rights and obligations of the parties with regard to the respective personal data of the party 'paying with data'. For the specific case of withdrawal of the consent for the processing of the consumer's personal data pursuant to Art. 7(3) GDPR this omission is expressly explained in Recital 40 of Directive 2019/770: 'These consequences should remain subject to national law.'

However, the wording of the provision on the consequences of the termination of the contract in Art. 16(2) and (3) Directive 2019/770 also deals with the handling of personal data and – in theory – non-personal data at the end of the contract, which is in the custody of the other party upon termination of the contract; the provision therefore concerns the typical settlement relationship at the end of the contract with regard to items transferred or otherwise obtained from the other party. Functionally this is similar to Art. 6(1) 2nd sentence DA discussed above,[30] where a similar principle underlies the duty to erase the data.

30 See *supra* II. 3.

Such a deletion is not explicitly required by Art. 16(2) and (3) Directive 2019/770 – nor is it required in the case of similar obligations arising from the consequences of the consumer's right to withdrawal under Art. 13(4) and (5) Consumer Rights Directive 2011/83/UE. This at least proves that the custody relationship between the consumer and the trader ends as soon as the contractual relationship that forms the core of the trader's performance ends. While the Directive obligates the trader to refrain from further use of nonpersonal data (with some detailed exceptions), obligations to return or delete this data are not expressly imposed.

For personal data, however, Art. 16(2) Directive 2019/770 and Art. 13(4) Consumer Rights Directive 2011/83/UE contain the familiar, rather enigmatic references to the obligations of the controller under the GDPR, with reference mainly to Artt. 12 to 21 GDPR. Here, the Directives seem – like general data protection law – to paint a picture of a special data restitution regime, including the right to data (re-)portability in Art. 20 GDPR and the obligation to erase the data in accordance with Art. 17 GDPR. However, the Directives do so – correctly – only in a clarifying manner and leave the consequences at the level of contract law undecided. These enigmatic references in Art. 16(2) Directive 2019/770 and Art. 13(4) Directive 2011/83/UE must therefore not be understood as imposing additional contractual functions on the data protection provisions of the GDPR.

These parts of the Directives thus show, that the 'consideration function' of the contracts covered by them, involves a kind of usage contract element, that is linked to some regulation of the custody for this data. However, most of the consequences of this use as part of the – actual or fictitious – consideration of these contracts must be dealt with by application of national law.

The German legislator has introduced the aforementioned[31] special provision in § 327q BGB, which, firstly, establishes a principle of abstraction (not only separation) between the obligatory and the privacy layer of the relationship in § 327q(1) BGB. Secondly, § 327q(3) BGB excludes any compensation for the trader, if the exercise of the data subject's rights by the consumer prevents the trader from using the data to generate further income. Only in long-term contracts for the supply of digital content or digital services does § 327q(2) BGB grant the trader a special right to terminate the contract for good cause, which mainly refers to an unbearable

31 See I.2.

reduction in income due to the consumer's – justified – data protection remedies.

b. Supply of data as supply of digital content to the consumer

The main objective of the Directive 2019/770 was to establish rules for the supply of digital products and remedies in the event of failure to supply them, as well as rules on the conformity of digital products and consumer remedies in case of lack of conformity. In addition, the Directive addresses situations where the digital product is modified. These rules also apply to cases where the consumer has a right under a contract with the trader to receive data as digital products. The term 'digital products' is not limited to software, media content, platforms or clouds, but also includes contracts for the supply of personal or non-personal data to the consumer.

The picture painted by the Directive in this regard represents the general concept, which European Union law has developed for contractual obligations to supply an object. The possibility of generalising the various provisions and deriving general principles from them is not only supported by other Directives with similar rules, such as the Consumer Sales Directive 2019/771[32] and the Package Travel Directive 2015/2302[33]. Rather, Art. 20 of Directive 2019/770 extends the principles of the entire Directive to B2B contracts by introducing a right of recourse in favour of the trader, who is liable to the consumer for a breach of contract attributable to an act or omission of a person in the chain of transactions. While the details of the remedies, actions and conditions of this recourse are to be determined by national law, the Directive establishes the right to a remedy as such

32 Directive (EU) 2019/771 of the European Parliament and of the Council of 20 May 2019 on certain aspects concerning contracts for the sale of goods, amending Regulation (EU) 2017/2394 and Directive 2009/22/EC, and repealing Directive 1999/44/EC, OJ No L 136, 22.5.2019, p. 28.

33 Directive (EU) 2015/2302 of the European Parliament and of the Council of 25 November 2015 on package travel and linked travel arrangements, amending Regulation (EC) No 2006/2004 and Directive 2011/83/EU of the European Parliament and of the Council and repealing Council Directive 90/314/EEC, OJ No. L 326, 11.12.2015, p. 1. See also the planned and essentially unchanged continuation of the general concept by the Proposal for a Directive of the European Parliament and of the Council amending Directive (EU) 2015/2302 to make the protection of travellers more effective and to simplify and clarify certain aspects of the Directive, COM/2023/905 final.

– together with the extension of the concepts of non-performance and conformity to the B2B sector.

The rules laid down in the Directive, in particular those regarding the conformity and non-conformity of the digital products supplied and the remedies available in case of breach by non-compliance, would also apply to contracts for the use of data if and to the extent that they are classified as the supply of digital products. This becomes particularly clear in places where the Directive refers to contracts that stipulate the continuous supply over a period of time, whether limited or unlimited, and distinguishes them from contracts that provide for a single act of supply.

If a contract for a continuous supply is terminated by the consumer due to a breach of contract by the trader before the end of the contract term, Art. 17(1) Directive 2019/770 then obligates the consumer to refrain from further using the digital product or making it available to third parties. Here, too, the typical consequences of a contract for use at the end of the period of use are specified – bearing in mind that this also extends to cases of single supply, but with the added need to protect the consumer's reliance on retaining the digital product.

These elements of the end-of-contract provisions contained in Art. 17 Directive 2019/770 may, to a certain extent, serve as a model for the general picture, that secondary European Union law paints for contracts for use of digital items, including personal and nonpersonal data.

4. Conclusions

Considerations of the individual legislative acts of the European Union, relating to contracts on the use of data, leads us to some preliminary conclusions on this particular type of contract:

This primarily includes the finding, that contracts for the use of data exist as a subject of European Union law and that European Union law provides at least some elements for the regulation of such contracts. However, these elements are not primarily contained in the GDPR. The regulation does not structure the relationship of use, but only co-regulates it in relation to data protection, mainly concerning the necessary element of custody in the event, that the data come under control of the data user, i.e. the Data Act third-party recipient.

The Data Act, on the other hand, lays down initial elements of the contract for use of data, in particular for the relationship between the IoT device user and the third-party recipient of the data. It is important to emphasise that the Data Act limits the availability of such contracts to temporary – but not necessarily fixed-term – contracts for use of the data and adds special provisions governing the relationship between the parties, including the initial start-up phase, the performance of the contract, and the obligations of the parties, as well as the ending and the settlement phase of this use relationship. The Data Act is supplemented regarding certain specific aspects of consumer contracts by the Directive 2019/770 on Digital Content and Digital Services, which deals with some synallagmatic consequences of 'paying' with rights to use data and establishes a model for the treatment of contracts for the temporary supply of data to consumers. These special provisions also contain requirements on data quality, which will need to be further developed in the future, in particular for the provision of personal and nonpersonal data to consumers in accordance with Directive 2019/770 and beyond the scope of that Directive.

IV. Ancillary duties and data contracts

The focus of research, legislation and case law relating to data processing and data contracts is on the processing for use and the processing services as the main subject matter of the respective contract for use or agency relationship. This situation of the central subject matter of the contract is likely to be the case in many large contracts for data processing, data intermediary services or data usage. However, this approach does not provide a complete picture of data contract law and its type of contract.

The main reason for this is that the practical relevance of data for the contracting parties is often a secondary issue. This applies even to the Data Act, insofar as it concerns contracts for the sale or rental of IoT devices, in particular in Artt 3 and 4 DA. In those relationships, the processing of the data generated during the use the IoT device will often be reduced to a minor issue.[34] And the same applies to contracts for the supply of digital content or digital services under the Directive 2019/770. Except for the supply of personal and nonpersonal data as the core performance of a trader to a consumer, this consumer protection directive regulates data contracts and data contract terms only as ancillary services or other ancillary aspects.

34 See *Schmidt-Kessel*, MMR 2024, 75, 82. Pure data processing in some cases excludes a contract from the scope of application of the data act, see *Schmidt-Kessel* in Bomhard/Schmidt-Kessel (eds.), Data Act, Art. 2(6) No. 22.

This finding leads to a certain tension between the regulatory requirements of data protection and data contract law, respectively data obligation law, of the European Union on the one hand, and requirements for contract design that do not fall under the data-centric perspective but are nevertheless subject to European Union legislation, on the other. These European regulations often do not fit the ancillary or mixed situation that arises in many contractual situations in practice and theory.

Art. 11(2) DA is a good example of this: As a consequence of certain breaches by the parties in the various relationships relating to data access (which are mainly dealt with in Chapter II of the Data Act), this provision provides for a number of special remedies, that are clearly aimed at treating data contracts as the core of a business relationship or consumer contract. The remedy of erasure of data made available and of all copies thereof pursuant to Art. 11(2)(a) DA would often not fit the entire contractual context and must be restricted or even excluded in cases where such data contract components are merely ancillary to the predominant parts of the contract. This applies all the more to the right to obtain the cessation of 'the production, offering or placing on the market or use of goods, derivative data or services produced on the basis of knowledge obtained through such data, or the importation, export or storage of infringing goods for those purposes" and the destruction of all infringing goods pursuant to Art. 11(2)(b) DA, which may be the reasonable remedy in pure data relationships, but must be adapted to a considerable extent if the data processing is only a subordinate element in other relationships. In contrast, other remedies under Art. 11(2) DA – namely obligations to inform or to compensate aggrieved parties – constitute a more general rule and are therefore also suitable in cases with an accessory character of data contract components.

These findings show (once again) that legislative rules and concepts for ancillary contractual obligations are necessary at the European level. In the absence of more general private law and contractual rules and legislation, European Union courts will have to answer the question of which principles of efficiency and equivalence are required when the data centric rules apply in situations that are ancillary to other contractual contexts.

V. Mixed contracts as the new normal

Even the concept of ancillary obligations does not always meet the regulatory requirements and expectations of market participants. This is because the decisive preponderant (or main) part of such contracts cannot always be clearly determined and the criteria for determining this preponderance are still open. For example, time shares and acquired or created values do not necessarily provide complete information about the intentions and expectations of the parties.

This lack of general rules for mixed contracts and similar mixed situations in European Union law becomes a threat for the functioning of private law in the internal market, if mixed situations become the new norm, when data control and data use are included in contractual relationship environments, covering all types of contractual subject matter, on all kinds of contractual objects. EU law appears to be developing its own approach to mixed contracts,[35] but the exact form of this approach and its legal consequences are not yet entirely clear:

Based on the familiar formula in Article 3(6) of Directive 2019/770 on Digital Content and Digital Services, a general principle for mixed contracts could read as follows: 'Where a single contract between the same parties includes a bundle of elements falling under one EU legislative act and elements relating to the provision of other services or goods, the legislative act shall only apply to the elements of the contract covered by that legal act.' The basic idea of contract types in Articles 3 and 4 DA could in any case be reconciled with such a formula. At first glance, the basic structure of EU contract law seems to tend to favour combined solutions rather than absorption solution in favour of traditional types of contracts. However, this question needs to be examined in more detail.

VI. General Conclusions

In summary, it can be stated that:

First, European Union law provides a multi-layered system for data contracts. The first layer, i.e. the data protection layer, deals mainly with the allocation of the positions of data, the subject and the controller, which is functionally similar to the legal allocation of rights *in rem* to property under property law. However, as in the field of intellectual and industrial property, this allocation follows rules that differ significantly from traditional property law on corporeal objects. In particular, the GDPR and EU

35 Cf. *Schmidt-Kessel* in Bomhard/Schmidt-Kessel (eds.), Data Act, Intro to Art. 3 No. 41.

data protection law requires this layer of allocation to be separated from the contractual balancing of interests on the second layer. At this second layer, mainly the provisions on access to and use of data (in particular of the Data Act but also established by certain other legislative acts of the European Union) apply; an autonomous system of data contract law and data law of obligations of the European Union is beginning to emerge. However, this autonomous system is calibrated on its main object, data, which causes a formative effect of the allocation of rights by data protection law on data obligation law and data contract law.

Second, European Union law establishes a set of rules for data services involving custody and agency relationships. The most important service providers covered by these rules are the data controller, within the meaning of data protection law, and the data holder, within the meaning of the Data Act, both of whom act as agents of the data subject and the user of the IoT device respectively. The main characteristic of this position is the duty to act in the interest and on behalf of the data subject or the user. European Union law thus creates a separate type of contract for services and custody relationships in the interest and on behalf of persons with better rights in the data. In addition, this special contract often comes across as a contract component for service and custody, which then forms part of the larger context of the contractual relationship.

Third, European Union law has begun to develop a basic structure for contracts for the use of data. This also includes an element of custody and service in the interest and on behalf of the person with the better right in the data i.e. the provider of the use, if the contract includes a control position of the data user. For these contracts, purpose limitation provides the most constructive principle, in addition to the custody elements (in the case of control by the data user), and leads to temporary contractual relationships and restitutionary obligations alongside the settlement at the end of the contract.

Finally, under European Union law such contracts or contractual elements of agency in the interest and on behalf of persons with better rights, as well as contracts for the use of personal or nonpersonal data, are often elements of a larger contractual structure. This includes purely ancillary processing and processing rights, as well as mixed contracts. Mixed contracts are likely the new norm in European Union contract law. European Union contract law tends to apply, to a certain extent, a kind of combination solution to this, whereby the specific and pointillistic regulatory elements, that then become part of the larger contractual structure, remain unaffected.

III.
The Value of Consumer Data in and Beyond the Data Act

Data Act Beyond Consumer Protection: The Fairness Problem

Teresa Rodríguez de las Heras Ballell[*]

I. Monetising and Mobilising Data Value in the Market: The Context

Contemporary societies and modern economies are heavily dependent upon data. Data-driven solutions, businesses, and decision-making pervade all sectors of the economy and promise immense benefits for society.[1] As non-rival (and non-excludable or excludable) goods,[2] data[3] can expand and replicate their value and utility for multiple purposes and unlimited uses and reuses without losing quality or dwindling quantity. However, the potential of data as public goods is not fully realised.[4] Serious market failures exist. Hence, instruments for monetising and mobilising data are limited and suboptimal. A well-functioning data market is then instrumental to an optimal allocation of data for the good of society. In its absence, data control is asymmetric, sharing of data value is not fair, and access to data is not properly representing the weight of contribution in data (co)generation. Therefore, promoting the sharing of high-quality, interoperable data fosters innovation, competition, and economic growth. Data sharing en-

---

* Full Professor of Commercial Law, University Carlos III of Madrid, Spain. President of the European Law Institute (ELI). Member of the Expert Group on B2B Data Sharing and Cloud Computing. The present contribution expresses only the personal opinion of the author and does not necessarily represent neither the opinion of the Expert Group nor the views of the European Commission.

1 OECD (2019), *How's Life in the Digital Age?: Opportunities and Risks of the Digital Transformation for People's Well-being,* OECD Publishing, Paris, https://doi.org/10.1787/9789264311800-en.

2 Data can be public goods (and non-excludable) or club goods (excludable). Duch Brown, N., Martens, B. and Muller-Langer, F. (2017). *The economics of ownership, access and trade in digital dat*a, JRC Digital Economy Working Paper 2017–01, European Commission, 2017, JRC104756.

3 Zins, Chaim (2007), *Conceptual Approaches for Defining Data, Information, and Knowledge,* Journal of the American Society for Information Science and Technology, 22 January 2007, 58 (4): 479–493.

4 European Strategy for Data: Communication from the Commission to the European Parliament, the Council, the European Economic and Social Committee and the Committee of the Regions, *A European strategy for data,* COM (2020) 66 final.

courages innovation and enhances competition in the aftermarket, foments the development of innovative and novel products and services, and even incentives the devising of sustainable practices and business models around or related to the main product market.

Data economy is not only enlarging in size and in amount, but also diversifying in terms of data-providing, data-collecting, and data-generating sources, devices, and actors. Then, while the volume of data and the variety of data sources increase, the need to remove any barrier to data sharing is more pressing and crucial to revert data asymmetries, dismantle data silos, and debilitate (or dilute) data monopolies. Hurdles and impediments could arise from market failures, wrong incentives to data-sharing promoting contract terms, sectoral practices hindering data sharing and/or devices' design that create, perpetuate, or lead to exclusive (*de facto*) control over data of those controlling rather the technical design than the value creation or generation process.

Connected products have upgraded data market to new dimensions. The increasingly popularity and expanding use of connected products have inundated the economy with unprecedent amounts and volumes of data. Data collected and generated by connected products present various characteristics. These products, systems, or devices massively and continuously transform into data (capable of digital processing) the physical world (*off-line*). The 'real world' can be permanently, 'recoded', 'de-and re-constructed' in enormous amounts of data. Actions, behaviours, preferences shown by use, environment conditions, and patterns observed or inferred from operation, use and surveillance feed data collection and data generation processes. These data can be collected on a permanent or regular basis and reach massive volumes. Personal and non-personal data are commonly combined and intimately commingled in mixed sets of data. These characteristics need to be taken into consideration to better understand how this potential data market works or could work. To the market failures common to data markets, the Internet-of-Thing-driven (IoT-driven) data market adds specific problems.[5] Wrong incentives in the market, design dependencies, lack of experience and practice, high transaction costs, and complexities in estimating, and assessing data value and data price dampen the potential of data monetising and leash the growth of data mobilising.

5 Kerber, W. (2023), *Governance of IoT data: Why the EU Data Act will not fulfill its objectives*, GRUR International, 72(2), pp. 120–135.

I.1. Goals and scope of the Data Act: the blurred distinction between personal and non-personal data

As the potential value of these data for individuals, businesses, the economy and the society may be outstanding, mobilising such data and properly allocating rights of access and use constitute a decisive policy.[6] Incentives for data sharing should be unlocked and adequate mechanisms for data sharing must be implemented or freed of constraints, inefficiencies, or impediments. Data Act[7] crystallizes these policy goals and deploys a data sharing strategy under fair, reasonable, and non-discriminatory terms. Essentially, the Data Act provides for two main mechanisms. First, it grants users the right to access and make available to a third party any product data or related service data (Art. 4 and 5 Data Act). So, the Data Act empowers users.[8] On the other hand, it relies on a contract-based model for the mobilisation of data. Under a triangular model, data sharing contracts make the data circulate among data holder, user, and date recipient/s. To that end, private law[9] rules and, in particular, contract law rules play a central role not only to unleash data sharing but also to attain fairness objectives.

Data Act establishes a harmonised framework to enable the availability, the access, and the use of data in a pervasive economy of connected products and related services. Therefore, rules specifying who is entitled, in which conditions and on which basis to use such product data or related service data, as well as right-allocating mechanisms, have to be laid down

6 An EU level action on the market has been called since the Building a European Data Economy' Communication in 2017, COM (2017) 9 final.

7 Regulation (EU) 2023/2854 of the European Parliament and of the Council of 13 December 2023 on harmonised rules on fair access to and use of data and amending Regulation (EU) 2017/2394 and Directive (EU) 2020/1828 (Data Act), PE/49/2023/REV/1, *OJ L, 2023/2854, 22.12.2023.*

8 Article 2 (12) Data Act: "'user' means a natural or legal person that owns a connected product or to whom temporary rights to use that connected product have been contractually transferred, or that receives related services." The Data Act complements consumer protection legislation and applies without prejudice to any Union law promoting the interests of consumers.

9 Private law is today experiencing an extraordinary revival revisited from various approaches that challenge a monolithic and simple construction of private law's role in society. Grundmann, Stefan, Micklitz, Hans-Wolfgang & Renner, Moritz (2022), *New Private Law Theory – A very Brief Introduction,* German Law Journal, 23, 801–804. Against such a backdrop, the reinforced role of private law, and in particular, contract law for data governance proves, or at least seems to corroborate, this revival.

(Recitals 4 and 5 Data Act). Deftly, the Data Act avoids pronouncing itself on the elusive question of data rights. Thus, it states that the Data Act should not be interpreted as recognising or conferring any new right on data holders to use data generated by the use of a connected product or related service (Recital 5, Data Act). In fact, without qualifying the situation from a data-right perspective, the Data Act seems to pivot on a cogenerated-data scenario. 'Data generation is the result of the actions of at least two actors, in particular the designer or manufacturer of a connected product, who may in many cases also be a provider of related services, and the user of the connected product or related service' (Recital 6 Data Act). That may provide various legal grounds for data rights; or more specifically factors to consider in weighting the contribution of parties in the co-generation of data (Part III, ALI-ELI Data Principles).[10] The data holder is the designer, the manufacturer and/or the provider of connected products and/or the related service; while the user is the data subject, the operator of the product, or the subject of the monitored behavior. Such an intimacy of the use of the product with the collected/generated data blurs the distinction or, at least renders rather complicate to distinguish, between personal data and non-personal data.

In fact, the Data Act explicitly recognises that it covers both personal data and non-personal data (Art. 1(2) Data Act). Should the data to be shared qualify as personal data, parties must ensure that there is a valid legal basis under the GDPR[11] for the data holder making the data available to the data recipient, and the data sharing contract will specify the modes of provision. If data are non-personal the contract itself provides the legal basis as well as the mode of data sharing.

The consequences of such a premise are rather obvious, but maybe the assumption is more evasive. Are data generated by the use of a product naturally, commonly, and primarily, personal data just because they are stemming from the user's actions in operating the product? Such a presumption, or simply assumption, may lead to overinclusion. In any case,

10 ALI-ELI Principles for a Data Economy: https://www.europeanlawinstitute.eu/projects-instruments/instruments/ali-eli-principles-for-a-data-economy-data-transactions-and-data-rights/.

11 Regulation (EU) 2016/679 of the European Parliament and of the Council of 27 April 2016 on the protection of natural persons with regard to the processing of personal data and on the free movement of such data, and repealing Directive 95/46/EC (General Data Protection Regulation) (Text with EEA relevance). *OJ L 119, 4.5.2016, 1–88.*

even if it is assumed that some data would be personal data while others would be non-personal, the proper distinction will be extremely intricate.

Product data are generated by the use of the product. Related service data represent user actions or events related to the connected product, recorded intentionally by the user or generated as a by-product of the user's action during the provision of a related service by the provider. Consequently, data are generated because the product has been designed to that end, while, it is the use, but also the mere idle consumption or the interconnection with other ecosystems, what enables the performance of the data-collecting and data-generating functions. Coping with the data protection requirements in this challenging scenario is becoming increasingly tedious and burdensome.[12] Therefore, it is not unreasonable to think further and maybe reconsider or, at least, revisit the, undoubtedly commendable, assumptions of the personal data protection. It is inevitable to wonder whether the notion of personal data is compatible with a densely interconnected economy and a profound transformation[13] of our original connection of digital life.[14] The blurring of the distinction between reality and virtuality; the blurring of the distinctions between human, machine and nature; the reversal from information scarcity to information abundance; and the shift from the primacy of entities to the primacy of interactions invite a further consideration, even radical, of the distinction, never conclusive nor unambiguous, between personal data and non-personal data.

The broad notion of personal data under the GDPR risks to absorb almost entirely the expanding data sphere generated by connected product and related services.[15] Despite the real or remote possibility of associating product-generated data with the user, and consequently with a data subject, certainly, numerous data are primarily related to environment, operation or

---

12 Schwartz, Paul M. and Solove, Daniel J., *The PII Problem: Privacy and a New Concept of Personally Identifiable Information* (December 5, 2011), New York University Law Review, Vol. 86, 1814, 2011, UC Berkeley Public Law Research Paper No. 1909366, GWU Legal Studies Research Paper No. 584, GWU Law School Public Law Research Paper No. 584, Available at SSRN: https://ssrn.com/abstract=1909366.

13 Floridi, Luciano (2015), *The Online Manifesto. Being Human in a Hyperconnected Era*, Springer, 2015, 1. The Online Manifesto was launched on 8 February 2013 and presented at an inaugural event in Brussels held by DG Connect, the European Commission Directorate General for Communications Networks, Content & Technology.

14 Simon, Judith & Ess, Charles (2017), *The ONLIFE Initiative—a Concept Reengineering Exercise*, Philosophy & Technology, 2017, 28. 10.1007/s13347-015-0189-8.

15 Purtova, Nadezhda, *The law of everything. Broad concept of personal data and future of EU data protection law*, Law, Innovation and Technology. 10 (1), 2018, 40–81.

performance. Frankly remote from the data subject in a certain way. More precisely, a part of product data and related service data appear to respond better to the logic of co-generated data.

Therefore, it can be questioned what is truly the real rationale behind the model deployed by the Data Act. Stacking on the success of the GDPR in establishing a solid and robust protection net for personal data, the Data Act is logically not expected to overlap in achieving the same goals, or simply dig deeper in the already fertile ground of personal data protection. As a matter of fact, the Data Act emerges in a context where the value of non-personal data is on the rise and highly recognised and appreciated as the primary fuel of reliable, accurate, and safe artificial intelligence (AI). Therefore, it seems that the ultimate aim is now to succeed in creating value by mobilising data and monetising data in a market and through contracts. Data value risks at being locked and captive if there is no incentive to share. Should market forces poorly work, legal rules need to (re-)create such a data market where data circulate and data value is effectively allocated. Fair data-sharing contracts, healthy practices, and technical design of connected products converge in bringing about a conducive environment.

Non-rivalry (and non-excludability, primarily) invites an ambitious, expansive, and multifaceted approach to data sharing. Data Act acknowledges the multiple fronts converging on data sharing and sets out harmonized rules on the making available of product data and related service data to the user of the connected product or related service, the making available of data by data holders to data recipients, and, in exceptional circumstances and for the performance of a specific task in the public interest, the making available of data by data holders to public sectors bodies.

I.2. Data Act and consumer protection: an initial assessment

It is our understanding that the Data Act is not intended to primarily be a consumer protection text. Certainly, the Data Act expand protective safeguards to consumers, when using connected products, as all the general measures, rules, and mechanisms available for consumer protection are preserved. The Data Act complements and is without prejudice to such Union law aimed to ensure a high level of consumer protection (Art. 1(9) Data Act). In fact, the Data Act's strategy might be described as the 'reverse' one. The regulation aims for governing principally B2B (Business-to-Business) data sharing by way of contracts. Mobilising data flows and breaking down data silos to unleash data potential and to create a fluid data market are the drivers of data sharing contracts.[16] But in fuelling party autonomy as the driving force of data sharing, the Data Act confronts a fairness challenge. Transactions costs, asymmetries, or gatekeeping strategies render fairness a common and key problem in the entire data ecosystem. Hence, Data Act addresses the fairness problem and provides for various solutions and tools.

Thus, the Data Act is not a text whose ultimate aim is to raise the level of consumer protection – that is nonetheless preserved and extended over the data sharing scenarios -, but to face same unfairness concerns in B2B transactions and export, accordingly, some fairness-enhancing solutions to B2B data sharing. On the one hand, empowering both consumers and businesses to have more control over any product data or related service data by with a right to access and make it available to a third party. That does not only drive circulation (mobilisation) but also allows monetisation as consumers and businesses can benefit from more options, more innovation and lower prices in aftermarket and secondary products and services. This right is granted to both consumers and business users. On the other hand, repairing market failures, allocating proper incentives, and deactivating counterproductive practices to combat unfairness. To that end, the Data Act provide for rules on unfair contractual terms in (B2B) data sharing contracts between enterprises (Article 13 Data Act) and non-binding model contractual terms on data access and use for B2B data sharing contracts to be developed and recommended by the Commission (Article 41 Data Act).[17]

The Data Act does not displace neither general contract law rules nor specific consumer protection rules. Consumer is not the principle actor in the Data Act but it is present and the need of protection is not ignored.

---

16 Contrary to the conventional disclosure paradox, information (data) is not always nonexcludable. In this context, contracts can play a fundamental role in building trust relationships and facing information asymmetries. Burstein, Michael J., *Exchanging Information Without Intellectual Property* (December 2012), Texas Law Review, Vol. 91, 227, Available at SSRN: https://ssrn.com/abstract=2038772.

17 The Expert Group on B2B data sharing and cloud computing contracts (E03840) – https://ec.europa.eu/transparency/expert-groups-register/screen/expert-groups/consult?lang=en&groupID=3840 – has the mission of assisting the Commission in its work on developing model contractual clauses for B2B data sharing and standard contractual clauses for cloud computing contracts. The author is member of the Expert Group. All views and opinions in this contribution are personal and do neither bind nor represent the European Commission or the Expert Group.

As Chapter II explicitly states, its provisions govern business to consumer and business to business data sharing. In this regard, consumer protection is not only assimilated but taken for granted. But this is not the novelty. More interesting and promising than the acknowledgement that a high level of consumer protection is to be ensured, is precisely the efforts to achieve fairness in B2B data sharing. Hence, in the next sections, the Paper explores the notion of fairness in data sharing, single outs the protective measures implemented by the Data Act, and pushes the merits of the regulation beyond consumer protection.

II. Parties in the Data Sharing Ecosystem: Consumers, Micro-and SMEs and Enterprises

The Data Act traces data sharing flows around three main actors: data holder, user, and data recipient, who can participate on an individual or multiple basis. The three notions are defined in the regulation (Art. 2(12)(13)(14) Data Act) as a natural or legal person. In this triangular scenario, the request from the user and the data sharing contracts operate in the form of bilateral interactions (to avoid the reference to a contract): user-data holder (U2H), user-recipient (U2R), holder-recipient (H2R). As noted above, without any additional qualification of the parties involved, the Data Act identifies, addresses, and aims to combat an unfairness problem. This problem emerges from several failures and impediments that are unrelated to the condition of the parties as typically classified in legacy regimes. In that regard, the regulation wisely confronts the problem by unveiling its sources and grounds as a structural and relational failure. Thus, the solutions are not stemming from the legacy classification of parties on the basis of their condition but from a functional, structural, and relational approach to the market. Under subsection II.1 below, the unfairness problem, as a structural, relational, and functional problem, is unravelled.

In a second layer, the Data Act adds a classification of the parties on grounds of their condition in a classical way. With a traditional and well-known approach, a consumer is defined as 'any natural person who is acting for purposes which are outside that person's trade, business, craft or profession' (Art. 2(23) Data Act), while with the term 'enterprise', it is defined a natural or legal person that is acting for purposes which are related to that person's trade, business, craft or profession. Nothing uncommon or unexpected, the distinction consumer-business (trader or enterprise) pivots on the duality 'outside', or 'related to' instead, the sphere of trade, business, craft or profession.

However, the inclusion of additional definitions for small enterprises and microenterprises (Art. 2(25)(26) Data Act) reflects the sensitiveness of the Data Act to weaknesses, asymmetries, and vulnerabilities that may bring about fairness problems and derive from the size of the enterprises involved.[18] There is not only a mere terminological recognition, but a substantive impact on the scope of application. Thus, Article 7 Data Act closes Chapter II with a subtle delineation, *ratione personae,* of the scope of application of the obligations related to data sharing both in business to consumer scenarios and in business to business ones. The obligations laid down in Chapter III do not apply to data generated through the use of connected products manufactured or designed or related services provided by a microenterprise or a small enterprise. The Data Act realises and acknowledges that imposing certain obligations as provided for the regulation to enterprises of reduced size could be overly burdensome and stifle innovation led by start-ups, and innovative micro- and small enterprises.

Therefore, the size and the condition of the enterprises are taken into account in the regulation with a twofold aim. On the one hand, (Recital 40 Data Act) to facilitate access to data for those entities that due to their reduced size (micro-, small, and medium size) or to less-developed digital capabilities have to struggle to obtain access to relevant data. Such an enabling objective is paired with efforts to ensure that the corresponding obligations are as proportionate as possible to avoid overreach. On the other hand, to avoid suffocating innovation of micro- and small enterprises and preventing market concentration by excluding, in certain conditions, micro- and small enterprises from the scope of the design obligation (Recital 41 Data Act).

As the rationale behind such exempting or limiting decisions is not to asphyxiate the innovation capabilities of a substantial part of the business

---

18 Directorate-General Internal Policies, Policy Department C, Citizens Rights and Constitutional Affairs, *SMEs in the European Contract Law*, Author: Martijn W Hesselink, *Background note for the European Parliament on the position of small and medium-sized enterprises (SMEs) in a future Common Frame of Reference (CFR) and in the review of the consumer law acquis*, June 2007, PE 378.300. Stuyck, Jules (2014). *Do We Need 'Consumer Protection' for Small Businesses at the EU Level?*. In *Varieties of European Economic Law and Regulation*, 2014, 359–370,10.1007/978-3-319-04903-8_17.

fabric in contemporary economies, significantly in the common market, the exclusion from the scope or the transitional period is not absolute but subject to certain conditions. Thus, the exclusion provided for by Article 7(1) Data Act shall not apply if the enterprise has a partner enterprise or a linked enterprise, within the meaning of Article 3 of the Annex to Recommendation 2003/361/EC, that does not qualify as a microenterprise or a small enterprise and where the microenterprise and small enterprise is subcontracted to manufacture or design a connected product or to provide a related service. In such cases, it is assumed that the enterprise who has subcontracted the manufacturing or the design to a microenterprise or a small enterprise is able to compensate the subcontractor appropriately. Then, there is no risk of unfairness or disproportionality in the compliance of obligations. Along the same lines, a transitional period is provided for in case that the enterprise is qualified as a medium-sized enterprise. As per Article 7(1), second paragraph, the same exclusion from the scope of Chapter II applies to data generated through the use of connected products manufactured by or related services provided by an enterprise that has qualified as a medium-sized enterprise under Article 2 of the Annex to Recommendation 2003/361/EC for less than one year and to connected products for one year after the date on which they were placed on the market by a medium-sized enterprise.

Under the same prism, but at the other end of the spectrum, the Data Act applies the notion of proportionality and aims to strike a real balance in the market by taking into account the unrivalled abilities to collect data of very large enterprises in the digital economy. Thus, it bridges the Data Act with the DMA[19] to spot those enterprises with considerable economic power amply based on data aggregation and data accumulation. Consistently, such prominent enterprises are not described by their size, as very large companies, but on the basis of their designation as gatekeepers in conformity with the DMA. The scope-delimiting solution of the DMA pivots on three elements: (i) the definition of the core platform service, (ii) the concept of the gatekeeper, and (iii) the substantial connection with the Union market. These elements embody the policy goals of the regulation: to capture those providers that, even if they are not necessarily dominant in competition

19 Regulation (EU) 2022/1925 of the European Parliament and of the Council of 14 September 2022 on contestable and fair markets in the digital sector and amending Directives (EU) 2019/1937 and (EU) 2020/1828 (Digital Markets Act) (Text with EEA relevance) PE/17/2022/REV/1, OJ L 265, 12.10.2022, pp. 1–66.

law terms, have an impact on the internal market due to their considerable economic power, and their role as a gateway for a large number of users to markets, services, or infrastructures. The combination of the features characterising gatekeepers is likely to create significant power imbalances in the market and lead to unfair practices that the DMA aims to prevent and repair.

The DMA applies to 'core platform services' (Art. 1.2 DMA), defined as any digital service included in the exhaustive list enumerated by Article 2.2 DMA: online intermediation services, online search engines, online social networking services, video-sharing platform services, number-independent interpersonal communication services, operating services, web browsers, virtual assistants, cloud computing services, online advertising services. Only these services qualify. Article 3 DMA sets out the quantitative and the qualitative criteria for the Commission to designate a provider of core platform services as a 'gatekeeper'.[20]

This means (Art. 5(3) and 6(2) Data Act) that a provider of core platform services designated as a gatekeeper cannot request or be granted access to users' data generated by the use of a connected product or related service or by a virtual assistant pursuant to the Data Act. Furthermore, the data flow towards such gatekeepers is not only blocked directly but also indirectly, or in a second round, by preventing third parties to whom data are made available at the request of the user (data recipients) from making the data available to a gatekeeper. The objective of the Data Act does not need, and in fact, it could be perverted, if gatekeepers can leverage the mechanisms of the regulation. Then, these enterprises cannot be directly benefitted from the granting of access, but they are not excluded from the market. These gatekeepers can provide data processing services to data recipients; obtain and use the same data through other lawful means; and enter into voluntary agreements with data holders.

As anticipated, the sensitiveness of the Data Act to unfairness in the market goes largely beyond consumer protection. Asymmetries other than the classical consumer-trader imbalance are unveiled. While consumer protection mechanisms might handle those arising in such a type of relationships, data sharing scenarios abundantly overflows the perimeters of consumer

20 In September 2023, six businesses as gatekeepers (Alphabet, Amazon, Apple, ByteDance, Meta and Microsoft) were designated as gatekeeps in relation to 22 core platform services. Subsequently, the designation of additional gatekeepers has been announced (13th May 2024) – Booking.com; as well as the initiation of a market investigation – social media platform X.

protection use cases. Therefore, the need for regulatory action is precisely more pressing and necessary in B2B data sharing. Proclaiming contracts as the vehicle for an optimal allocation of data value is not self-sufficient. There, an unfairness problem is discovered and needs to be combatted.

II.1. The unfairness problem in the B2B data sharing market: a structural, relational, and functional problem

The primary question to address is why there is an unfairness risk in the B2B data sharing market. A study[21] complementing and contributing to the impact assessment of the (then, proposal for a) Data Act[22] sets the background and provides basic premises and key assumptions.

Contract law is the main driver for data sharing but leads to unfairness and underutilisation should market failures prevent parties from sharing data in free, competitive, transparent, and fair conditions. Market failures range from lack of competition and data monopoly situations, to gatekeeping-enabling value chains, or non-disputable data ecosystems or markets. As in other markets or sectors, data market can be distorted by market players holding a dominant position and imposing imbalanced conditions in the sharing, provided that there is any incentive for the dominant holder to deal and share, rather than retaining the data and holding the position. Should innovation and competition in the principal market or in connected markets depend upon data access, a substandard level of data sharing ruins the potential of data as non-rival and non-excludable economic goods.

Thus, the first type of market failure is related to this asymmetric position of market players within a scenario of high levels of data concentration.[23] Data can reinforce tipping, raise barriers to entry barriers and

---

21 European Commission, Directorate-General for Justice and Consumers, Graux, H., Somers, G., Van Camp, S. et al., *Study on model contract terms and fairness control in data sharing and in cloud contracts and on data access rights – Final report*, Publications Office of the European Union, 2022, https://data.europa.eu/doi/10.2838/174720.

22 Impact Assessment report and support studies accompanying the Proposal for a Data Act available at https://digital-strategy.ec.europa.eu/en/library/impact-assessment-report-and-support-studies-accompanying-proposal-data-act.

23 Crémer, Jacques, Montjoye, Yves-Alexandre, Schweitzer, Heike, *Competition Policy for the Digital Era:* Final Report, Luxembourg 2019, Publications Office of the European Union, 2019.

increase the economic power of large data holders that can benefit from strong network effects and economies of scope and scale in data. To identify and adequately categorize this failure is key to ideate and devise an effective and fit-for-purpose intervention. Whether competition-law type measures[24] are sufficient and efficient, or ex-ante regulatory measures should be, solely or in combination, provided for.[25] While the spotlight on the dominance may direct the attention towards measures attacking or mitigating market power, the data unavailability or scarcity problem may be instead rather aggravated by unbalanced or unfair terms.

A second type of market failure is not necessarily provoked by more or less traditional market dominance situations but rather be triggered by gatekeeping scenarios. Strategic positions in the value chain may raise barriers in the data flow and erect such data holders in gatekeepers creating bottlenecks and imposing unfair conditions to downstream participants. Interestingly, in these cases, the data holder deploying strategical gatekeeping strategies does not necessarily occupy a dominant position and, however, it can foreclose the development of connected markets, corelated activities, or ancillary services. This adverse effect in narrowing down or locking side or related markets is particularly damaging for competition and innovation. The non-rivalrous use potential of data is seriously compromised and missed.

These market failures can cross-cut the data ecosystem or surface with particular intensity and seriousness in specific niches or sectors. The market fails to effectively mobilise data value and avoids an optimal allocation of data. Although contracts are the primary mechanisms for enabling data sharing, party autonomy is leading to underperformance and suboptimal data sharing.

Lack of competition, non-disputable markets, and gatekeeping strategies explain, at least, one side of the identified problem: suboptimal level of

---

24 Graef, Inge, *Market definition and market power in data: The case of online platforms*, World Competition Law and Economics Review, 38(4), 2015, 473–506; Martens, B, *An economic policy perspective on online platforms*, JRC Technical Report 2016/05, 2016; Stucke, M. and M. Grunes, *Debunking the myth over big data and antitrust*, Antitrust Chronicle, 2015, 5; Tucker D. R. and H. B. Wellford, *Big mistakes regarding big data,* Antitrust Source, American Bar Association, 2014.

25 Assuming, and to the extent that, the level of data sharing in the market is proved to be a problem and provided that (free) contractual arrangements between the market players do not suffice. Kerber, Wolfgang, *Rights on Data: The EU Communication 'Building a European Data Economy' From an Economic Perspective*, 2017, https://papers.ssrn.com/sol3/papers.cfm?abstract_id=3033002.

B2B data sharing. Whereas they also lay the problematic foundations for the second side of the identified problem: the unfairness risk. The resultant imbalance of negotiating power and the existence of weak incentives for data sharing of those dominant or gatekeeping data holders precipitate conditions conducive to possible unfair clauses in data sharing contracts.

In conjunction with other policy interventions, such as the fairness control over contractual terms related to data access and use between enterprises, the model contractual terms (MCT) to be developed pursuant to Article 41 Data Act play a contributory role in unleashing the full potential of data in the Union by aiming at deactivating or mitigating, at least, the unfairness risk (*infra* III).

II.2. - Consumers in the Data Act

The more natural placeholder for consumers in the possible data sharing scenarios would seem to be the position of the user. The user is placed in the hinge position of the data sharing model underlying the Data Act. Data are generated, collected, and retrieved by connected products and related services while used and operated. More specifically, the Data Act defines 'product data' as data generated by the use of a connected product that the manufacturer designed to be retrievable, by a user, data holder or a third party, including, where relevant, the manufacturer; and 'related service data' as data representing the digitisation of user actions or of events related to the connected product, recorded intentionally by the user or generated as a by-product of the user's action during the provision of a related service by the provider. Thus, the use of these products and services is the driving force of this data-generating machinery. For the purposes of generating, collecting, and retrieving data through connected products and related services, the user plays a pivotal role, as data collected by or representing actions, events, or behaviours are triggered by the use, provided that the product is designed to collect, generate or retrieve such data. That leads to the logic of data co-generation.

The user is not always a consumer though. Furthermore, there are various relationships converging on the use of the connected product where the user may interact with different actors in relationships that may be of varying character.

The analysis needs to start with the definition of 'user' in the Data Act. The user is the 'natural or legal person that owns a connected product or to whom temporary rights to use that connected product have been contractually transferred, or that receives related services', while the consumer is always defined as a natural person in the terms indicated above. Under the definition of the Data Act, the user can be a consumer via-à-vis the vendor of the product, the lessor, or the provider of the service. But in such cases, the user is a consumer for the purposes of the contract for the purchase, lease or rent of the product. Nonetheless, these actors might not be necessarily and in all scenarios the data holder. The U2H (User-to-Holder) data sharing contract is to be entered into by the user and the data holder, that may be, for instance, the manufacturer. It may be questioned whether the user is to be treated as a consumer in such a data-related relationship. Certainly, the definition of consumer as the natural person acting outside their scope of trade, business or profession can be easily extended over the data-related relationship. Less convincing might be to assume an asymmetric relationship in the interaction between the user and the data recipient (U2R). Or, at least, acting for purposes outside trade, profession or business might not be always the case in the U2R relationship as it might depend upon the aims and agreed purposes of the data sharing agreements.

Uncertainties may arise, for various relationships can overlap. On the one hand, the pure data sharing relationship. On the other hand, other non-data-related relationships that could frame the data sharing or serve as the transactional context within data sharing takes place. Therefore, it might be an overreaction to presume that as the user is a consumer in the contract for the purchase, rent or lease of the connected product, such a condition would pervade all relationships deriving from that use. Naturally, that assumption may be the best solution to ensure a high level of consumer protection and, by all means, it is not refused in this Paper. Nonetheless, it should be based on solid grounds and be justified. Either on the basis of a principle of accessory that would render the subsequent contracts dependent upon the qualification of the main contract for the purchase, rent or lease of the product, or pursuant to a case-by-case analysis of the position of the parties in each relationship.

Differentiating the contractual relationships overlapping or converging in the data sharing scenarios that the Data Act contemplates is instrumental to allocate the obligations that the regulations sets out.

The first obligation that the Data Act provides for is a design obligation (Art. 3(1) Data Act). 'Connected products shall be designed and manufactured, and related services shall be designed and provided, in such a manner that product data and related service data, including the relevant metadata necessary to interpret and use those data, are, by default, easily, securely, free of charge, in a comprehensive, structured, commonly used and machine-readable format, and, where relevant and technically feasible, directly accessible to the user'. Such a design obligation (with the exceptions explained above) is stipulated by the law and is intended to apply solely to those enterprises who are responsible for designing, providing, or manufacturing the connected product or the related service. In fact, the obligation is imposed to those enterprises who are engaged in such stages of the manufacturing, and commercialization process. Thus, distributors, authorized representatives or, for instance, retailers might not be in a position to influence in the design, or in the provision conditions so as to comply with such a design obligation. Interestingly, it may be traced this obligation in subsequent stages of the value chain. Could non-compliance with this design obligation be deemed as a lack of conformity in the value-chain contracts concluded to reach the end user? Should the suppliers in ulterior stages of the value chain be responsible for ensuring that the design obligation is complied with by manufactures and developers?

By providing for a design obligation, the Data Act contributes to consumer protection, as well as it inserts into the value chain for connected products and related services a legal requirement that extensively benefits B2B data sharing too.

It is crucial to link this design obligation with the obligation to inform provided for by the second and the third paragraphs of the same Article 3 Data Act. Unlike the provider of the related service (Art. 3(3) Data Act), the seller, rentor or lessor is not necessarily (albeit it may happen) the designer, the manufacturer or the provider (Art. 3(2) Data Act). However, the information obligation is allocated on them as it has to be complied with by the contracting party before concluding a contract for the purchase, rent or lease of the connected product. The seller, the rentor or the lessor can only provide the required information in a clear and comprehensive manner if they have that information that should be then provided first by the manufacturer or the provider. Pursuant to Article 3(2) Data Act, at least, the following information shall be provided to the user: (a) the type, format and estimated volume of product data which the connected product is capable of generating; (b) whether the connected product is capable of generating data continuously and in real-time; (c) whether the connected product is capable of storing data on-device or on a remote server, including, where applicable, the intended duration of retention;

(d) how the user may access, retrieve or, where relevant, erase the data, including the technical means to do so, as well as their terms of use and quality of service.

Should the duty to inform be allocated on the vendor, the rentor, or the lessor, it may be discussed whether they effectively comply with such an obligation by simply ensuring that the connected product includes the required information. That could be available in different media, either via product interfaces (what entails that the information might not be displayed before the contract is concluded), accompanying notices (what might remind, nonetheless the differences, the old format of shrink-wrap licenses)[26] or external sources (so the user is referred to consult such information in sites, apps or other digital addresses). Would these options be compliant with the Data Act? As the obligation is defined as an 'obligation to inform', is then an active obligation on the vendor, the lessor, or the rentor, that implies a direct duty to render such information available in the context of the contractual relationship? Despite the fact that these operators might not be the data holder, are they held responsible not only for the provision but also for the completeness, accuracy, and compliance with the comprehensibility requirements?

This information duty can easily be construed as an enlargement and reinforcement of the typical pre-contractual information duties underpinning consumer protection. It is perfectly aligned therewith and backed by the same rationale.

As an alternative to the design obligation to render data directly accessible by the user from the connected product or related service, an obligation

26 Provided that the relationship between the user and the data holder (U2H) amounts to be a data sharing contract. It was discussed whether the request from the user as provided for by the Data Act, might not necessarily be assimilated or inserted into a contract as such. Literature on shrink-wrap agreement is ample and primarily focussed on copyright. Einhorn, David A., "Shrink-wrap Licenses: the Debate continues", 38 *IDEA,* num. 3, 1997–1998, pp. 383–401; Lemley, Mark A., "Intellectual Property and Shrink-wrap Licences", 68 *Southern California Law Review,* 1994–1995, pp. 1239–1294; Baker, Darren C., "NOTE. *ProCD v. Zeidenberg:* Comercial Reality, Flexibility in Contract Formation, and Notions of Manifested Assent in the Arena of Shrinkwrap Licences", 92 *Nortwestern University Law Review,* 1997–1998, pp. 379–433; Puhala, Karen, "The protection of computer software through shrink-wrap license agreements", 42 *Washington & Lee Law Review,* 1985, pp. 1347–1380; Kaufman, Page M., "The Enforceability of State "Shrink-Wrap" license statutes in light of *Vault Corp. v. Quaid Software, Ltd.*", 74 *Cornell Law Review,* 1988–1989, pp. 222–244; Minassian, Apik, "The Death of Copyright: Enforceability of Shrinkwrap Licensing Agreements", 45 *UCLA Law Review,* 1997–1998, pp. 569–609

to make available such data is provided for (Art. 4(1) Data Act). Thus, data holders shall make readily available data, as well as the relevant metadata necessary to interpret and use those data, accessible to the user without undue delay, of the same quality as is available to the data holder, easily, securely, free of charge, in a comprehensive, structured, commonly used and machine-readable format and, where relevant and technically feasible, continuously and in real-time. This shall be done on the basis of a simple request through electronic means where technically feasible. So, the obligation to make data available is paired with and triggered by the right granted to the user to request such data. The right to request the making data available in such conditions is clearly aimed to empower the user via-à-vis the data holder. It is not stemming from a consumer protection aspiration, albeit it is undoubtedly empowering consumers as well. The focus is on the user regardless of their condition.

Interestingly, Article 4(4) Data Act prevents data holders from making the exercise of choices or rights by the user unduly difficult via the structure, design, function or manner of operation of a user digital interface or a part thereof. This provision refers, in particular, to design or functional features of the interface through which the user can exercise their rights and options that may subvert or impair the autonomy, decision-making or choices of the user. As explicitly mentioned in the recitals (Recital 38), that includes manipulative techniques, commonly called *dark patterns.* practices in digital interfaces that steer, deceive, coerce, or manipulate consumers into making choices that often are not in their best interests. Reference to dark patterns bridges again the Data Act with the consumer-protection realm and spotlights a conspicuous interaction with unfair commercial practices in business-to-consumer (B2C) relationships. The definition and rules governing unfair business-to-consumer commercial practices are mainly set out in the Unfair Commercial Practices Directive 2005/29/EC (UCPD)[27], but there are other relevant rules scattered in legislation on consumer protection, privacy and data protection, advertising and commercial communications, and competition rules. UCPD focuses

27 Directive 2005/29/EC of the European Parliament and of the Council of 11 May 2005 concerning unfair business-to-consumer commercial practices in the internal market and amending Council Directive 84/450/EEC, Directives 97/7/EC, 98/27/EC and 2002/65/EC of the European Parliament and of the Council and Regulation (EC) No 2006/2004 of the European Parliament and of the Council ('Unfair Commercial Practices Directive') (Text with EEA relevance). OJ L 149, 11.6.2005, pp. 22–39.

on business to consumer (B2C) practices. Commercial practices are widely defined by Article 2(d) UCPD as comprising 'any act, omission, course of conduct or representation, commercial communication including marketing, by a trader, directly connected with the promotion, sale or supply of a product to consumers'. As the ECJ has held, this notion is intended to cover any commercial practice directly connected with the promotion, sale, or supply of a product[28] (including services as well)[29] to consumers. A practice directly related to the promotion, sale, or supply of products has been interpreted as extending over any commercial practice before, during or after a commercial transaction relating to any goods or service.[30] Given the operation of data sharing under the Data Act, it is the data holder who could be deploying unfair commercial practices via-à-vis the user while designing, making available, or enabling the operation of interfaces, decision-making processes, or mechanisms for the user to exercise their rights and select their options.

That may constitute a manifestation of unfair commercial practice if the user is a consumer. But the Data Act seems to go further. The provision is not restricted to consumer transactions. Hence, it is again a protective effect of the regulation in the data sharing beyond consumer protection.

III. Combating unfairness in data sharing: beyond consumer protection

The Data Act looks further the horizon of consumer protection. With the aim to counter the unfairness risk in the data sharing market, the regulation relies on two main instruments to fairly and effectively mobilise and monetize data value.

As described above, one of these instruments is the development of model contractual terms (MCT). As per Article 41 Data Act, the Commission shall develop and recommend non-binding model contractual terms on data access and use. Such MCT should contain, in particular, terms on reasonable compensation and protection of trade secrets. On 19 November 2025, the Commission has adopted the Communications C(2025) 7750 final-to approve raft Commission Recommendation on non-binding model

28 Mediaprint Zeitungs-und Zeitschriftenverlag, C-540/08, EU:C:2010:660, par. 17 and par. 21.
29 CHS Tour Services, C-435/11, EU:C:2013:574, par. 27.
30 Perenicová y Perenic, C-453/10, EU:C:2012:144.

contractual terms on data access and use and non-binding standard contractual clauses for cloud computing contracts (with Annexes), annexed hereto.[31]

With the mission[32] of assisting the Commission in the work of developing the MCT (and the SCC[33]), the Expert Group on B2B Data Sharing and Cloud Computing Contracts is created.[34]

While the unfairness control laid down in Article 13 Data Act is obviously directed to counter such risk, the role attributed to MCT in the fairness-promoting strategy may require more elaborate analysis and further explanation.

The joint analysis of the impact assessment report, the support studies of the initial proposal of the Data Act, and the final text of the regulation allow to sketch the multiple-function role of MCT in the policy intervention. The succinct statements of Recital 111 of the Data Act and the concentrated and brief wording of its Article 41 condense, nonetheless, the four drivers guiding the policy role of MCT.

---

31 https://digital-strategy.ec.europa.eu/en/library/draft-recommendation-non-binding-model-contractual-terms-data-access-and-use-and-non-binding.

32 Expert Group on B2B Data Sharing and Cloud Computing Contracts, Terms of Reference: "3. Tasks
The expert group shall assist the Commission by: analysing existing B2B data sharing models and practices, identifying problems and commonalities and recommending to the Commission a general horizontal set of balanced model contract terms for B2B data sharing that could be applicable for sharing data across sectors, including for data generated by machines and the use of products and related services;
analysing data sharing practices in some sectors where there is a need for model contract terms and recommending to the Commission model contract terms tailored for these sectors;
analysing existing practices for cloud contract terms and recommending to the Commission a general set of standard contractual clauses for cloud contracts.
issuing recommendations/suggestions to the Commission on other subjects related to fair contractual relations in B2B data sharing as follow-up to the Data Act and Cloud Marketplace, following a proposal by the Commission services."

33 As previously developed for the transfer of personal data: Commission Implementing Decision (EU) 2021/914 of 4 June 2021 on standard contractual clauses for the transfer of personal data to third countries pursuant to Regulation (EU) 2016/679 of the European Parliament and of the Council (Text with EEA relevance), C/2021/3972, *OJ L 199, 7.6.2021, 31–61.*

34 Register of Commission Expert Groups, Expert Group on B2B data sharing and cloud computing contracts (E03840): https://ec.europa.eu/transparency/expert-groups-register/screen/expert-groups/consult?lang=en&groupId=3840&fromMeetings=true&meetingId=48306.

First, promoting data sharing by recommending MCT, albeit non-binding and voluntary, can instil fairness objectives in the market. The presumption is that the MCT are drafted to achieve certain fairness objectives. Thus, once the parties have identified a common or compatible economic purpose and mutual benefit in sharing data, by utilizing the MCT, parties would naturally pursue and attain the 'embedded' fairness objectives. As per Article 41 Data Act, MCT would provide parties with terms to conclude contracts with 'fair, reasonable and non-discriminatory contractual rights and obligations'. In that regard, contractual terms would be modelled to achieve such fairness objectives, so parties could simply align with them.

The binding or non-binding character of the MCT and the possibility of the parties to depart from the set of MCT as a 'fair contract model' shall determine the effectiveness of MCT in imbuing market practice with such fairness goals.

Second, by resorting to MCT in their dealings, parties would significantly reduce transaction costs in negotiating, drafting, valuating, and performing. This is probably the most visible benefit of MCT as a policy intervention in a market afflicted by limited contractual practice, little experience in data sharing, lack of expertise in the matter, and even certain imbalances in the negotiating power. The longed-for reduction of transaction costs might, however, be attained at the cost of 'over-standardising' contracting praxis, 'corseting' party autonomy, or even relegating the very economic interests that parties do seek in their business negotiations. Mindful of such undesired effects in the market, a MCT-based policy strategy needs to carefully consider on which conditions the model terms should operate.

While opting for their possible binding character more intensely interferes into parties' autonomy, promoting flexibility and voluntariness with non-binding MCT inevitably raise doubts about the actual effect of the cost-reduction objective insofar as negotiation and drafting costs may abruptly reappear, and be even exacerbated, if parties have to discuss the application of the MCT, agree on their use in the contract, and subsequently select the applicable terms and renegotiate the remaining ones where, if possible, an agreement to use the MCT has not been reached. The possibility that parties can either not apply the MCT or substantially alter their terms in the final agreement question puts, to a certain extent, in jeopardy the ultimate aim of ensuring by MCT fairness objectives, as parties could elude them either by renegotiating the model terms individually or by readjusting the fairness equilibrium of the entire contract. Besides, should

MCT be non-binding and voluntary the risks of imbalance in the negotiating power of the parties are not totally eliminated. Certainly, it cannot be ignored that the existence of MCT alleviate asymmetries and can empower the disadvantageous party with a yardstick to measure the reasonableness of the counterparty's proposal and with a benchmark to start and conduct negotiations. Hence, while MCT represent a more effective tool to reduce transaction costs rather than to achieve fairness objectives in data sharing contracts, the actual use of MCT in the market may, nonetheless, lead to satisfying *de facto* outcomes related to both policy goals.

Third, MCT provide a *practical tool* to help enterprises, in particular, SMEs to conclude data sharing contracts. Recital 111 highlights this role of MCT as a practical tool. With this descriptive term, the role of MCT seems to distance from pure policy goals and fairness objectives and perform more practical functions. MCT are presented to as to serve as educational, helpful tools that assist enterprises, specially of small size, in their contracting practice. This role is not *per se* rooted into fairness objectives, unless improving SMEs' knowledge on data contracts and fortifying their data contracting skills are deemed indeed rebalancing mechanisms. In fact, the value of MCT as a practical tool for SMEs, in particular, directly connect with the lack of expertise and the limited data-sharing practice as drivers of the identified market failures and triggers of the policy intervention.

The educational value and the role as a practical tool can be particularly enhanced with suited drafting and formatting strategies. In certain terms, and where it is required or relevant, the MCT can provide options for the parties to choose in their drafting of the agreement. Options are to serve as real substantive or material alternatives, purely alternative drafting versions, or mechanisms to adapt the MCT to different sectors or transactional contexts.

For instance, in delimiting the scope of the agreement the parties can refer to detailed Annexes (option 1) or describe or list the data covered by the contract in one of the contractual terms. That is essentially a drafting option without substantial impact on the agreement.

Or, the MCT can contain as an option a clause stipulating the compensation for additional support or a penalty clause (or liquidated damages). Here, these options help the parties to exercise their party's autonomy within the perimeters of the MCT and still benefit from the benchmarking value of pre-drafted terms that, if parties agree on the matter, can be incorporated into the contract. By providing these clauses as optional, the MCT sign that stipulations governing such issues are not essential and the parties can find their own equilibrium of interests. Particularly advisable is the use of options in those clauses, normally general clauses, where there is not preferred option in terms of fairness but they must simply reflect the free agreement of the parties.

Finally, with the use of options the MCT get a modular shape. Flexibility and adaptability to needs, sectors or circumstances. A good example might be where the MCT contain options for data recipients qualifying as SMEs.

Drafting and material options as well as (additional) optional terms imbue MCT with an adequate adaptability feature and, in a certain way, reinforce its potential value as a toolkit for the parties.

Besides, considering the identified lack of experience in data sharing in the market and little practice among the enterprises more exposed to unfairness risks, in principle those of more modest size, accompanying explanations, commentaries, and/or illustrations would enlighten its educational purpose. Thus, the MCT would turn into a contractual guidance where parties can find not only model contractual terms, but also a guide to understand the extent, assess the consequences, and construct the MCT for ensuring an informed contractual decision. While the MCT literally materialize the mandate of the Commission pursuant to Article 41 Data Act, a guidance format may go beyond and exceed expectations. In particular, it should be critically assess whether the wording of the commentaries may risk to become recommendations.

Yet, Recital 111 of Data Acts provides another perspective on the potential role of MCT that intimately relate with the fairness aspirations. When used widely and integrally, the recital states, MCT influence contractual praxis and drive contractual relations towards fairer data access, use, and sharing practices. It is an interesting construction of the role of MCT that assumes a medium/long term impact on the market, a silent and progressive effect on commercial practice, and a natural and pervasive permeation of the fairness objective embedded in the MCT in the contracts more and more frequently concluded under or inspired by the MCT. This perspective takes a distance from the market functioning and the parties' behaviour and proposes a low level of intervention. It relies on a continuing accommodation of the market and the contracting practices to MCT that would naturally become a benchmark.

The idea that MCT encapsulate a 'fair contract model' is particularly intriguing. Article 13 Data Act provides for a definition of unfair contractual term based on gross deviation from good commercial practice in data access and use.[35] Subsequently, in the following paragraphs, Article 13 Data Act specify contractual terms that, considering its object or effect, shall be, in particular, unfair, and terms that shall be presumed unfair for the purposes of the fairness control defined in paragraph 3. As MCT may distil best practices in the market they could become a yardstick to measure fairness. Should MCT be conceived and accepted as good commercial practice, they would play an extremely valuable role in giving shape and content to the standard of good commercial practice. Nonetheless, that would not immunize the contract concluded by the parties using the MCT from judicial scrutiny and possible total or partial voidance. Therefore, as expounded below, the interplay of the MCT with the applicable legislation, both at national level and EU one, and with the exercise of party's autonomy.

A proper understanding of the sources of and the basis for the unfairness risk is crucial for the formulation of effective solutions. Therefore, it well worth wondering whether non-binding MCT for B2B data sharing serve the policy objectives and how deal with the unfairness problem in B2B relationship. The question cannot be adequately answered without acknowledging and incorporating into the analytical framework a third vector that crosses data market. Little, undeveloped, and non-elaborate market practice for data sharing. This factual state of play brings about two dealings-hindering factors: high transaction costs and high uncertainty. A pernicious combination of low experience, little market practice, high uncertainty, and significant transactions costs to manage hinders economic interaction and can even paralyse contracting. Albeit not exclusively, these factors do specially impact SMEs less prepared to handle uncertainty, inexperience and transaction costs in a competitive manner.

The value of the MCT initiative and its effectiveness in achieving the policy goals increase significantly where the problems of transactions costs, limited praxis, and uncertainty are included into the equation. The development of MCT for businesses, of any size, to rely on and utilize in their data sharing contracts is certainly a highly-effective fit-for-purpose solution. The beneficial effects to raise a data market and enable and accelerate data transactions are evident and substantial. MCT prove to be a practical, influential, and market-creating tool to achieve the policy goals.

---

35 Article 13(3) Data Act:
"A contractual term is unfair if it is of such a nature that its use grossly deviates from good commercial practice in data access and use, contrary to good faith and fair dealing".

All the above proves that MCT can play an important role in facing and mitigating unfairness risk in data sharing. In that regard, the idea of providing market with MCT embeds one of the main rationales behind Data Act. With the goal to mobilise and monetize data value, Data Act trusts Contract law. Contracts are the primary driver to make the data market fluidly, abundantly, and effectively flow. But the risk of unfairness is to be addressed and alleviated. Data Act takes on such a mission with the deployment of several tools aimed at facing the fairness problem. The control over unfair contractual terms in B2B data sharing together with the MCT are interwoven with other measures that may have a flavour of consumer protection in the Data Act and with all the safeguards in other legislation that are preserved. In fact, it is interesting to note that various models for MCT shall not be drafted separately to cover B2B and B2C situations. No special model terms shall be included to address consumer protection concerns. MCT are drafted to primarily instil fairness in B2B transactions. On top of them, protective measures provided for by specific legislation can be stacked. In particular, consumer protection legislation would apply to MCT where there is a consumer to be protected. Thus, rules on unfair contract terms and unfair commercial practices shall complement the mechanisms to restore fairness in the data sharing market where consumers are involved.

But Data Act succeeds in going further consumer protection. The fairness problem is indeed a structural, functional and relational problem that requires a more ambitious approach where market failures are observed and addressed with a broader perspective.

Beyond the EU Data Act: Value of IoT Data, Market Failures, and Consumer Choice in the B2C Sector

*Wolfgang Kerber and Karsten K. Zolna**

The recently enacted EU Data Act has introduced significant changes of the governance of IoT data (Internet of Things), which so far is dominated by IoT manufacturers. This includes new rights of users to access and share IoT data as well as a new contract which data holders (manufacturers) need for getting permission to use non-personal IoT data from the users. This article analyzes from an economic market failure perspective the problems that consumers face with regard to getting meaningful control over the generation, collection, use, and sharing of their non-personal and personal IoT data. It is shown that, in B2C contexts, serious market failures exist with regard to the terms of the "licensing" contracts of personal and non-personal IoT consumer data (buy-out contracts, adverse selection), which can lead to a too large collection and sharing of IoT data as well as to not enough choice for the consumers. After presenting a broad overview about the current policy discussion about a minimum of choice for consumers in competition law and data protection law (German Facebook case, new Opinion of EDPB about "consent or pay" on online platforms, Art. 5(2) DMA, and opt-out solutions in California privacy law), the last part of the article explores and analyzes a wide range of different policy options for granting consumers more choice about the collection, use, and sharing of their IoT data (consumer empowerment). One of these policy solutions would give consumers the right to use their IoT devices also without having to "license" to data holders IoT data that are not necessary for the functionality of these devices, which also might lead to "consent or pay" solutions in IoT governance. Other policy solutions would give consumers more direct de facto control over their IoT devices and their IoT data, which also might require more technical interoperability and standardisation.

---

* Wolfgang Kerber, Professor of Economics (kerber@wiwi.uni-marburg.de); Karsten Konrad Zolna, Teaching and Research Assistant (karsten.zolna@wiwi.uni-marburg.de); Marburg Centre for Institutional Economics (MACIE), School of Business & Economics, University of Marburg (Germany).

I. Introduction

The fast diffusion of an increasing number of IoT devices for consumers like connected cars, smart home devices, virtual assistants, fitness trackers, and smart watches will generate a huge amount of data.[1] Most of this data is personal data of consumers and therefore subject to EU data protection law that grants a set of rights to the consumers as data subjects. In December 2023, the EU legislator has enacted the Data Act (DA), whose chapter II introduced an additional layer of rules for data generated by the users of IoT devices, which covers both personal and non-personal data.[2] This paper will focus entirely on the governance of IoT data in B2C situations, although the DA applies also to B2B situations. The objective of this paper is to analyze the problems consumers can be expected to face even after implementation of the DA regarding the governance of their IoT data, especially with regard to their control over the generation, collection, use, and sharing of their IoT data, and about getting a fair share from the value of their consumer data.

So far, the discussion about chapter II of the DA has shown that still many open questions exist regarding the implementation of the DA, which relate to unclear provisions, lacking enforcement mechanisms, as well as legal uncertainty about the relationship between the DA and other laws, like data protection law and trade secret law. Even more important are, however, serious concerns about a lack of effectiveness of the DA for achieving its objectives.[3] After a brief explanation of the IoT data governance

1 Sector inquiry into consumer Internet of Things. Final report, COM(2022) 19 final, 2, and the accompanying Commission Staff Working Document, SWD(2022) 10 final.

2 Regulation (EU) 2023/2854 of the European Parliament and of the Council of 13 December 2023 on harmonised rules on fair access to and use of data and amending Regulation (EU) 2017/2394 and Directive (EU) 2020/1828 (Data Act) (hereafter: DA).

3 See for literature on the enacted DA the articles in Sattler/Zech (eds.), The Data Act: First Assessments (2024), and Lohsse/Schulze/Staudenmayer (eds.), The Data Act – a Cornerstone for the European Data Economy, Nomos 2024; Hennemann/Steinrötter, Der Data Act – Neue Instrumente, alte Friktionen, strukturelle Weichenstellungen (2024), NJW, 1; Schmidt-Kessel, Heraus- und Weitergabe von IoT-Gerätedaten (2024), MMR, 75; Antoine, Datenzugangsrechte im finalen Data Act – Fortschritt, Rückschritt, neue Fragen? Schlüssel zur Förderung datengetriebener Geschäftsmodelle? (2024), CR, 1; Wiebe, Der Data Act – Innovation oder Illusion? (2023), GRUR, 1569; Eckardt/Kerber, Property Rights Theory, Bundles of Rights on IoT Data, and the EU Data Act (2024), European Journal of Law & Economics, 113; Becker, IoT-Daten als Gemeineigentum – Der Data Act als digitale Utopie (2024), RDi, 615; Hennemann/Ebner/Karsten/Lienemann/Wienroeder, Data Act. An Introduction, (2024), Nomos; Specht-Rie-

problems that the DA wants to solve with the introduction of new mandatory rules, we will summarize in this introduction briefly the main concerns about the effectiveness of the rules of the DA with a focus on consumers as users of IoT devices.

What are the problems that should be solved by the provisions of ch. II of the DA? Manufacturers of smart IoT devices can get through their own technical design exclusive de facto control over all data that is generated by the IoT devices, which usually are sold to their users, both in B2C and B2B contexts. The DA claims that this leads to not enough access to this data (1) for the users of these devices, and (2) for many other firms which would like to offer complementary services to the IoT device users (e.g. repair services) or to develop new services and products with the help of this IoT data (data-driven innovation). This lack of access to and sharing of IoT data would lead to negative effects on innovation and competition on secondary markets and to an under-utilization of IoT data for innovative activities and research in the entire data economy. Particularly important for this paper is that the DA also claims that the exclusive control of the manufacturers over the IoT data can lead to negative effects on the choice of consumers, e.g., regarding service providers, and an unfair sharing of the value of data that are generated through the use of the IoT devices of consumers. Therefore, the main objectives of the DA are more unlocking of IoT data for innovation and competition (on secondary markets), more empowerment of the users of IoT devices (meaningful control over IoT data and more choice), as well as a fair sharing of the value of their IoT data.[4] The DA intends to solve the problems primarily through the introduction of two instruments:[5] (1) New rights for the users of IoT devices to access, use, and share the IoT data with third parties (Art. 4 and 5 DA), and (2) a new mandatory contract between the data holders and the users about the

menschneider/Hennemann (eds.), Data Act, Data Governance Act: DA, DGA (2025), 2. Aufl., Nomos; Tombal/Graef, The European Data Act. A Horizontal Building Block for the Data Economy? (2025), Van der Sloot/Monti/Bostoen, From Regulating Human Behaviour to Regulating Data, Open Press Tilburg University, 131; von Hagen, Internet of Things Data within the Context of the Data Act: Between Opportunities and Obstacles (2025), Gsenger/Sekwenz, Digital Decade, Nomos, 371.

4 Additionally, the DA also wants to preserve the incentives to invest in data-generating IoT devices. See European Commission, Draft DA, Explanatory Memorandum (2022) 2.

5 In addition, all IoT devices have to be designed in such a way that IoT data are easily accessible to the users and to third parties with whom the users want to share the data (Art. 3 DA).

use of the generated non-personal IoT data by the data holders (Art. 4(13) DA).[6] However, there are serious concerns about the effectiveness of these two new instruments in B2C contexts.

With regard to the new user rights for access, use, and sharing of the IoT data, the data sharing mechanism of Art. 5 DA might be most important because through sharing data to independent service providers on secondary markets, e.g. for repair services, consumers might get more choice between service providers and can profit from more competition on these markets.[7] However, the DA has made this path for third parties to get access to this IoT data difficult and expensive due to too many hurdles, restrictions, unresolved legal issues, and high transaction costs. The need for bilateral negotiations about "reasonable compensation", technical protection measures, trade secret problems, the often too narrow scope of the shared data and the lack of solutions for technical interoperability with the IoT device (e.g., access to proprietary software) for providing, e.g., repair services, are likely leading to a weak and ineffective data sharing mechanism. Therefore, much skepticism exists whether the new user rights of the DA will lead to much unlocking of IoT data, and therefore to more innovation, more competition, and more choice for consumers.[8]

Thus, the second key instrument might be much more important for consumer empowerment. Whereas before the DA the data holders were free to use, share and monetize the non-personal IoT data, the new Art. 4(13) DA stipulates that the data holders can use the non-personal

6 The processing, use, and sharing of personal IoT data is subject to EU data protection law.

7 It is doubtful whether consumers can get significant benefits from the right to access and use their IoT data directly.

8 See for this critique Kerber, Governance of IoT data: Why the EU Data Act will not fulfill its objectives (2023), GRURInt, 120, 125; Kerber, EU Data Act: Will new user access and sharing rights on IoT data help competition and innovation? (2024) Journal of Antitrust Enforcement, 234, 237; Wiebe (fn.3), 1578; Podszun/Offergeld, The EU Data Act and the access to secondary markets. Study for the Ludwig-Fröhler-Institut für Handwerkswissenschaften, 2022, https://doi.org/10.2139/ssrn.4256882; Krämer, Improving the economic effectiveness of the B2B and B2C data sharing obligations in the proposed Data Act, CERRE Report (November 2022). It is an open question whether the aim in the final version of the DA to enable also the emergence of "liquid, fair and efficient" data markets based upon such shared data, e.g. also through data intermediaries, can be achieved. See recital 33 and Art. 6(2)(c) DA about allowing the reselling of such IoT data with the permission of consumers. See Eckardt/Kerber, Designing the Bundle of Rights on IoT Data: The EU Data Act (2024), Sattler/Zech (eds), The Data Act: First Assessments, 3, 5.

data only based upon a contract with the users of the IoT devices. This has been characterized as a far-reaching change of the bundle of rights on IoT data, attributing the non-personal IoT data to the users of IoT devices. This implies theoretically a strong position of the consumers, because without their consent to this data use contract the data holders are not allowed any more to use this non-personal IoT data.[9] Since, however, the DA relies on freedom of contract regarding these data use agreements, serious concerns have emerged in the discussion about the effectiveness of this instrument for giving the consumers more control over their IoT data and an appropriate share of their value. The consumers might suffer with regard to this data use contract from the same information and behavioral problems as they are well-known regarding consent about the processing of their personal data. In addition, it is widely expected that the data holders will directly bundle the sale of the IoT device with the data use contracts, in which the consumers have to agree to a far-reaching collection, use, sharing, and monetizing of the IoT data. This can imply that their rights on the IoT data might be directly contracted away when buying the IoT device (buy-out contracts). Therefore, consumers might not be capable to use such a contract for getting meaningful control over their non-personal IoT data, and the ensuing asymmetric allocation of the rights on this IoT data might not give them a fair share of their data's value.[10] These problems can emerge in a similar way both for non-personal IoT data (under the new regulation of the DA) and for personal IoT data (under the data protection rules of the GDPR).[11] The consumers would only be left with their non-waivable IoT

9 For this very far-reaching change in the bundle of rights on IoT data, see Eckardt/Kerber (fn.3), 127; Eckardt/Kerber (fn.8); Hennemann/Steinrötter, Data Act – Fundament des neuen Datenwirtschaftsrechts? (2022), NJW, 1481, 1483; Wiebe (fn.3), 1570; Schmidt/Kessel (fn.3), 78; Lienemann/Wienroeder, V. Data Licence Agreement and User's Right of Access (Art. 4) (2024), Hennemann et al. (fn.3), 71, 78; Sattler, Artikel 4, (2025), Specht-Riemenschneider/Hennemann (fn.3), Rdnr. 12.

10 See Specht-Riemenschneider, Der Entwurf des Data Act (2022), Multimedia und Recht – Beilage, 809, 820; Krämer (fn.8), 9; Kerber (2023, fn.8), 132; Kerber (fn.3), 128; Specht-Riemenschneider/El-Rifaai/Mehnert/Bodemann, IoT-Data sharing in B2C: How to better serve the consumer (2024), Lohsse et al. (eds), Private Law and the Data Act, 59; Lienemann/Wienroeder, V. Data Licence Agreement and User's Right of Access (Art. 4) (2024), Hennemann et al. (fn.3), 71, 75.

11 Regulation (EU) 2016/679 of the European Parliament and of the Council of 27 April 2016 on the protection of natural persons with regard to the processing of personal data and on the free movement of such data, and repealing Directive 95/46/EC (General Data Protection Regulation) (hereafter: GDPR).

data rights according to Art. 4 and 5 DA, which might also be weak and largely ineffective (as discussed in the last paragraph).

The described concerns in the last two paragraphs would imply that both key instruments of the new DA might be largely ineffective for helping consumers with regard to the governance of their IoT data. Thus, this paper has the objective to analyze from an economic perspective whether and to what extent serious market failures regarding the data use contracts (for personal and non-personal data) exist on the market for IoT devices, what the implications are for the choice of consumers and the sharing of the value of data, and what future policy options exist for better solving these problems, especially with respect to more consumer autonomy (empowerment) and more choice regarding their IoT data and IoT devices.

From an economic perspective, it is important that these data use contracts for IoT data can be seen as a component of the payment of consumers to the manufacturers (combination of monetary payment and data). In section II, we will show that the concerns about market failure problems with regard to the data use contracts in IoT contexts are justified. Competition between IoT device manufacturers with regard to the terms of the data use contracts cannot be expected to work well, which will support the hypothesis that in markets for IoT devices the emerging data use contracts will lead to not enough choice for consumers and a too extensive collection, use, and monetization of their IoT data through the data holders.

This would not only be economically inefficient, but can also be seen as a violation of the basic principle of consumer autonomy (consumer sovereignty) with regard to their IoT data. It can be in particularly problematic due to the intrusive surveillance character of many IoT devices as they collect a huge amount of personal data about the private behavior of consumers, especially in private homes and cars. Therefore, there exists the challenge of finding suitable future policy options in order to ensure at least a minimum standard of choice for consumers about the generation, collection, use, and sharing of their IoT data. This surveillance dimension of IoT devices has not sufficiently been taken into account in the discussion about the governance of IoT data yet. It is, however, an important additional argument for strengthening the empowerment of consumers over their IoT data and their IoT devices.

In section III, we will see that this question of choice regarding personal data has emerged in recent years prominently in different discussions and policy decisions, both in data protection law and competition policy. One very controversial current discussion refers to the so-called "consent or pay" models, through which consumers are faced with the choice of paying for a service either with personal data or with a monetary price. We will give an overview about these policy discussions about choice of consumers regarding personal data, both for understanding better the relevance and economic difficulties of mandated choice options, and for a better development of ideas about innovative policy options for more choice with regard to the governance of IoT data.

In the final main section IV about future policy options beyond the existing DA, we explore a wide range of different policy solutions for either better compensation of the consumers in return for not getting a fair share of the value of their IoT data, and, in particular, for ensuring that they have more control and choice over the generation, collection, use, and sharing of their IoT data. One option can be that consumers also get a right for using IoT devices without having to provide data that are not necessary for its functionality. Other discussed policy options would give consumers also more control over their IoT devices.

II. Market failure problems on the markets for non-personal and personal IoT data in B2C IoT contexts

II.1. Economics of IoT data governance and the data use contracts about IoT data

The economics of IoT devices differ from the economics of large digital platforms: Services, such as the social media platform Facebook or the search engine Google, are usually offering services for "free", i.e. a monetary price of zero, in exchange for the collection and use of personal data, mostly for the purpose of behavioral advertising. In contrast, IoT devices, such as connected cars, are usually sold for a monetary price, which often can cover all the investments into their development, their production and their operating costs. For manufacturers it is therefore in general not necessary to get additional revenues from monetizing the IoT data.[12] However, the data

12 The initial proposal of the DA emphasized the incentives of manufacturers to invest in data-generating IoT devices and tried to justify the strong position of data holders with the need for maintaining these incentives. For arguments that such an incentive problem does usually not exist, see Kerber (2023) (fn.8), 128–130; Martens, Pro- and anticompetitive provisions in the proposed European Union Data Act, Working

can – at least partly – be very helpful for improving their IoT devices, for further innovation, or also for additional revenues through their monetization. As far as consumers agree that data holders can collect, use, share, and perhaps also monetize IoT data in the two separate data use contracts about personal and non-personal IoT data, data holders can process the IoT data accordingly. This would imply that consumers are paying for the IoT device and its services with a combination of a monetary price for the device and an additional "data price" by granting data holders the right to use the IoT data according to the terms of these data use contracts. Economically, such data use contracts can be interpreted as data licensing contracts, even if data holders usually do not pay any (monetary) licensing fees to the users.[13] As far as the use of the generated IoT data is directly necessary for the functionality of the IoT devices, this use of the data by the data holders is also in the interest of the consumers. This is, however, different for those (often large amounts of) generated IoT data that are not necessary for the functionality of the devices, but can be used by the data holders for their own benefit, e.g. to develop new products or generate additional revenues through monetizing them. Important is also that the manufacturers as data holders can and will usually bundle the sale contract for the IoT device with those data use contracts. In other words: The consumers have only the choice of buying the entire bundle (IoT device and data use contracts) or of refraining entirely from buying the IoT device from this manufacturer. This also usually implies that the consumers cannot use the IoT devices without having agreed to such data use contracts.[14]

How would a well-functioning market work regarding these data use contracts about IoT data? The basic idea of the data use contracts between the user of IoT devices and the data holder is that both parties come to an agreement about the collection, use, and monetization of non-personal and personal IoT data by the data holders, in which the interests of both parties are taken properly into account. In contrast to large digital platforms, it can be in general assumed that the manufacturers on IoT device markets are in competition with each other regarding price and quality of their

---

paper 01/2023, Bruegel. An additional option is that the manufacturers can also offer more functions on the basis of subscriptions, e.g. with a monthly fee.

13 See Hennemann/Steinrötter (fn.9), 1483; for differences to licensing contracts in IP law see Becker (fn.3), 625.

14 See Specht-Riemenschneider et al. (fn.10), 76; Lienemann/Wienroeder, V. Data Licence Agreement and User's Right of Access (Art. 4) (2024), Hennemann et al. (fn.3), 71, 75.

devices.[15] In a well-functioning market, economists would assume that in such a situation there exists also competiton with respect to the terms and conditions of the data use contracts. Manufacturers might differ in their interests to collect, use, and perhaps monetize IoT data. The same holds in particular for the consumers, who might have different preferences in terms of how much, with whom, and what kind of IoT data should be collected and shared. Many consumers might have strong privacy preferences and others might not. Some consumers might want to insist on getting a share of the value of their IoT data, whereas others might not care about this. In such situations of heterogeneous preferences, economists would assume that different firms would offer different terms in their data use contracts in competition with each other or that they would offer directly an explicit choice between different options for these data use contracts for a better matching with preferences of consumers. This could also include monetary payments of the data holders (as licensing fees) for the collection and use of IoT data, either through direct monetary payments or in form of a lower price for the IoT device. Thus, in well-functioning competition processes, a variety of different data use contracts for non-personal and personal data (and with more or less options for choice) can be expected and would fulfill better the heterogeneous preferences of consumers about privacy, choice, and data sharing (including with whom and for what purposes).[16] Economists would interpret such an outcome as an increase in consumer welfare and more economic efficiency.

With regard to the discussion about the DA, it should be noted that user rights for access, use and sharing of IoT data (as legally required through Art. 4 and 5 DA) would be offered voluntarily in the data use contracts in well-functioning markets, if the consumers would want such rights. Therefore, a mandatory introduction of these rights, which are also designed as rights that cannot be waived in contracts between data holders and consumers, would not be necessary and justifiable from an economic perspective. This implies that the DA itself already seems to assume that the market does not work well and that therefore some market failures exist.[17]

---

15 This is the reason why market power problems on the market for IoT devices were not a topic in the discussions about the DA.

16 This would also include to what extent the firms would offer their customers more or less choice regarding the generation, collection, and sharing of IoT data, including the terms for termination of these data use contracts.

17 In contrast to B2C situations, it was very controversially discussed for B2B contexts whether a general market failure exists and whether therefore such mandatory rights

What types of market failures can emerge regarding such data use contracts about IoT data in B2C situations? In a first step, we summarize briefly the results of the general market failure discussion regarding markets for personal data with a main focus on information and behavioral problems (section II.2). In a second step, we analyze this market failure problem with a specific focus on data use contracts for non-personal and personal IoT data, which – as we have seen – might be a part of the overall price that consumers pay for IoT services (section II.3). A brief summary and intermediate conclusions can be found in the final section II.4.

II.2. Market failure problems on markets for personal data

From an economic perspective it can be argued that through the principle of informational self-determination and through a far-reaching freedom of contract about allowing others to collect, use, and share personal data by giving consent (Art. 6(1)(a) GDPR), EU data protection law has de facto established a market for personal data. Despite the broad opinion in the data protection community that personal data should not be seen as tradeable commodity,[18] EU law has, in the meantime, accepted legally that services can be paid both with money and with "licensing" personal data.[19] Therefore, from an economic perspective, markets for personal data exist and, in fact, have existed already for a long time.

However, the law, and especially data protection law, has so far not sufficiently considered that these markets suffer from several serious market failure problems:[20]

can be justified. See Metzger/Schweitzer, Shaping markets: A critical evaluation of the draft Data Act (2023), Zeitschrift fur europäisches Privatrecht, 42, 56. In the final version of the DA, these user rights have been made waivable in B2B situations, which leads back to a situation of freedom of contract. See Eckardt/Kerber (fn.8), 17.

18 See most recently EDPB, Opinion 08/2024 on Valid Consent in the Context of Consent or Pay Models Implemented by Large Online Platforms – Adopted on 17 April 2024, 29.

19 See Ebner/Wienroeder, IV. SME-Exemption (Art. 7), Product Design, Service Design, and Informational Duties (Art. 3) (2024), Hennemann et al. (fn.3), 49, 59 with reference to Art. 3(2) Digital Content Directive and Sec. 327 German Civil Code.

20 See Kerber, Digital markets, data and privacy: Competition, law, consumer law and data protection (2016), GRUR Int, 639; Kerber/Zolna, Konsumentensouveränität und Datensouveränität aus ökonomischer Sicht (2022), Augsberg/Gehring (eds.), Datensouveränität. Positionen zur Debatte, 45, 58–70; Metzger/Schweitzer/Wagner, Daten-

(1) If market power exists, e.g., through market dominance or gatekeeper positions of the large tech firms, the lack of competition can lead to an excessive collection and use of personal data as well as to an insufficient choice for the consumers. In turn, this can further manifest economic power positions through data accumulation.[21]
(2) Individual consent decisions about personal data do not take into account positive and negative data externalities, i.e. that either the consent to provide personal data by one individual can allow inferences about other individuals with negative effects on their privacy (negative data externality),[22] or, vice versa, the denying of consent by an individual might not take into account that the use of its personal data might have positive effects on others or on the society, e.g. with regard to health data for medical research (positive data externalities).
(3) Most well-known, however, are information and behavioral problems of individuals regarding their decisions about consent to data-processing contracts.

In the last twenty years, manifold research and broad discussions have emerged about the information and behavioral problems of consumers with regard to giving consent to the processing of their personal data and about protection of their privacy.[23] Non-transparent, long, and unintelligible privacy terms leading to high transaction costs, behavioral manipulation

schutz und Datenmarkt: Grundzüge einer Marktordnung für die europäische Datenwirtschaft (2023), ZfPW, 227, 236–259; Specht-Riemenschneider: Datenschutzrecht als Verbraucherschutzrecht – Zum Erfordernis der Behebung vielfältiger Marktversagen auf Datenmärkten durch Anpassungen des materiellen Datenschutzrechts (2023), Buchner/Petri (eds), Informationelle Menschenrechte und digitale Gesellschaft, 7.

21 See Robertson, Excessive data collection: privacy considerations and abuse of dominance in the era of big data (2020), Common Market Law Review, 161; Kerber/Zolna, The German Facebook case: the law and economics of the relationship between competition and data protection law (2022), EJLE, 217, 235.

22 See Choi/Jeon/Kim, Privacy and personal data collection with information externalities (2019), Journal of Public Economics, 113; Acemoglu/Makhdoumi/Malekian/Ozdaglar, Too Much Data: Prices and Inefficiencies in Data Markets (2022), American Economic Journal: Microeconomics, 218; see also Gómez Pomar/Artigot Golobardes, Data as an asset and data trade (2025), De Franceschi/Schulze/Staudenmayer (eds.), The Value of Consumer Data in the Digital Economy.

23 See Norberg et al., The Privacy Paradox: Personal Information Disclosure Intentions versus Behaviors (2007), Journal of Consumer Affairs, 100; Kokolakis, Privacy attitudes and privacy behaviour: A review of current research on the privacy paradox phenomenon (2017), Computers & Security, 122; Luguri/Strahilevitz, Shining a light on dark patterns (2021), Journal of Legal Analysis, 13; Martini/Drews/Seeliger/Wein-

through biased choice architectures (dark nudging), and consent fatigue are only some of the most important issues in that regard. In addition, consumers cannot assess the potential harm through multiple privacy risks ensuing from the sharing their personal data. Therefore, it is very hard or even impossible for consumers in many situations to make rational cost-benefit decisions about agreeing to data-processing contracts with regard to the use of their personal data.[24] Various policy attempts to increase the transparency of processing personal data for more well-informed decisions and to fight behavioral manipulation have so far not been very helpful for giving consumers more meaningful control over their personal data to protect their privacy in an effective way.[25] As a consequence, individual consent decisions about the use of personal data might not be an effective instrument for consumers to protect their privacy and to control data processing activities due to these information and behavioral market failures.[26]

Can competition between firms lead to terms and conditions for processing personal data, which are aligned with the preferences of the consumers? The main problem is that the above-described information and behavioral problems imply that it is very hard and often impossible for consumers to compare the terms from different firms, which might also collect and use different data and share it with many different partners for different purposes. Although, in the meantime, most consumers know that they are also paying with their personal data, they cannot really understand the "data price" they are paying. Consumers know well what a monetary price of € 10 means, i.e. what they can buy with € 10, and that € 20 is 100 % higher than € 10. Therefore, comparing monetary prices is not difficult when shopping in supermarkets or online. Such a metric, however, does not exist regarding paying with "licensing" contracts for their personal data. Since the "data price" they pay is not salient for consumers, they cannot

---

zierl, Dark patterns. Phänomenologie und Antworten der Rechtsordnung (2021), Zs. für Digitalisierung und Recht, 47.

24 See Hermstrüwer, Informationelle Selbstgefährdung, 2016, 93; Schweitzer, Neue Machtlagen in der digitalen Welt? Das Beispiel unentgeltlicher Leistungen (2017), Körber/Kühling, Regulierung – Wettbewerb – Innovation, 269, 276; Metzger/Schweitzer/Wagner (fn.20), 246–257.

25 See as brief overview e.g. Metzger/Schweitzer/Wagner (fn.20), 244.

26 See e.g. Solove, Privacy Self-Management and the Consent Dilemma (2013), Harvard Law Review, 1880.

compare the "data price" offers from different companies, and, thus, will tend to ignore differences in "data prices" in their consumer decisions.[27]

This again leads to the consequence that it will often not be a profitable strategy for firms to offer more privacy-friendly solutions, i.e. to collect and use fewer personal data, for attracting more consumers. Instead, firms have an incentive to pursue a strategy of collecting, using, and sharing more personal data (and perhaps as much as possible), because the additional revenues make them more competitive and the consumers do not react due to this market failure problem. This is certainly one of the main reasons why competition between firms regarding more favorable privacy terms, does in general not work.[28] Therefore, competition in such data-related markets will often lead to a "race to the bottom" with regard to the protection of privacy, i.e. the least privacy-friendly solutions will survive in the market. From an economic perspective, this is very similar to the well-known "adverse selection" problem, in which due to information asymmetries about the quality of a product or service, only low-quality offers can survive in a market.[29] From an economic perspective, it is not surprising that competition cannot solve the market failures of information and behavioral problems.[30]

27 For a very skeptical view whether data as a price for otherwise free services can fulfill the same role as monetary prices on markets due to the lack of transparency of such data prices, see Schweitzer (fn.24), 275–291; she also discusses the innovative idea to use Art. 6(1)(f) ("legitimate interest") as an instrument for "regulating" when the processing of personal data should be allowed and when not (ibid., 281); see also the discussion in Metzger/Schweitzer/Wagner (fn.20), 237–241.

28 For a long time there has been much hope that competition would also lead to more privacy-friendly terms with regard to the collection and use of personal data. See for this discussion e.g. Esayas, Competition in (data) privacy: 'zero'-price markets, market power, and the role of competition law (2018), International Data Privacy Law, 181.

29 See Becker, Ein Recht auf datenerhebungsfreie Produkte (2017), JuristenZeitung, 170, 174; Metzger/Schweitzer/Wagner (fn.20), 237, 243; for "adverse selection" as a market failure see Akerlof, The market for lemons: Quality uncertainty and the market mechanism (1970), Quarterly Journal of Economics, 489.

30 See also the conclusion of Schweitzer (fn.24), 304: "Der 'Datenpreis' ist für Nutzer nicht transparent. Er wird daher auch durch Wettbewerb nicht kontrolliert."

II.3. Market failure problems for data use contracts about personal and non-personal data of IoT devices

What do these very serious problems through market failures regarding contracts about personal data imply for the data use contracts about non-personal and personal IoT data between the data holders of IoT devices and the consumers? First, we can assume that also in an IoT environment consumers have the same information and behavioral problems, and that they are also unable to understand the "data price" they are paying through these licensing contracts. Understanding what kinds of personal IoT data are generated through IoT devices and how they can be used can even be more difficult for most consumers. In addition, they might also have only a vague idea about the non-personal IoT data and their value, to whose use they agree in the data use contract according to Art. 4(13) DA. Secondly, the fact that in IoT contexts consumers usually will pay with a combination of a clear monetary price for the IoT device and a very unclear "data price" might lead most consumers to look only at the monetary price and ignore the specific terms in the data use contracts.

This again will imply that also competition between IoT device manufacturers will not work well with regard to these two data use contracts for non-personal and personal data, because manufacturers might not have incentives for offering terms and conditions in the interest of the consumers. Therefore, similar "race to the bottom" problems and "adverse selection" effects will emerge as discussed in the last section II.2. As a consequence, the bundle of contracts (sale contract and the two data use contracts) offered by the manufacturers will often entail data use contracts that lead to a too far-reaching generation, collection, use, and sharing of personal data, and, presumably, also to total buy-out contracts with regard to non-personal IoT data.[31] Through the bundling of these contracts by the manufacturers, consumers might often have no (or not enough) choice regarding the collection and use of their IoT data, resulting in significant negative effects on their consumer autonomy, their privacy, and the fulfilling of their preferences.

However, the wide-ranging differences between the IoT devices in functionality and field of application, the extent and type of generated IoT data, and the business models of IoT device manufacturers require more

31 See Specht-Riemenschneider (fn.10), 816–820; Kerber (2023, fn.8), 132; Lienemann/Wienroeder, V. Data Licence Agreement and User's Right of Access (Art. 4) (2024), Hennemann et al. (fn.3), 71, 75; for data in connected cars see also Metzger; Digitale Mobilität – Verträge über Nutzerdaten (2019), GRUR, 129, 134.

differentiated analyses and assessments, which cannot be done here. We want, at least, point to a few important aspects:

(1) Important is the ratio between the revenues from selling an IoT device for a monetary price and the potential benefits and revenues from the use, sharing and monetization of the IoT data for the manufacturers. If the share of the revenues through the sale of the IoT products (e.g. refrigerators) is very high, then the problems might be very different from other cases, in which the generated IoT data (e.g. in the case of fitness trackers) might be much more important for the profitability of the business model.
(2) Another factor is whether the IoT device is an expensive durable good (like connected cars), leading to a long-term lock-in of the consumers (also with regard to the data use contracts), or whether it is a comparatively cheap product, which the consumers can easily refrain from using, e.g. by switching to another inexpensive competing device. In the case of an expensive durable IoT device, it can be assumed that consumers might look deeper into the specifics of the data use contracts. However, it is also much harder for consumers to make rational decisions about benefits and costs of these devices because their services might evolve much over time (through further innovation).
(3) The assessment also depends on the type of the IoT device, how privacy-sensitive the generated, collected and shared IoT data (e.g. in the case of health data) is. It can also be important how valuable the personal and non-personal IoT data of different types of IoT devices is, and whether the manufacturers are mostly interested in the IoT data for improving their products and for innovation, or whether they want to monetize the data in various ways, e.g. also for the purpose of targeted advertising.[32]

Does the result that these market failures do not lead to enough choice for the consumers and lead presumably to a too large collection, use and sharing of IoT data (buy-out contracts) also to the conclusion that the consumers will not participate in the value of their IoT data? The unequal bargaining situation between data holders and consumers regarding these

32 There can also be differences regarding the consumers. Privacy-oriented consumers might be much less concerned regarding their non-personal than their personal data, i.e. they worry less about the terms of the data use contract according to Art. 4(13) DA. If, however, consumers would like to participate in the value of their IoT data, then this might be very different.

contracts would suggest such a conclusion. However, from an economic perspective this is not so clear if price competition on the IoT device markets still exists. If the IoT manufacturers as data holders could reduce their costs for producing and operating their IoT devices through various benefits from collected IoT data, then competition economists would usually assume that this might also lead to lower (monetary) prices for the IoT devices due to price competition. In the ideal world of the model of perfect competition, the cost reduction would lead to a corresponding reduction of the market prices of the IoT devices. In turn, there would be an increase of the consumer rents on these markets. Although real-world markets do not work so well as in the model of "perfect competition", paying higher "data prices" through the two IoT data use contracts might lead to lower monetary prices for the IoT devices, which would give the consumers in an indirect way some compensation for their IoT data. However, there might also be problems with price competition, for example, through various forms of oligopolistic pricing or price collusion between manufacturers. Therefore, it is an open question whether and to what extent price competition might lead to lower prices and therefore some sharing of the value of the IoT data with the consumers. Empirical research might help for analyzing this issue, and the answer might also be different for different types of IoT devices and IoT consumer data.

II.4. Intermediate results and conclusions

Our analysis has shown that due to information and behavioral problems with regard to the two data use contracts for non-personal and personal IoT data, it cannot be expected that consumers can use these two contracts effectively for getting meaningful control over their IoT data. This can lead to a too large generation, collection, use, and sharing of IoT data, which is not necessary for the functionalities of these devices. This result supports the serious concerns that the two data licensing contracts might not reflect sufficiently the preferences of consumers with regard to their IoT data, especially also with regard to protecting their privacy. Through the bundling of the data use contracts and the sale contract of the IoT devices, a very asymmetric allocation of the rights on the use, sharing and monetizing the personal and non-personal IoT data between data holders and consumers can emerge, e.g. through far-reaching buy-out contracts. It might, however, be possible that through competition regarding the price of the IoT devices, consumers can benefit to some extent indirectly from the value of their IoT data. Overall, more empirical research is necessary, also for enabling more differentiated assessments of the implications of market failures for different types of IoT devices.

What are basic policy strategies for dealing with governance problems of IoT data from the perspective of consumers? In the following, we will look at two policy strategies with different objectives:

(1) Compensation: One strategy would focus on the question whether IoT users would get a fair share of the value of their consumer data (as one of the objectives of the enacted DA). If the market failure on IoT data markets in B2C contexts leads to a too large collection and use of IoT data, then it could be argued that the consumers as users of these devices should at least get a fair compensation for this IoT data. This could require that IoT data holders might have to pay additionally a fair monetary compensation to the consumers.
(2) More choice: The second strategy would focus on policy options strengthening the choice of users of IoT devices through introduction of minimum standards of choice about the generation, collection, use and sharing of personal and non-personal IoT data. Ensuring that consumers have more choice would protect and increase consumer autonomy (or consumer sovereignty). It increases as well the chances from an economic perspective that the data use contracts would fit better to the preferences of the consumers, also with respect to the protection of their privacy, and especially due to the surveillance risks of IoT devices. Therefore, from an economic perspective, it can be argued that strengthening the choice of consumers has significant advantages compared to only compensating them to some extent in case of wrong and inefficient market outcomes.

Before exploring the wide range of policy options that can be applied under both strategies in section IV, the following section III will show that in recent years the topic of establishing a minimum standard of choice for data subjects with regard to personal data has emerged as an important new issue in legal cases and policy discussions in competition law and data protection law. This discussion has so far not influenced the discussion about the governance of IoT data and the DA.

III. New discussions about minimum standards of choice regarding personal data

III.1. Introduction

These discussions about choice for consumers have their roots partly in data protection law with its high requirements of "voluntary" consent. According to the "tying prohibition" of Art. 7(4) GDPR, the tying of "consent" for the processing of personal data that is not necessary for providing a service might not be allowed, because denying consent should not lead to a detriment for the data subject. Consent might also not be voluntary in case of an "imbalance of power", e.g. through market dominance. In the German Facebook case, this has become relevant in competition law, because here the German Federal Cartel Office (FCO) imposed an additional choice regarding consent for the combination of collected personal data from different sources as a competition law remedy, which then also was the model for a similar obligation for gatekeepers in the recently enacted Digital Markets Act (Art. 5(2) DMA). The issue of sufficient choice regarding the use of personal data by platforms has also emerged in data protection law with a controversial discussion about "consent or pay" models with respect to behavioral advertising and the question of the need of a third (less personalized) option ("equivalent alternative") without monetary payment (new Opinion of the EDPB) and compliance investigations of the Commission against gatekeepers with regard to Art. 5(2) DMA. Therefore, the issue of a mandatory minimum standard of choice for the processing of personal data has emerged both in competition policy and data protection law.

III.2. Competition law, market dominance, data protection law, and choice

In 2019, the FCO made a decision that Meta (then Facebook) abused its dominant position on the German market for social media through an infringement of the GDPR.[33] Users, who would like to use the social media platform Facebook, were forced to agree to terms of services which allowed Meta not only to collect consumer data across different platforms owned by Meta (like Instagram or WhatsApp) and from third-party websites using

33 See Federal Cartel Office (FCO), decision B6–22/16 (6 February 2019).

services offered by Meta, but also to combine all this data in one user profile. Based upon §19 of the German competition law (GWB), the FCO argued that Meta with its market dominance cannot force its users to agree to such an unlimited collection and combination of their personal data, because such a consent cannot be considered freely-given, leading to an infringement of the GDPR. Such a behavior was therefore not only considered to be exclusionary towards its competitors, but in particular exploitative towards the users and their control over their data. Consequently, the FCO issued an innovative competition law remedy: It requested Meta to give users an additional and explicit choice with regard to the combination of the collected data from different sources. In other words, users cannot be forced anymore to accept all these practices only for using the social media platform of Facebook. As far as the consumers do not explicitly agree to the data combination, this remedy leads to an "internal unbundling" of Meta's data sets. In the following legal proceedings, the German Federal Court of Justice, the Bundesgerichtshof (BGH), backed the decision and remedy of the FCO in 2020, albeit with a slightly different argumentation.[34] This decision of the BGH can be interpreted as claiming that Meta has to give users a minimum standard of choice with regard to collection and combination of their personal data.[35]

The FCO case and its remedy appears to have inspired Art. 5(2) in the EU Digital Markets Act, which tries to deal with the huge economic power of large gatekeeper platforms with its objectives of contestability and fairness.[36] Art. 5(2) not only restricts significantly the data combination abilities of a gatekeeper across all its core platform services (CPS) and its other products and services, but also hinders it to use data collected via third-party services for advertisements, unless the gatekeeper obtains an additional valid consent from its users for such data combinations. In other words, gatekeepers are in particular obliged to grant their users a

---

34 See Bundesgerichtshof (BGH), Order of 23.06.2020, Case KVR 69/19. It emphasized, on the one hand, both the exclusionary and exploitative effects of the abusive behavior of Meta and, on the other hand, Facebook's quasi-unavoidable role for the majority of its users, leading to a violation of the constitutionally protected right to informational self-determination in Germany.

35 See, for further detail, the discussion in Kerber/Zolna (fn.21), 239–240.

36 See European Commission, Regulation (EU) 2022/1925 of the European Parliament and of the Council of 14 September 2022 on contestable and fair markets in the digital sector and amending Directives (EU) 2019/1937 and (EU) 2020/1828 (Digital Markets Act) (2022), OJ L 265 (hereafter: DMA).

real choice with regard to different types of data combination practices. However, different to the FCO case, the main concern of Art. 5(2) DMA refers to the potential effects of such data combination practices on the objective of the contestability of markets.[37] Gatekeepers, such as Meta, might receive unfair advantages from their ability to process and combine user data across many different sources, which can reduce the contestability of the markets for advertising or for social media platforms. Therefore, granting users an additional choice with regard to the combination of their personal data is seen as an instrument to not further manifest the gatekeeper position and to keep (or to make) such markets contestable. It is, however, very unclear, whether giving users such a choice will have positive effects on contestability and competition.[38] More of interest for the literature so far has been the question under which circumstances a gatekeeper will receive valid consent according to EU data protection law for these data combination practices.[39] Particularly interesting is that recital 37 DMA claims that a gatekeeper has to offer also users denying consent "[a] less personalised alternative [which] should not be different or of degraded quality compared to the service provided to the end users who provide consent [...]".[40] In the most recent discussion Art. 5(2) DMA has increasingly been seen as a possible instrument for strengthening both competition and data protection, although its effectiveness remains unclear.

Since the Meta decision of the German FCO was the first competition case which included directly data protection law, it also triggered an entirely new (and international) discussion about the relationship between compe-

37 See DMA (fn.36), recital 36. Many commentators, however, deem Art. 5(2) DMA to pursue also the goal of fairness by strengthening the control of users about their data. See e.g. Louven, DMA Art. 5 Rn. 15–39 (2023), BeckOK InfoMedienR, 41. Ed. 1.8.2023, paras. 15–17; Podszun, DMA Art. 5 Abs. 2 (2023), HK-DMA/Podszun, 1. Aufl. 2023, para. 11.

38 The precise effects of Art. 5(2) DMA on competition have not been discussed in the literature in greater detail yet. See Kerber/Zolna (fn.21), 243, who argue that this provision can only have positive effects on competition, if many users would deny consent to the combination of their data.

39 See e.g. Botta/Borges, Compliance with the DMA obligations: The prohibition of data combination under Art. 5(2) DMA (2024), Ruiz Peris/Estevan de Esquada (eds.) New European Competition Trends in Digital Markets, 259; D'Amico, The DMA's Consent Moment and its Relationship with the GDPR (2025), European Journal of Risk Regulation, 16(1), 170.

40 DMA (fn.36), recital 37.

tition law and data protection law.[41] It also shifted the focus on the question whether (and how) also data protection law could include concepts of market power and market dominance. Data protection laws, such as the GDPR, intend to strengthen the position of consumers as data subjects and control firms with regard to their data processing practices, but, so far, they do not consider any market power related criteria.[42] Nevertheless, the GDPR acknowledges that wherever a consumer is facing a so-called "imbalance of power", consent might not be deemed to be freely given. Both the literature and recent court decisions deliver new insights on how exactly to take this "imbalance of power" into consideration, which could help to imply certain aspects of market power. One example is the idea of using the existing concept of a "special responsibility" of a dominant firm in competition law also in data protection law. This could require that a dominant firm might have to follow a higher data protection standard.[43]

Particularly important, however, is the recent CJEU decision in the German FCO Meta case in June 2023.[44] Firstly, it confirmed that the German FCO can take the violation of data protection law into account in its application of competition law. Secondly, it clarified that the fact that a firm has a dominant position does not automatically imply that consent of users is invalid (due to an imbalance of power), but that such a position can be an important aspect when determining whether consent is valid according to the GDPR. Thirdly, it specified clearer the requirements of a real choice in such cases: "... those users must be free to refuse individually, ..., to give their consent to particular data processing operations not necessary for the performance of the contract, without being obliged to refrain entirely from using the service offered by the online social network operator, which

41 See Douglas, Digital crossroads: the intersection of competition law and data privacy, Report to the global privacy assembly digital citizen and consumer working group, July 2021; Kerber, Competition policy and data protection law: The complexity of its interplay from an economic perspective (forthcoming 2025), Ioannidou/Mantzari (eds), Research Handbook on Data, Privacy and Competition Law (Edward Elgar); for an explicit economic analysis see Kerber/Zolna (fn.21), 222–229.

42 See for a more detailed discussion Kerber/Zolna (fn.21), 232–234.

43 See Graef/van Berlo, Towards Smarter Regulation in the Areas of Competition, Data Protection and Consumer Law: Why Greater Power Should Come with Greater Responsibility (2020), European Journal of Risk Regulation, 674; D'Amico, Market power and the GDPR: Can consent given to dominant companies ever be freely given? (2023), European Papers, 611.

44 See Court of Justice of the European Union (CJEU), Order of 04.07.2023, Case C-252/21 (2023), paras. 140–154.

means that those users are to be offered, if necessary for an appropriate fee, an equivalent alternative not accompanied by such data processing operations".[45] Therefore, both the Meta decision of the CJEU and Art. 5(2) DMA help to specify a minimum standard of choice for consumers with regard to their personal data.

III.3. Tying prohibition in data protection law, "consent or pay" models, and the EDPB Opinion 08/24

So far, we have focused primarily on situations where consumers might lack appropriate choice options due to market power problems. The GDPR, however, intends with Art. 7(4) to control whether consent can be considered freely given if "[...] the performance of a contract, including the provision of a service, is conditional on consent to the processing of personal data that is not necessary for the performance of that contract." This suggests that consumers should not be forced to agree to any data processing activities which are not necessary for the actual service or for the actual functionality of a product. Important is that this "tying prohibition" does not require a market power position of firms, and therefore can also be relevant for firms under effective competition. However, there is still large legal uncertainty about the criteria and the scope of its application.[46]

This legal uncertainty becomes also visible in the current debate about the application of "consent or pay" models by different types of services. One prominent example are the so-called "pure" subscriptions for online services of newspapers, which give users often the choice between either paying a (monthly) subscription fee without tracking and behavioral advertising, or accepting to be tracked and targeted with behavioral advertising without a monetary payment. The legality of such "pure" models is not finally clear yet, but some national data protection authorities seem to be open-minded towards this solution as long as the price for the alternative option appears to be appropriate in the market.[47] It can, however, be ques-

45 See CJEU (fn.44), para. 150.

46 See for this discussion Sattler, Personenbezug als Hindernis des Datenhandels (2020), Pertot (ed.) Rechte an Daten, 49, 74–79.

47 See e.g. the French Commission Nationale de l'Informatique et des Libertés (CNIL) and the German Datenschutzkonferenz (DSK): CNIL, Cookie walls : la CNIL publie des premiers critères d'évaluation (2022), https://www.cnil.fr/fr/cookie-walls-la-cnil-publie-des-premiers-criteres-devaluation; DSK, Beschluss der

tioned whether the prices for the "pure" subscriptions are not too high. Usually only a minority decides to choose the tracking-free alternative. Thus, despite some level of competition in these markets, the prices for the "pure" alternatives seem to be prohibitively high (i.e. reflecting no realistic alternative), leading most consumers to accept to be tracked and to be faced with targeted advertising.[48] This discussion has raised the question of a need for controlling the price for the option without behavioral advertising.

In November 2023, Meta also decided to apply such a "consent or pay" model for using its services.[49] This was a reaction to a decision by the European Data Protection Board (EDPB) in October 2023, which de facto prohibited Meta to rely for behavioral advertising on any other legal basis than consent.[50] In consequence, users of Facebook and Instagram faced in their browsers a screen where they could either choose to continue with data collection and targeted advertising without paying a monthly fee, or choose to pay €9,99/month to avoid any personalized advertising.[51] Both the specific implementation and the use of such a "consent or pay" model by Meta received much criticism. As consumers might not have a realistic choice due to the high price and due to lack of realistic alternatives to both platforms, doubts were raised about the model's compatibility with the GDPR.[52]

After a request of several national data protection authorities, the European Data Protection Board (EDPB) published in April 2024 an Opinion about the requirements for the application of "consent or pay" models by

---

Konferenz der unabhängigen Datenschutzaufsichtsbehörden des Bundes und der Länder vom 22. März 2023: Bewertung von Pur-Abo-Modellen auf Websites (2023), https://www.datenschutzkonferenz-online.de/media/pm/DSK_Beschluss_Bewertung_von_Pur-Abo-Modellen_auf_Websites.pdf.

48 See, also for further empirical analyses about the implication of "pure" and "Pay or OK" models in the European Union and their economic consequences, Müller-Tribbensee/Miller/Skiera, Paying for Privacy: Pay-or-Tracking Walls (2024), https://dx.doi.org/10.2139/ssrn.4749217.

49 See Meta, Facebook and Instagram to Offer Subscription for No Ads in Europe – Original publication of October 2023 (2024), https://about.fb.com/news/2024/11/facebook-and-instagram-to-offer-subscription-for-no-ads-in-europe/.

50 See EDPB, Urgent Binding Decision 01/2023 requested by the Norwegian SA for the ordering of final measures regarding Meta Platforms Ireland Ltd (Art. 66(2) GDPR) – Adopted on 27 October 2023.

51 See Meta (fn.49).

52 See e.g. D'Amico/Pelekis/Teixeira Santos/Duivenvoorde, Meta's Pay-or-Okay Model: An analysis under EU Data Protection, Consumer and Competition Law (2024), Technology and Regulation, 254.

large online platforms, such as Meta, with regard to receiving valid and freely given consent for the purpose of behavioral advertising.[53] The EDPB did not generally reject "consent of pay" models by large online platforms, but emphasized that firms still need to respect in their "consent or pay" models the data minimization principle as well as fairness considerations (no exploitation of power imbalances, no implementation of deceptive "dark patterns", etc.). For the question of a minimum standard of choice it is particularly interesting that the EDPB states that, in order to satisfy the requirements for valid consent, large online platforms might need to offer their users more than two options.[54] In its Opinion the EDPB, more specifically, suggests that there should be also an equivalent alternative of the service available without any tracking for behavioral advertising and without any costs. Instead, "simple" advertisements, e.g. contextual ones, could be used in this "third option". Further requirements for valid consent, such as granularity for different purposes, should also be respected. The claim of the EDPB for the need of such a third option of an "equivalent alternative" without behavioral advertising and without a monetary payment is controversially discussed in the literature.[55]

However, not only the EDPB favors an extension of choice through this type of "third option", which uses fewer personal data and does not charge consumers for an equivalent service. This approach is also favored by the Commission in its enforcement of Art. 5(2) DMA regarding the combination of personal data from different sources by gatekeepers. According to the Commission, Meta's binary "consent or pay" advertising model is not compliant with the DMA as it granted users neither the "[...] specific choice to opt for a service that uses less of their personal data but is otherwise equivalent to the 'personalised ads' service", nor did it "[...] allow users to exercise their right to freely consent to the combination of their personal data".[56] The missing "third option" is used by the Commission as one argument to prove the second infringement of lacking valid consent, as

53 See EDPB (fn.17).

54 See EDPB (fn.17), 18–21; important is that the opinion of the EDPB formulates only guidelines, i.e. the specific application of these requirements needs to be conducted on a case-by-case basis by data protection authorities.

55 For a critical position see e.g. Kühling, Wann sollen Nutzer für Onlineplattformen zahlen?, FAZ, 6 May 2024.

56 European Commission, Commission finds Apple and Meta in breach of the Digital Markets Act, Press release, 23 April 2025 (2025), https://ec.europa.eu/commission/presscorner/detail/en/ip_25_1085.

offering only binary solutions would result in certain detriments to users who would like to refuse consent to behavioral advertisements (e.g. being forced to pay a monthly fee or to stop using Facebook and Instagram).[57] Thus, in particular gatekeepers, such as Meta, who will need to comply with both the DMA and the special GDPR requirements formulated by the EDPB,[58] might be significantly affected in their business models and need to adapt their processes with regard to receiving valid consent from their users.

III.4. More choice: Recent developments in Californian privacy law

The CCPA (California Consumer Privacy Act) was introduced in 2018 as a part of the Cal. Civ. Code (Californian Civil Code) and was amended by the CPRA (California Privacy Rights Act), which came into force in 2023.[59] The latter established the California Privacy Protection Agency (CPPA) as first data protection authority in the US, introduced additional consumer rights, a clear definition of consent with regard to processing of sensitive data, and the possibility to send a preset opt-out preference signal to firms with regard to data collection.[60] All these amendments bring the CCPA closer to the standards of the European GDPR. A significant difference is that Californian privacy law is based on an opt-out principle instead of the European opt-in principle regarding the processing of personal data. However, according to Cal. Civ. Code § 1798.125, this opt-out principle is complemented by a non-discrimination principle, i.e. firms are not allowed to discriminate consumers who exercise their data protection rights. This implies that if consumers want to use a certain product or service and refrain from related data processing (through opt-out), they should in consequence neither suffer from any price-related harms nor from any harms

---

57 European Commission, Decision of 23.04.2025, Case DMA.100055 – Meta – Article 5(2), paras. 189–202.

58 For the relationship between DMA and GDPR, see e.g. Botta/Borges (fn.39), 264–277.

59 See for a detailed overview about the amendments Determann, Kaliforniens erste Datenschutzbehörde – dank Volksentscheid: California Privacy Rights Act (CPRA) verschärft California Consumer Privacy Act (CCPA) und gilt auch für deutsche Unternehmen (2021), ZD 2021, 69.

60 See Kühling/Schwartz, Daten gegen Leistung. Konvergenz von kalifornischem Recht und DSGVO? (2023), DuD, 749, 750.

that are not related to prices (e.g. loss in quality of a good or even a denial of this good).[61]

There exists, however, an exception to this "non-discrimination principle" that allows firms to treat consumers differently as long as it is reasonably related to the value of the data of consumers. In other words, consumers who decided to opt-out can be charged with a higher price for a product or can be provided with a lower quality of a service that is more or less equivalent to the value a firm loses by not receiving the data of these consumers. In addition, as long as it also reasonably relates to its value of the respective data, firms are also allowed to offer consumers financial incentives (i.e. a compensation) for sharing their personal data. This exception to the "non-discrimination principle" leads to solutions that are similar to "consent or pay" models (as discussed above in section III.3): Firms can offer their standard products and services with their standard data processing practices, but also claim a certain "price" in case consumers decide for opting-out of data collection.

Important is that the firms have to justify the level of this "price", as it may not be higher than the value a firm gets from gathering the consumer's data. Hence, the Californian "non-discrimination principle" contains a de facto price regulation, which, due to its independency of any market power concepts, can be applied very broadly. Nevertheless, it is clear that for its successful implementation it is essential to find pragmatic solutions for determining an adequate price. Such guidelines were developed in 2023 by the new Californian data protection authority CPPA, which offer not only illustrative examples for non-discriminatory cases, but also in total eight economic calculation methods which each can be used by firms for justifying any price differences.[62] The calculation methods are for example related to the average value or the marginal value of consumer data, while other methods consider the related expenses or the related profits. It is important to note that all these methods are related to the value of consumer data for the specific firm and its specific business model, and not to a potential market price. The eighth method formulated by the CPPA is more or less a placeholder, as it allows firms to apply "any other practical and reasonably reliable method of calculation used in good faith". Thus, such a broad range

61 See Kühling/Schwartz (fn.60), 750.

62 The relevant articles § 7080 and § 7081 of the CCPA regulations can be found here: https://cppa.ca.gov/regulations/pdf/cppa_regs.pdf, 58–61.

of potential calculation methods can make it clearly easier for firms to find plausible solutions for offering alternative options to consumers.

Current discussions in the literature show both problems and advantages of the "Californian solution".[63] Determining the value of consumer data for justifying different prices will be hard and the guidelines for the calculation methods look still rather vague and unclear. However, it will be very interesting to see how the firms will experiment with different calculation methods, and what also in Europe can be learnt from the experiences with this Californian solution, e.g. with respect to discussions about controlling prices in the case of mandated options without the collection of data or behavioral advertising. Making it mandatory for firms to use publicly known methods to justify their prices in "consent or pay" schemes might increase the transparency of their price-setting and the awareness of consumers about the value of their data, which might also strengthen the sovereignty of consumers.[64] However, Californian consumers might still end up in many cases with unattractive alternative options, which will lead the majority to accept data-intense products and services. It will be interesting to see the effects of the Californian solution on both firms and consumers.

Particularly noteworthy in the Californian version of "consent or pay" solutions as minimum standards of choice regarding personal data is, first, that with the combination of the opt-out and the non-discrimination principle a far-reaching right seems to have been established to buy products and services without the need to allow processing of personal data. It is, secondly, also not limited to cases of market dominance or gatekeeper power, i.e. consumers in markets with strong and weak competition might receive an alternative option with respect to data collection.[65]

III.5. Choice of consumers regarding personal data: Some critical reflections

In this section III we have seen important recent developments both in data protection law and in competition law that try to ensure that consumers

63 See e.g. Rose, The commodification of personal data and the road to consumer autonomy through the CCPA (2021), 15 Brook. J. Corp. Fin. & Com. L. 521; Serrato, How Much Is Your Data Worth? CCPA's Data Valuation Requirement Explored (2022), 59 San Diego L. Rev. 621; Donahue, Financial Incentives: The Fault in California's Privacy Framework (2023), 56 Loy. L.A. L. Rev. 411.

64 See Kühling/Schwartz (fn.60), 752–754.

65 See Kühling/Schwartz (fn.60), 754.

have at least a minimum level of choice regarding the collection and use of their personal data. This discussion focusses, on the one hand, on the huge collection of personal data through digital platforms with market power (consumer profiles and behavioral advertising). Here the German competition authority in its Meta case decision, and, more broadly, Art. 5(2) DMA want to ensure that consumers at least have an additional choice regarding the combination of their personal data from different sources in cases of a dominant position (Art. 102 TFEU) or a gatekeeper position (as defined in the DMA). Data protection law, on the other hand, might go further by requiring that voluntary choice would imply that consumers should also have the choice to use a service without having to provide personal data that are not necessary for the service. This has led to the discussion of solutions that offer a choice to pay either with personal data or with a monetary price ("consent or pay"). Whereas in the EU it is still unclear to what extent consumers should have such a choice if there is competition between the service providers and no market power exists, in Californian privacy law consumers always seem to have an opt-out option regarding personal data, i.e. they have a choice to buy a product or service both with and without the collection and use of their personal data. Both in EU and California this leads to questions about controlling the level of the monetary price if non-necessary personal data are not provided. It is, however, California that has seriously started developing methods for implementing that. With regard to very large online platforms and gatekeepers, in the EU both data protection law and DMA have additionally extended the discussion about choice through demanding an additional third option for consumers, which would allow them to use an equivalent service with less use (or combination) of personal data and without paying a monetary price. Therefore, partly already far-reaching regulations exist about a minimum standard of choice for personal data.

Having a choice between paying with personal data (and behavorial advertising) or with a monetary price has been discussed in the EU controversially for a long time. One position rejects entirely the approach that personal data should be tradable and that it is possible to pay with personal data (e.g. due to privacy as a fundamental value), another critical position emphasizes the problem that poor people might feel that they have no choice than "paying" with their personal data.[66] Independent from this more fundamental critique to a market approach regarding personal data, we have seen in section II that serious market failures can arise with regard to decisions of consumers regarding their personal data, which also might be relevant for a regulated minimum standard of choice, like "consent or pay" solutions. Whereas mandatory "consent or pay" solutions (including a third option) might help consumers in "imbalance of power" situations, it is less clear to what extent it also can solve information and behavioral problems of consumers regarding such a choice. Will consumers understand well what such a choice means and can consumers be sufficiently protected against behavioral manipulation strategies of digital firms for nudging them to certain choice options, especially to accept the current option with the provision of data? However, having always a choice between a monetary price for a service or paying with data can also lead to learning processes of consumers about the value of their data, which might help to reduce the market failure problems discussed in section II. But these questions suggest that mandatory "consent or pay" solutions might require additional regulations, e.g. with respect to the design of choice architectures and also regarding the size of the monetary price for the option to pay only with money.

IV. Future policy options for governance of IoT data in B2C contexts: An exploratory discussion

IV.1. Introduction

After this overview about recent developments in data protection law and competition policy about granting consumers a minimum standard of choice with regard to their personal data, this section IV returns to the results of our market failure analysis with regard to the data use contracts in B2C IoT contexts in section II: Even with competition between IoT device manufacturers and the implementation of the DA, it cannot be expected that the instrument of data use contracts (for personal and non-personal

66 See e.g. an open letter of 28 NGOs and consumer rights organizations arguing against "pay or okay"/"consent or pay" in general: noyb et al., 'Pay or okay' – the end of a 'genuine and free choice' (2024), https://noyb.eu/sites/default/files/2024-02/Pay-or-okay_edpb-letter_v2.pdf. For a discussion of social aspects with a special emphasis on the Californian situation, see Donahue (fn.63), 450–455.

data) will enable consumers to get sufficient control over their IoT data, have enough choice for fulfilling their preferences about the governance of this data, and get a fair share of its value. This section will explore additional regulatory policy options for solving these problems. In a first step (section IV.2), we will briefly discuss the policy option to grant consumers directly a fair compensation for their data by the data holders. Mostly, however, we will focus on policy options which try to ensure that consumers have more choice over their IoT data and IoT devices (section IV.3). As economists we will not analyze which of these options might already be possible de lege lata, e.g. also through different interpretations of existing laws (including the DA), and which need a change of the law (de lege ferenda), e.g. through new regulations.

IV.2. Direct compensation for personal / non-personal IoT data

Due to the market failure problems, which – also through the bundling of the data use contracts with the sale contract – can lead to a too large collection, use, and sharing of personal and non-personal IoT data, the concerns that the consumers do not get a fair share for their data are justified. From that perspective, it might be an interesting policy option to mandate data holders to compensate the consumers in an appropriate way for the use and monetisation of their IoT data.[67]

Introducing an obligation that data holders have to pay a monetary compensation for their use, sharing, and monetizing of IoT data directly to the users can also be interpreted as a mandatory regulation of licensing fees or remuneration for IoT data.[68] This is a difficult task that raises many questions:

(1) As discussed in section II.3, there might be already some indirect compensation through potentially lower prices via price competition for the IoT devices. However, any mandatory licensing fee is an additional cost for the manufacturers, which can lead to higher prices of the IoT

67 It is not possible here to delve into the complex question what a fair sharing of the value from IoT data might mean. It is one of the open questions in the discussion about the DA.

68 According to Becker (fn.3), 621, the DA does not require that the users get a remuneration for the licensing of their IoT data to the data holders. See also the discussion about remuneration of non-personal data in Specht-Riemenschneider et al. (fn.10), 92.

devices as it would reduce the extent of the indirect compensation through price competition. In any case, it is very hard to assess to what extent the processing of the data of consumers might have led to lower prices, and how much should be paid for the uncompensated part.

(2) For what kind of data should be paid compensation? Should it be only for IoT data that are not necessary for the functionality of the device and lead therefore to additional benefits and revenues for the data holders? Or should it be paid for all collected and processed IoT data?

(3) How should these fees be calculated? Should the compensation be calculated as a monthly lump sum licensing fee (e.g. a few Euros per month) or be directly proportional to the amount of collected data, which might be proportional to the use of the device by the consumer?[69]

(4) Should the compensation be linked to the specific value these manufacturers draw from the data or should it rather be seen as a general price for collected IoT data (as a standardised licensing fee), independent from their specific use? It depends very much on the business model of IoT device manufacturers, how much value they draw from the data.[70]

(5) The administration and compliance costs of such a compensation system will presumably be very high compared to the expected size of such fees.

These are only some of the questions that can be raised. Overall, we are skeptical whether such a regulation would lead to an effective compensation mechanism that would lead to an increase in the fairness of sharing the value of the IoT, especially if also the costs of this regulation is taken into account.[71]

---

69 As a reminder, the monthly subscription fees for consumers using a service (like Meta's social media services Facebook or Instagram) are lump sum fees independent from the extent of use of this service.

70 Should the consumers also directly participate in the revenues that data holders can get through monetizing the IoT data of the consumers? From an economic perspective, data sharing contracts of data holders with third-parties can also be interpreted as sub-licensing contracts: Why should consumers not get a direct share of these sub-licensing fees? How should the option be taken into account that consumers could have licensed the data also to other firms if the contracts were not bundled by the data holder?

71 For the approach to establish a "collecting society for data" in analogy to copyright law, see Specht-Riemenschneider et al. (fn.10), 93 (with further references).

IV.3. More choice: Minimum standards of choice for users of IoT devices in B2C contexts

IV.3.1. Reasons why consumers do not have sufficient choice regarding their IoT data and IoT devices

In section II, we argued that due to market failures consumers do not get enough control over their data and the IoT device. This lack of choice, however, is also a consequence of the following two strategies of IoT device manufacturers, which also complement each other in strengthening their exclusive control over the IoT device and IoT data.

(1) *Technical-factual control through data holders:* Manufacturers of IoT devices are largely free to technically design their devices in a way that gives them exclusive de facto control over the device and the generated IoT data.[72] Although the DA obliges the data holders to give access to raw and preprocessed IoT data to users (Art. 4 DA) and, via the users' request, also to third parties as data recipients (Art. 5 DA) ("data accessibility by design"), the DA also seems to give data holders a large discretionary scope how they make the data available. Data access can be made also only through in-situ access or in combination with technical protection measures: This can ensure that the IoT data will never leave the technical-factual sphere of the data holders when users are exerting their data access and sharing rights of Art. 4 and 5 DA. Therefore, it is very unclear whether users or third parties can get a copy of this data into their own technical-factual sphere, if data holders do not want this.[73] This limits significantly the choice of users, and

72 For an analysis from a property rights theory perspective of using technical design for exclusively "capturing" data and its application to IoT devices, see Eckardt/Kerber (fn.3), 119–121; for the general importance of technical factual control see Specht-Riemenschneider, Diktat der Technik. Regulierungskonzepte technischer Vertragsgestaltung am Beispiel von Bürgerlichem Recht und Urheberrecht, 2019.

73 For the issue of whether data holders are free to offer only "in-situ" access or whether users (should) have a right to get a copy of the data, see Kerber (fn.8), 124; Specht-Riemenschneider (fn.10), 66–68; Lienemann/Wienroeder, V. Data Licence Agreement and User's Right of Access (Art. 4) (2024), Hennemann et al. (fn.3), 71, 83–85; Sattler, Artikel 5 (2025), Specht-Riemenschneider/Hennemann (fn.3), Rdnr. 24. Very surprising are the recently published "Frequently Asked Questions. Data Act" (13 September 2024) of the European Commission, which claims that the data holders can decide in their own interest how they make the IoT data available (see the answers to the question 14 and 19). It is not clear whether this is legally

indirectly also the data recipients, how to use the data. In addition, data holders usually also have to some extent remote control over the IoT device, which implies that they can factually decide what data are generated and collected, as well as stop remotely the operating of the device ("bricking"). The consumer as owner of an IoT device has therefore usually only very limited options of de facto control over the IoT device and its generation of data.[74]

(2) *Strategy of bundling contracts:* If the manufacturers of IoT devices bundle the data use contracts for personal and non-personal data with the sale contract, consumers will only have the choice between agreeing to the entire bundle of contracts or refraining from buying and using the IoT device (take-it-or-leave-it situation). These data license contracts can entail also the generation, collection, use, sharing, and monetizing of IoT data, which are not necessary for the functionality of the IoT device.[75] Then consumers would not have the choice option to buy an IoT device that processes only data which are necessary for its functionality. So far, user as owners of IoT devices do not have the right to use their device without having to agree to data license contracts with the data holders, i.e. they can be forced to pay for the IoT services also with personal and non-personal data.[76] As long as bundling of the contracts

---

compatible with the final version of the DA. Such a large discretionary scope of the data holders could also make strategies impossible that users circumvent the data-sharing mechanism of Art. 5 by directly transmitting the data to other firms. See for this strategy Boeselager/Jaenicke, The Data Act as a design for (non-personal) industrial data markets (2024), Lohsse et al. (eds), Private Law and the Data Act, 231, 238–242), and Sattler (fn.73), Rdnr. 22.

74 See Specht-Riemenschneider et al. (fn.10), 66–68, and for "bricking" ibid, 77; Becker (fn.29), 178; for a more fundamental critique of the manufacturers of IoT devices and their relations to IoT users without referring to the DA, see Noto La Diega, Internet of Things and the Law (2023), 275–340.

75 In the final version of the DA, it was clarified that only the users have the right to monetize the product data from their IoT devices (recital 26) for better incentivizing the users to share the data, also for enabling "liquid, fair and efficient" data markets. Users can monetize these product data via data holders and other firms, e.g. data intermediaries. See Eckardt/Kerber (fn.3), 15. With regard to bundling the interesting question is whether data holders can also include directly this monetization of product data by the users in its bundle of contracts, i.e. that the users, if they want to buy a device, also have to monetize their product data through the data holder (and whether the data holder has to pay any remuneration for that).

76 For the legal situation that also after the implementation of the DA such bundling of contracts is not prohibited, although there might be some so far unclear limits through Art. 7(4) GDPR for personal data, see Specht-Riemenschneider et al. (fn.10),

is allowed, it will also remain unclear whether a termination of the data use contracts by the consumers is possible without risking to lose the functionality of the device via "bricking".[77] As a consequence, the data holders can maintain this bundling and these data license contracts for the entire life-time of the IoT device, even if a consumer resells this device (see below section IV.3.3). Depending on the average life-time of IoT devices, the monetary price for the device, and the data use contracts, the lock-in of the consumers can be significant. It does not seem as if the DA is able to help the consumers against this lock-in situation and the bundling strategy of manufacturers.

However, it should be kept in mind: If the markets and competition between IoT device manufacturers would work well, then consumers might not need to accept IoT devices with so much de facto control and bundling of contracts, because manufacturers would be under competitive pressure to offer such devices also with much more choice, less far-reaching bundling, and less de facto control of the IoT device by the manufacturers. This also implies that the need for mandatory rights for more choice – as discussed in the following sections – might be different in different IoT contexts, also because the extent of these market failures and the business models might differ.

IV.3.2. A right for data collection-free IoT devices: A case for applying "consent or pay" models in B2C IoT contexts?

With regard to the bundling problem, it can be asked whether "consent or pay" models (as discussed in section III) can be an interesting policy solution for the governance of IoT data. What would this imply? Instead of having to accept the entire bundle of the sale contract and far-reaching ("buy-out like") data use contracts, consumers might also have a right to choose between this usual bundle of contracts and an alternative bundle of contracts, which does license personal and non-personal IoT data to data holders only as far as it is necessary for the functionality of the IoT

76, 88–91; Lienemann/Wienroeder, V. Data Licence Agreement and User's Right of Access (Art. 4) (2024), Hennemann et al. (fn.3), 71, 75; Becker (fn.29), 620.

77 Lienemann/Wienroeder, V. Data Licence Agreement and User's Right of Access (Art. 4) (2024), Hennemann et al. (fn.3), 71, 75.

device.[78] Depending on the relevance of the benefits of licensing the non-necessary IoT data for the business model of the IoT device manufacturers, the question can be raised whether the data holders should then be allowed to charge a higher price for the IoT device if the consumers chose this alternative with less data and only limited data use contracts. This then could result in the application of a variant of the "consent or pay" model for IoT devices, in which consumers could choose between paying with the usual combination of a monetary price and personal and non-personal data or only with a somewhat higher monetary price. Therefore, they would not be forced to pay also with their data if they want to use, e.g., a connected car or a smart TV.[79]

Such a solution would be very close to older concepts of "data free" or "data poor" digital products and services, as e.g. in Becker's concept of a right for "datenerhebungsfreie Produkte" in 2017.[80] This concept did only focus on personal data, but emphasized the need of a free choice of consumers between a digital device with the usual collection of data and a device with the same basic functionalities but without collecting personal data that are not necessary for its functionality.[81]

Becker also acknowledges the potential need that the manufacturer of both products with and without the collection of (non-necessary) data might charge different prices.[82] It is surprising that his proposal as well as the "consent or pay" approach have so far not been seriously considered in the context of IoT data governance and the discussion about the DA. An important exception is Specht-Riemenschneider's analysis of the DA from a consumer perspective, in which she strongly supports an approach of granting the consumers a minimum standard of choice in form of a

78 Otherwise, the consumers remain free in their decisions what they want to do with this personal and non-personal IoT data and can decide, in particular, not to share the personal IoT data for protecting their privacy or to licence the non-personal IoT data to other firms, e.g. for monetizing it by themselves. The IoT data necessary for the functionality can also have the purposes of safeguarding cyber security or preventing fraud etc.

79 Since such a "consent or pay" model could then also be applied to non-personal IoT data, the data holders would also have to offer two different data use contracts according to Art. 4(13) DA.

80 See Becker (fn.29), who already 2017 deeply analyzed the data governance issues, which have emerged in IoT contexts; see also Becker, Reconciliating data privacy and trade in data – A right to data-avoiding products (2017), ZGE/IPJ, 371.

81 See Becker (fn.29), 175.

82 See Becker (fn.29), 179.

right for buying and using also an IoT device, which does not generate and collect data that are not necessary for its functionality.[83]

What are the implications, advantages and problems of applying the "consent or pay" approach to the governance of IoT data and the two data use contracts about personal and non-personal data?

(1) Since no tying prohibition exists regarding this bundling of contracts by the data holders, consumers do not yet have such a right to choose between the usual data-collecting IoT devices with and without far-reaching data use contracts. Introducing therefore such a right could be a big step for more choice of consumers (also with respect to their privacy).
(2) Also here the question can arise whether and to what extent the manufacturers should be allowed to set a higher price for the IoT device, if consumers choose not to license non-necessary IoT data to the data holders. Important, however, is that for many IoT devices the revenues from monetizing the IoT data might be relatively small compared to the price of the device. Therefore, getting additional revenues from using and monetizing non-necessary data is not necessary for developing and manufacturing such IoT devices.
(3) Since, however, there will also be cases where a price difference can be justified (and might be necessary), the question arises whether this difference should be controlled to a certain extent. It is clear that this also would be difficult, both conceptually (e.g. regarding the criteria) as well as practically. It might be interesting to see to what extent the Californian approach could provide some help.
(4) An additional complication can be that IoT devices often offer different levels of functionalities, partly via additional subscription options which also generate different sets of data that can be collected and used by the manufacturers. This might require pragmatic solutions, because otherwise this can lead to too many alternative options and much too complicated choice tableaus, especially for the consumers.

While some consumers might be rather open-minded towards IoT devices, other consumers might perceive them as surveillance instruments, which collect a huge amount of data about consumers and are often unavoidable. Therefore, having a regulation which requires, for example, that IoT device manufacturers might have to offer an option that does use only personal

83 See Specht-Riemenschneider et al. (fn.10), 96.

and non-personal data that are necessary for the functionalities of the device, might be a very interesting policy option for introducing a minimum standard of choice for consumers of IoT devices. This might lead also to the application of "consent or pay" models in B2C IoT contexts. Due to the differences between various types of IoT devices, such an approach would need much deeper analysis from a legal and economic perspective. It can be expected that such "consent or pay" solutions might be appropriate or necessary for some IoT devices but not for others.

IV.3.3. Minimum standards of choice for users of IoT devices: More granular choice and termination rights

General discussion about rights on more granular choice

Such general "consent or pay" models, as they have been discussed in data protection law or with regard to their application to IoT devices in the last section IV.3.2, are only one way of limiting the bundling strategy and ensuring that consumers have at least some choice. But they might also be a crude and insufficient instrument, as consumers might have much more differentiated preferences about what IoT data should be generated, collected, used, and shared with whom. As described in section II.1, firms might have in well-functioning IoT device markets incentives to offer much more granular choice options for matching better what consumers want. Due to market failures, however, such choice options might not be provided on markets.[84] Therefore, it might be important that consumers should have directly much more granular rights regarding their IoT data.

However, neither data protection law nor the DA give consumers granular rights with regard to data processing activities by IoT device manufacturers. Data protection law does not ensure that consumers have a right to choose how data holders use their personal data for each purpose at a granular level, and such a right does not exist at all for non-personal IoT data. Thus, the question arises whether consumers should get more far-reaching granular rights over their data which cannot be contracted away through data use contracts for personal and non-personal data. It is clear that the question whether to introduce more far-reaching granular minimum rights about choice over IoT data might depend also much on

84 Examples might be that consumers would like to have the right in a connected car that no data are collected about their driving behavior or that for certain car trips the car does not collect and transmit location data for protecting the driver's privacy.

the type of IoT device and the type of data. It would therefore also require much more research.

Problems regarding rights of consumers to terminate data use contracts, reselling used IoT devices, and the long-term adaptation of data use contracts

Very important questions refer to rights of consumers to terminate data use contracts without losing the ability to use the IoT device and to problems in the case of reselling their devices (e.g. a used car). It is usually assumed by legal scholars that in addition to the data use contract for personal data, also the data use contract for non-personal IoT data (Art. 13(4) DA) can be terminated by the users. However, it is not clear whether the data holder can then stop operating the IoT device ("bricking") if one or both of the data use contracts have been terminated.[85] If the IoT device is only usable with such contracts a termination of data use contracts by consumers might lead theoretically to renegotiations. The consumers, however, will have only a very weak bargaining position, i.e. terminating one of these contracts is de facto no option if they still want to use the device. A similar problem arises in the case of reselling the IoT device. If such a strict bundling is legal, then any buyer of the used device also has to accept the terms of the data use contracts of the manufacturers in order to use the device. Therefore, a consumer can only buy a used IoT device, like a connected car, if he or she also accepts the data use contracts of the data holders, which therefore can de facto remain valid for the entire life-time of the IoT device.

In turn, giving consumers more choice would imply to give them effective termination rights (e.g. after a period of two years) that would also ensure that they can use (at least core functions of) their IoT devices without such data use contracts after termination (or, as buyers of used devices, in the case of not agreeing to the data use contracts). Such a solution can lead to complex legal and economic questions, but might also lead to genuine renegotiations. It will limit to some extent the negative effects of the bundling strategies of the manufacturers on consumers, but can also influence the business models as the data holders can lose (to some extent) their exclusive contractual control over the future IoT data stream.

85 For a deep analysis of the legality of bricking under different circumstances, see Specht-Riemenschneider et al. (fn.10), 77–88. Based upon this discussion, it might be that under such circumstances "bricking" the IoT device might be legal if this was made transparent at the point of the sale of the device. The authors claim that, e.g. the German legislator should clarify more for which purposes "bricking" is allowed (ibid., 88).

However, difficult problems regarding the long-term governance of IoT devices between data holders and users will arise anyway for durable IoT devices, e.g. connected cars. Since, due to technological and economic change, the generated data of a durable IoT device and how they can be used, shared, and monetized will often change significantly over time (e.g. through software updates with additional and changing functionalities), the data use contracts for both personal and non-personal data will need to be adapted regularly during the life-time of the device. Since the consumers as owners of these devices are locked-in, difficult questions will arise, whether the extent and the changes of these contracts are still fair and what will happen if consumers do not agree to these changes. These are typical problems of long-term contractual relationships, which require legal solutions that we cannot discuss here.

However, "consent or pay" solutions for IoT devices, as discussed in section IV.3.2, might help to some extent with problems related to termination of data use contracts and the reselling of devices. If a consumer as owner of an IoT device wants to terminate a data use contract or if a buyer of a used device does not want to accept an existing contract, there would always exist the option to switch to the version without non-necessary IoT data and additional payment. This solution would be an interesting compromise, as it would allow choice for the consumer who can opt-out from the data use contracts, and simultaneously protect the business model of the data holder who would get over the entire life-time of the device either the IoT data or some payment.[86]

IV.3.4. More far-reaching solutions for the control of consumers over their IoT devices and IoT data

So far, our discussion was based on the currently most used governance model for IoT devices in which the manufacturers have far-reaching tech-

86 However, if we do not want manufacturers to make de facto such long-term contractual arrangements, which are often also not understandable for consumers and in which the data holders could capture at least the value of all data through buy-out contracts for the entire life-time of the IoT device, then the combination of such effective termination rights with the possibility of "consent or pay" models should not be allowed. This raises again the general question about the extent of limitations for buy-out contracts with regard to such data use contracts, e.g. also through more consumer protection.

nical-factual control over these devices and their operation (as described above in section IV.3.1). However, if we take the objective of more consumer empowerment and consumer autonomy with regard to IoT devices seriously, then it might be necessary to think also about further policy options which would give the consumers directly also more factual control over the IoT devices and the IoT data. This implies that consumers cannot only claim rights to have control over the functionality of the devices based upon contracts with the data holders, but would also have more de facto control over the device and the generation, collection, and sharing of the IoT data through the technical design of the device.[87]

More de facto control over IoT devices and IoT data for users

For example, in the concepts for a right to data collection-free (or data collection-poor) IoT devices, it has been discussed that the two versions of products can also differ with regard to their technical design, i.e. one of these versions could give the consumers also more de facto control over the IoT device.[88] A particular interesting option is the proposal about a so-called "legacy switch", i.e. that the device has a mechanical switch, which allows the consumer to disable directly the connectivity of the device, its microphones, its sensors etc.[89] The decisive idea is that choice via a mechanical switch cannot be overridden by software.[90] Another option is giving the product a modular design, allowing the user the choice to use it either as an analogue product, with only basic functions (and a limited generation and collection of necessary data), or with additional functions (and more collection and processing of IoT data).[91]

The question who has the technical-factual control can also be discussed with respect to the generated IoT data. So far, IoT devices are often de-

87 It should be kept in mind that manufacturers of cars did never have any factual control over the operation of a traditional (unconnected) car, because it was entirely within the technical-factual sphere of its owner. This is different with connected cars, which can be technically remotely accessed and controlled by the manufacturers, e.g. also for "bricking" the car.

88 See Becker (fn.29), 178.

89 See for this proposal Ohm/Kim, Legacy switches: A proposal to protect privacy, security and the environment from the Internet of Things (2023), Ohio State Law Journal, 101, 120–131.

90 A small example is that some Lenovo Thinkpad notebooks have a mechanical switch for shutting the built-in camera.

91 See for a position emphasizing the importance of more such de facto control and discussing these options Specht-Riemenschneider et al. (fn.10), 88–91.

signed in such a technical way that all relevant generated IoT data are transmitted directly to proprietary servers of the manufacturers who then have exclusive de facto control over them (as it is also assumed in the DA). However, IoT devices might also be designed technically in a way that the generated data are stored and processed in the device itself, with no transmission of data to the manufacturers and direct control of the user over the data. Although the DA introduces the principle of "data accessibility by default" (Art. 3(1) DA) for the user, it is according to the DA not the user, but still the data holder who has the technical-factual control over the generated IoT data. Although the DA is attributing the generated IoT data to the users, we have seen in section IV.3.1 that the manufacturers have a large discretionary scope for deciding how they can make this data accessible to the users (and also to data recipients). If they rely only on in-situ access and require technical protection measures, then the accessed and shared IoT data will never leave the technical-factual sphere of the data holders. Therefore, an important policy option would be to clarify legally that users have a right to get a copy of the data in their own technical-factual sphere, which they can use and share with anybody.[92] This also would not only increase the choice options of the consumers, but could also have positive effects on data sharing, competition, and innovation on secondary markets and the development of thriving independent data markets, e.g. through data intermediaries (DGA).

Technical interoperability, competition, and consumer choice on secondary markets

The exclusive control by the manufacturers over the IoT devices is also important for the question whether consumers can choose independent service providers, e.g. for repair and maintenance services: These firms often need not only access to IoT data for their services, but also technical access to the IoT device for being able to provide such services (technical interoperability). Since many manufacturers pursue the strategy to design their IoT devices technically as closed systems, in which they have exclusive

92 See Specht-Riemenschneider (fn.10), 31; Drexl et al., Position Statement of Max Planck Institute (Data Act) (2023), para 66, available at: https://papers.ssrn.com/sol3/papers.cfm?abstract_id=4136484; Kerber (2023) (fn.8), 124; Eckardt/Kerber (fn.3), 132; Lienemann/Wienroeder, V. Data Licence Agreement and User's Right of Access (Art. 4) (2024), Hennemann et al. (fn.3), 71, 83–85; Sattler (fn.73), Rdnr. 35–38.

control over the technical access to the IoT device, other service providers cannot get access to the device without the manufacturer's permission. Important is that not even the consumers as owners of the devices can give such technical access to other firms.[93] This enables the manufacturers to foreclose such independent service providers from these secondary markets, which limits the choice of consumers.

It was one of the objectives of the DA to enable more competition on these markets and to give consumers more choice. In particular, it was the new user right for sharing IoT data with third parties (Art. 5 DA) that should break up the exclusive control of manufacturers over IoT data and enable independent service providers to enter secondary markets. If this data sharing mechanism would work well, manufacturers would lose their ability to foreclose service providers from these markets due to a lack of access to data.[94] However, no mechanism exists at all for solving the problem of the lack of technical access to the IoT device for providing these services.[95] Since the DA does not address this problem of technical interoperability, e.g. by giving consumers also the right to give technical access to other firms, it is still an unsolved problem that leads to less competition, innovation, and consumer choice. Such problems of lacking technical interoperability could, for example, be solved through additional sectoral regulations.[96]

Choice of consumers on the data holder position

In the last section, we already discussed the policy option that data holders should not be allowed to strictly bundle sales and data use contracts for the entire life-time of IoT devices. This would imply that consumers could also make data licensing contracts directly with other firms, which would allow competition between firms for making data use contracts about such IoT data. Nevertheless, we could even go one step further. First, it is important to note that the data holder concept in the DA is a rather unclear and

93 Manufacturers usually refer to safety and security concerns but these problems can also be solved differently.

94 However, in section I, it was already mentioned that the data sharing mechanism is often too ineffective for solving this problem (see the literature in fn.8).

95 For example, for providing remote repair and maintenance services, it might be necessary to get access to proprietary software of the manufacturer or to install own software on the IoT device for additional services.

96 See below our example of governance of connected cars.

elusive concept. The DA implicitly assumes that only the manufacturer can decide who the data holder is, without explicitly discussing this issue.[97]

The following questions can be asked: Why should it not be possible that a user as the owner of a device can decide who the data holder is? The data holder, who often operates the IoT device as a service, could also be interpreted as an agent for the user as principal.[98] And, furthermore, why does the DA not consider the possibility that users (here: the consumers) have a right to switch with their IoT data to another service provider as data holder? With regard to the data portability right of Art. 20 GDPR, there has been a long and extensive discussion that this right could facilitate the switching of consumers between digital platforms, which then might lead to more competition between platforms through reduction of switching costs. Strengthening Art. 20 GDPR was therefore seen as a possibility for enabling more competition between platforms.[99]

Thus, it would be an interesting policy option to clarify legally that the user should have the right to decide who the data holder is.[100] This might also imply that the user can switch to other service providers who can operate the IoT device. It is clear that there might be problems of technical feasibility, but these problems might differ subject to the type of the IoT device. In turn, such a policy could lead for certain products to a new market with competition between service providers for operating IoT

97 See e.g. Lienemann/Wienroeder, V. Data Licence Agreement and User's Right of Access (Art. 4) (2024), Hennemann et al. (fn.3), 71, 73; Schmidt-Kessel (fn.3), 77. With regard to additional related services it might be possible that the user can choose the service provider and then also the data holder. But the manufacturer can decide with its bundle of contracts whether the user can decide between different providers of related services or not.

98 See, in particular, Schmidt-Kessel (fn.3), 81, who characterizes the legal relationship between user and data holder as "Geschäftsbesorgung".

99 See Krämer/Senellart/de Streel, Making Data Portability more effective for the Digital Economy (2020), CERRE report (June 2020).

100 It seems so far to be legally very unclear how the data holder position can change. Can a current data holder "sell" its data holder position to another firm or does the user have to agree to such a change in the data holder position? See Kerber (fn.8), 130, where for the initial very data holder-friendly DA proposal of the Commission it was argued that the data holder position with its control over future IoT data streams might be tradable, with the danger of leading potentially to new forms of data concentration (now with regard to IoT data).

devices and for the position as "data holders", giving at the same time the consumers the power to decide who should provide this service.[101]

It would be a large step for more control of consumers over (the operation of) their IoT device and their data if they could decide who the "holder" of their IoT data is. It would also allow the consumers to get de facto control over their IoT data. In turn, this would also open the important option for consumers to give the data holder role to data trustees, either for monetizing the data in their interest or for making the IoT data available for different purposes of public interest, e.g. by donating it to recognised data altruism organisations (DGA). It is clear that introducing a right of the consumer to decide on the data holder position changes the architecture of IoT governance in a significant way, opening up in turn the perspective to very different alternative governance structures for IoT devices and IoT data.

Alternative IoT governance structures: The discussion on connected cars

For other architectures of governance of IoT devices, it is very interesting to look at the early policy discussion about "access to in-vehicle data" in connected cars in Europe.[102] The European car manufacturers have developed the "extended vehicle" concept, which implies that the manufacturers get exclusive control over all generated IoT data and over the technical access to the cars but leads to large problems for competition on secondary markets, innovation, and the choice of consumers. In early policy discussions in 2016 and 2017 about access to "in-vehicle" data, also two other alternative options were discussed: The first one is the so-called "On-Board Application Platform" (OBAP), which, due to a different technological approach, would give the consumers directly de facto control over the generated car data and the technical access to the cars. This would have required as a different technological solution some standardisation of telematic platforms, which

101 It is clear that this concept might not be compatible any more with the "data holder" role in the current DA.

102 See for the following discussion TRL, Access to In-Vehicle Data and Resources – Final Report, 2017; Kerber, Data Governance in Connected Cars: The Problem of Access to In-Vehicle Data (2018), JIPITEC, 310; Martens/Mueller-Langer, Access to digital car data and competition in aftersales services (2018), Digital Economy Working Paper 2018–06, JRC Technical Reports; Wiebe/Helmschrot/Kreutz, Studie zur Notwendigkeit und Ausrichtung von spezifischen Datenzugangsregelungen im Bereich des vernetzten Fahrzeugs in der Automobilwirtschaft. Study for Bundesnetzagentur (2023).

has been seen as feasible by experts. This would have enabled to design connected cars as much more open systems, allowing for more access to data and technical interoperability, which can lead to more competition, innovation, and consumer choice. The second option is the so-called "shared server", which means that the car IoT data would not be under the exclusive control of the car manufacturers, but under the governance of a data trustee which could give non-discriminatory access to other stakeholders and consumers in the broader ecosystem of connected driving. An independent study commissioned by the European Commission in 2017 came to the conclusion that both of these alternative governance systems would be superior to the "extended vehicle" concept of the car manufacturers.[103]

Although the Commission has acknowledged this problem for competition and consumer choice in the automobile sector since 2017, it has until today not solved the problem through an appropriate update of the already existing sectoral "type approval regulation for motor vehicles", despite several announcements of the Commission about such plans and the most recent policy initiative in March 2022 after the publication of its DA proposal (with a main focus on solving the above described lack of technical interoperability problem).[104]

This example shows that also other very different (and perhaps superior) IoT governance structures are possible than the approach of the DA, which, despite its new user rights and the new contract between consumers and data holders, is surprisingly close to the "extended vehicle" concept of the European car manufacturers. Especially the On-Board Application Platform as a different technological solution would allow much more far-reaching choice for consumers over the IoT device and the IoT data.[105]

---

103 See TRL (fn.102), 11–16. For a proposal of a specific data trustee solution for the governance of data in connected cars see Specht-Riemenschneider/Kerber, Designing Data Trustees – A Purpose-based Approach, Konrad-Adenauer-Stiftung (2022), 53–73.

104 See European Commission, Call for evidence for an impact assessment (Access to vehicle data, functions and resources), Ref. Ares(2022)2302201 – 28/03/2022 (2022); Kerber/Gill, Revision of the Vehicle Type-Approval Regulation: Analysis and recommendations (21 June 2022), available at: http://dx.doi.org/10.2139/ssrn.4174028.

105 See the policy recommendations in Wiebe/Helmschrot/Kreutz (fn.102), 93–99. From an economic perspective, it can be argued that the choice of a wrong technological design by the car manufacturers can itself be seen as a market failure, see Kerber (fn.102), 322, and Eckardt/Kerber (fn.3), 121 ("inefficient choice of technologies").

V. Conclusions

One of the big problems of the Data Act is that it wanted to establish the same mandatory rights and rules for the governance of IoT data in B2B and B2C situations, although the extent and type of market failures is very different. Whereas in B2B situations it is very unclear whether any general market failure exists, which could justify such a far-reaching regulation, the specific market failure problems of information and behavioral problems in B2C contexts have not been taken seriously although they are not surprising at all from a consumer protection perspective. Introducing the new data use contract between consumers and data holders (Art. 4(13) DA) based upon a pure freedom of contract model has ignored what we know for a long time in research about consumer behavior and consumer protection.

Therefore, this paper started with concerns that even after the implementation of the DA the governance of IoT data in B2C situations would lead due to such significant market failures to negative effects on consumers with respect to their control and choice over their IoT data as well as to unfair sharing of the value of their consumer data. In section II, we have seen that these concerns are justified. With respect to both data use contracts for personal and non-personal IoT data, consumers, due to information and behavioral problems, cannot understand the "data price" they are paying through agreeing to these contracts. This tends to lead to "race to the bottom" and "adverse selection" effects regarding the terms of the data use contracts, implying a too large collection and use of IoT data by the data holders and not enough choice for consumers for fulfilling their preferences and protecting their privacy. Especially also through the bundling of sale and data use contracts by the data holders, consumers very often cannot choose IoT devices without having to agree to a far-reaching collection and use of their personal and non-personal IoT data (buy-out contracts), because no firm on the market is offering other options (with less or no data collection).

From that perspective, it was very interesting to see in section III that we have currently an intense discussion in competition law and data protection law about granting consumers a minimum standard of choice with respect to the processing of their personal data. Particularly important, also from an economic perspective, are "consent or pay" models which give consumers the choice to get a service also without having to provide non-necessary data, albeit perhaps with an additional price. Although these "consent or pay" models are very controversially discussed from a data protection perspective, introducing a right for consumers to choose between IoT devices with and without collection and use of non-necessary data would be a very important step for granting consumers at least a minimum standard of choice with respect to their IoT data, which so far does not exist. Such solutions are close to already existing concepts in which consumers should have a right to choose a data collection-free IoT device (Becker, Specht-Riemenschneider). They deserve to be discussed much more in the context of IoT data governance.

This suggestion is one result of our broader exploratory discussion in section IV about future policy options for giving consumers more control and choice over their IoT data and IoT devices. We could analyze and discuss only some policy options from the wide range of possibilities of how such a minimum standard for consumer autonomy in IoT contexts could be designed and established. "Consent or pay" is only one step in such a direction. Developing solutions for ensuring that consumers have also more granular options for deciding on the generation, collection, use, and sharing of their IoT data might be another important step. Key issues are also whether consumers can terminate data use contracts (and still use their IoT devices), and whether they might even have some control about who the data holder is (including switching data holders, e.g. in favor of data trustees). All of these options would require that the possibility of manufacturers to bundle these contracts have to be limited through additional rules and (non-waivable) rights of consumers. However, it might also be necessary to increase the de facto control of consumers over their IoT devices and data, which can also require regulatory solutions at the technological level. Regulatory solutions for more technical interoperability and standardisation might also help to open IoT governance systems that have been technically designed by manufacturers as closed systems. This could give consumers more control over their IoT data and IoT devices, and could also have manifold positive effects on competition and innovation.

Overall, there is much scope for strengthening the control and choice of consumers over their IoT data and devices both de lege lata and de lege ferenda, e.g. also through additional sectoral or device-specific regulations (both on the EU and Member State level). However, what we have not discussed in this paper is the question, whether more control of consumers over the generation, collection, use, and sharing of IoT data can also lead to negative effects on other objectives, like, e.g., innovation, because less data might be collected, shared and used by firms or society.[106] Therefore, tradeoff problems can exist, which could not be analyzed in this paper and require a complex normative analysis.

106 See, for example, Eckardt/Kerber (fn.3), 130.

IV.
The Determination of the Value of Data

Data as an asset and data trade

Fernando Gómez Pomar and Mireia Artigot Golobardes**

I. Data as a cornerstone of markets and as an asset allowing its holder to take profit-maximizing actions

The development of big data along with increasingly sophisticated, mathematical techniques and computational capabilities has changed, and will continue to change business models, social interactions, urban landscapes, and perhaps political structures in societies.

The development of new industries and business opportunities and the disruption that digital innovations entail in many economic activities have been possible only because data was in abundance. Data is the raw material necessary for the ascent and growth of AI-based technologies and the tech industry in its current form. It has also become an almost inescapable tool for firms in the digital environment to understand and know who their clients and consumers are and how they are likely to behave. The joint use of data and AI is also increasingly common in the toolbox of public administrations to decide how public investments should be designed, to write and implement a range of policies (from epidemiology and health to criminal justice and prison population management), as well as for assessing how certain public policies perform.

Data, hence, is not only an essential component of technological development and innovation, but data processing has become a very valuable activity for companies and public administrations to "improve" their operations.

Agents – public or private – who generate data, are typically different from those who eventually process it and are often different from those who ultimately demand services based on that data.

The value flows from data generation, processing and use -together with other inputs and technologies- for increasing business profits or enhancing/evaluating the performance of public policies affect various agents and

* Universitat Pompeu Fabra, Barcelona, Spain.

in different ways. The actors generating data are generally not the ones that process it to offer services to third parties such as companies or public agencies operating on this data-supported services and solutions. As a result, new types of interactions and business models have emerged along the entire process: first, data obtained by one company might be sold to another party in exchange for a monetary payment – direct trade/sale of data; second, new industries and segments where services based on data are offered by companies who neither generated the data nor will directly use the data – indirect trade of data. The pervasiveness of data use in many successful business models in several areas (from retail to energy, from healthcare to travel and leisure) and the concerns for individual privacy have raised many important concerns about data markets and also data intermediaries.[1]

Some of these issues may be linked to very specific beliefs or preconceptions. One that appears to be widely shared by policymakers and scholars in the field of privacy protection points at the fact that firms maximize the value of the data they obtain through selling it to third parties. In other words, it is not uncommon to consider that direct data sales by firms or agents collecting data is the preferred channel to monetize the data that companies obtain in the course of their business activity. And this channel will be exploited in endless pursuit of profit maximization. However, when one looks at the figures, the economic return from data either through processing, economic use or sale of data, the concerns may seem, at least at this point in time and in the current level of maturity of data markets, somewhat overrated. Direct data sales do not clearly emerge today as the prevailing form of transforming data into firm revenue. As an illustration, in 2020, three of the major players in the digital economy and some of the big collectors of data from their users' online behavior such as Google, Meta and Amazon, obtained all or a large portion of their net profit from advertising.[2] In contrast to what is frequently assumed, these three very

---

1 See, for example, Regulation (EU) 2022/868 of 30 May 2022 on European data governance and amending Regulation (EU) 2018/1724 (Data Governance Act), OJ L 152, 3.6.2022, p. 1–44 on the regulation and supervision of data intermediation services and Regulation (EU) 2023/2854 of 13 December 2023 on harmonised rules on fair access to and use of data and amending Regulation (EU) 2017/2394 and Directive (EU) 2020/1828 (Data Act) OJ L, 2023/2854 regulating contracts on access to and sharing of data.

2 Roberto Corrao, Joel P. Flynn, and Karthik Sastry (2022), Nonlinear Pricing with Under-Utilization: A Theory of Multi-Part Tariffs. Available at SSRN: https://ssrn.com/

large players do not seem to widely engage in direct data sales – selling consumers data for payment- but they rely on indirect data exploitation through the sale of targeted advertisement to advertisers, like Google and Meta do, or through the sale of sponsored marketplace listings to retailers, like Amazon does.[3]

Google, Meta and Amazon – all three regarded both as gatekeepers under the DMA[4] and very large online platforms or search engines under the DSA[5] – are not the only three market players that maximize the revenues through indirect data trade. Other firms also favor indirect monetization of data, engaging in a range of selling activities concerning various products based on processing data such as, for example, data reports, analytics, and intelligence, analytics-based consulting services or through providing products (software) or services (IT solutions) complementary to data.[6]

These examples illustrate the interaction between online and offline markets whereby the major driver of these products originates in online markets, but the ultimate product is acquired and used in offline activities.

Data, hence, has an economic substance that goes well beyond its value as a contractual object per se but rather as the raw material for new goods and services – digital and non-digital – that enhance the activity of private – and eventually also public – agents in online or offline activities. The participation in data markets, nevertheless, requires companies to either possess data directly or to be indirectly able to use their customer´s data.

With respect to direct data exchanges, there is already some empirical evidence[7] – in the US – from which interesting observations and implications may be drawn. For example, with respect to subject matter of data exchanges, most data (80 %) is composed of customers' data, and a

---

abstract=3817175 or http://dx.doi.org/10.2139/ssrn.3817175, noting that the percentage of revenues from advertisement is 98 % for Google, 100 % for Facebook, and is 60 % for Amazon.

3 See Amazon, for example, regarding sponsored products https://advertising.amazon.com/solutions/products/sponsored-products?ref_=a20m_us_fnav_lngsw_en-us.

4 The European Commission, on September 6th 2023 designated 22 companies as gatekeepers under article 3 of the DMA (https://ec.europa.eu/commission/presscorner/detail/en/ip_23_4328).

5 Article 33 of Regulation (EU) 2022/2065 of 19 October 2022 on a Single Market for Digital Services (DSA), PE/30/2022/REV/1, OJ L 277, 27.10.2022, p. 1–102 (hereinafter DSA).

6 Barbara H. Wixom, Cynthia M. Beath, Leslie Owens, Data Is Everybody's Business: The Fundamentals of Data Monetization (Management on the Cutting Edge) (2023).

7 Morad Elsaify, Sharique Hasan (2021), Data exchanges among firms, *Digital Business*, Volume 1, Issue 2.

significant part of that fraction is personal data affecting consumer activity, financial status, and other features. At the same time, the larger portion of direct data trade focuses on bilateral data sharing between participating firms, and only smaller portions are one-way data sharing agreements and direct data purchases. This suggests that a pre-condition for companies to participate in direct data exchanges is to be already data rich. Further, most data exchanges take place between firms in the same industry and with data science capabilities, which suggests that participation in the data market requires a degree of technical ability and the capacity to integrate data into one or more business models.

Hence, it seems that most data exchanges take place between large firms, operating within the same industry, and already in possession of large data capabilities. These prerequisites seem to suggest that data markets exhibit noticeable barriers to entry that lead those firms who intend to be participants in those markets to have a non-trivial level of technical ability concerning data, the integration of data in a given business model, and sizable investments in AI capabilities.[8]

These requirements seem to hold regardless of whether the demand for data is driven mostly by the purpose of reducing the firm´s production or organizational costs[9] or increasing the firm's revenue from the sale of the firm's products and services to its customers.[10]

---

8 The requirements of size and technical capabilities of companies participating in the market for processing data seems to be confirmed by the major sources of personal data coming from the data subject´s online activity. The five most popular online activities of adult internet users in the United States as of November 2021 were text messaging or instant messaging (93 %), using email (91 %), social networks (74.6 %), online financial services (74 %) and consumption (74 %). Four out of these five activities take place within Meta – Whatsapp, Facebook – or Google – email – products, who not only have the technical abilities but also have enough users to generate vast amount of data from data subjects that enable them to sell advertisement and other products to third parties. See https://www.statista.com/statistics/183910/internet-activities-of-us-users/ (author Ani Petrosyan, Dec 12, 2023 (last visited October 25th 2024).

9 Kristina McElheran et al. (2024), AI adoption in America: Who, what and where, *Journal of Economics & Management Strategy* 33(2), show that investments in AI complement investments in robotics.

10 This would include B2C interactions, and both when the larger revenues may arise from better or more valuable products or services, from better selection of customer base, or from enhanced abilities to extract willingness to pay from clients.

II. Economic elements of data exchanges in data markets

Data as the object of a transaction (that is, in the context of direct data exchanges) is shaped by the special nature and characteristics discernible in data: first, data shares some of the characteristics of a public good; second, data is the lifeblood of AI;[11] third, the collection, processing and use of data show significant externalities; and fourth, the valuation of data assets is remarkably complex.

These special features are explained and developed in the following sub-sections.

1. Data as a public good

Economic theory posits a fundamental distinction between public and private goods. This classification is not due to the composition of the goods, the combination of factors of production that lead to their creation and distribution, the way they are used, or the public or private nature of the agent producing or consuming them. Rivalry and exclusion are the dimensions underlying the above dichotomy. Private and public goods are different in the capacity of owners to limit and exclude others from the enjoyment of the good.[12] From that perspective, public goods are those the consumption of which is non-rival, and where there are no feasible ways to exclude access of those agents who do not contribute to the production of the good or pay the price of access. Non-rival consumption means that the consumption of that good by one of the agents does not prevent and affect the consumption of the same good by others. That is, the consumption of the good by one agent does not diminish the use or enjoyment of the same asset by another agent.[13] On the other side, public goods are -to a large extent at least- non-excludable, which means that the producer of the good is typically in a bad position to prevent others -especially, unauthorized others- from using or consuming the good.[14] Lack of exclusion may result in the presence of free riders: agents who will be able in practice to use the good, in this case, data,

11 Daron Acemoglu (2021), Harms of AI, NBER Working Papers 29247, National Bureau of Economic Research, Inc.
12 Hal R. Varian (2010), Intermediate Microeconomics: a Modern Approach. Chapter 36, pp. 695–716, 8th edition, New York:W.W. Norton & Company.
13 *Id.*
14 *Id.*

without neither generating it nor paying the purchase price for it. Private goods, in contrast, are characterized by rival and exclusionary consumption (a meal in a restaurant, an apple in a supermarket, the surgical actions of a surgeon, or the legal services of a defense lawyer in a civil case).

Traditional examples of public goods fit into the picture of non-rivalry and no -or very imperfect- exclusion of those who do not pay or shoulder the costs of producing the good: an educated citizenship, military security, extensive and safe transport infrastructure, or well-preserved environment or scenery. All of these goods share in common that the consumption by one agent does not exhaust the amount of the good to be consumed by others -it is still available for others to consume- while at the same time, the enjoyment of any of these goods is hard to prevent even *vis-à-vis* those agents who have not contributed directly or indirectly to their production.

Data shares these two defining properties of public goods – it is non-rival and non-excludable. Data is non-rival because the consumption of data or the use of a data set by a given individual, firm, or entity does not decrease the use or enjoyment of that same data set by anybody else. Technology allows to use data an infinite number of times, by an unlimited number of users, and for an unlimited number of purposes. It shows no erosion nor congestion in its use. The number of firms or agents using data sets does not decrease or diminish the use by any of other subject seeking this use.

An interesting result draws from the non-rival nature of data and data sets: if the costs stemming from data production and usage are constant, the higher the use of data and data sets by multiple users and agents would maximize the return from the asset and would increase social welfare. Hence, given an existing dataset, adding up demand for data and datasets would increase the value of the asset for the entire user population. For example, a same data set of labeled images of human tissue may be used by multiple med-tech firms for improving a diagnostic algorithm[15]. Similarly, the same data set of 1,000,000 cars being driven 1,000 km each can be used by car manufacturers to train different algorithms to increase safety decisions in automated cars or in vehicles driving in autonomous mode. In both cases, any additional use of the data set by a new firm would be benefi-

15 For the importance of image recognition in the development of neural networks in AI, Arvind Narayanan and Sayash Kapoor, *AI Snake Oil. What Artificial Intelligence Can Do, What It Can't, and How to Tell the Difference*, Princeton University Press (2024), p. 109 and ff.

cial for society while not diminishing or decreasing the individual value of the use of the data set. Figure 1 shows this feature of the equilibrium.

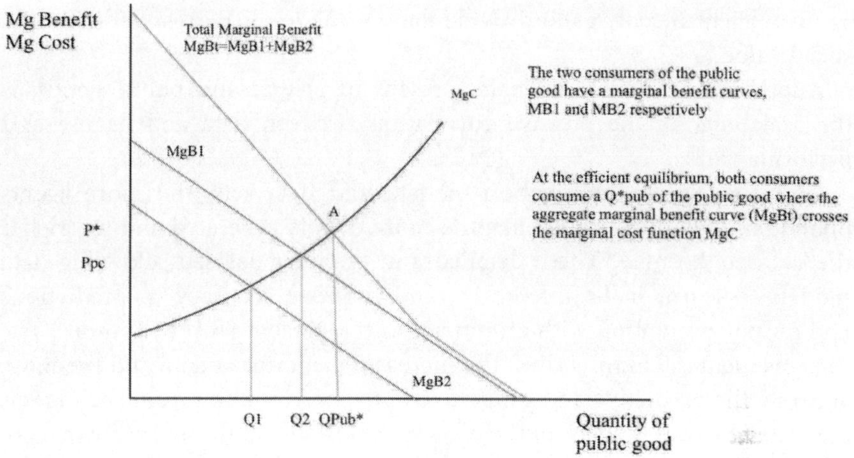

FIGURE 1 – Efficient provision of a public good

The use of data by individual firms and agents is also largely non-excludable. Excluding or limiting agents to use available data is as of today remarkably complex. This statement is not meant to imply that data may not be "private" and have an "owner" or "title-holder" who may want to limit the use of his or her data by others, nor that firms are unable to encrypt large packages of data – raw or processed –, thereby excluding others from the use of such data. However, the actual level of exclusion of unauthorized users, when feasible, depends on the technological capabilities of the agent aspiring to exclude others, as well as on the field of economic activity and type of use intended. Big firms or tech giants are perhaps, to a large extent, able to exclude others from the use of their data. However, individuals often have a hard time in protecting their personal data and excluding others from its use.[16] Small and medium-sized firms will probably display very heterogenous aptitudes to exclude unauthorized users from accessing and taking advantage of the data they generate.

16 Assuming they take steps to protect their data as much as they claim they value their privacy. See Patricia A. Norberg, Daniel R. Horne, and David A. Horne (2007). The privacy paradox: Personal information disclosure intentions versus behaviors. *Journal of Consumer Affairs,* 41(1), 100–126. https://doi.org/10.1111/j.1745-6606.2006.00070.x.

The limited capacity to exclude others from the use of data raises the familiar free- rider problem: agents use data they do not produce nor pay for.[17] All this results in large degrees of unauthorized uses of data as well as insufficient incentives to provide data at the levels corresponding to its social value

Another characteristic of data, present in private and public goods, is the scalability of the positive correlation between data and its use and performance.[18]

With respect to the creation of data and data sets, the more agents operate in digital environments, the more data is generated and the richer the datasets become. These detailed and granular datasets allow big data models to learn, make inferences, and improve accuracy in predictions and output generation with an impact in the present and the future.[19] The improvements stemming from the increasing amount of data and the more accurate the predictive and generative outcomes resulting from the models are, extend to every agent in the economy, not only to those directly part of the data set or directly using it.

There is a positive correlation between the amount of data and the richness of datasets and the accuracy of big data models to learn, infer, and produce predictions and generate content (text, images, code, etc). This positive correlation shows positive economies of scale between the production of data and data sets and the benefits from their use. The more data points are included in a dataset, in general one would expect higher quality in the output resulting from the data.

However, the contribution of each additional data point to the dataset increases the accuracy of big data models at a decreasing rate. While each new additional data point contributes positively to the accuracy of the big data or AI model, the additional, enhanced performance of the model decreases with each additional data added in the dataset. That is, there are decreasing economies of scale in accuracy on the amount of data.[20]

---

17 Hal R. Varian (2010), Intermediate Microeconomics: a Modern Approach. Chapter 36, pp. 699–701, 8th edition, New York:W.W. Norton & Company.

18 Charles I. Jones and Christopher Tonetti (2020). Nonrivalry and the Economics of Data, *American Economic Review*, 110 (9): 2819–58.

19 Daniel Alexandre Bloch (2018), Machine Learning: Models and Algorithms, Quantitative Analytics < https://ssrn.com/abstract=3307566>, Chapter 1.

20 Hal R. Varian H (2019), Artificial intelligence, economics, and industrial organization, in Ajay Agrawal, Joshua Gans, and Avi Goldfarb (eds.) The economics of artificial intelligence. An agenda. The University of Chicago Press, https ://

2. Data is the lifeblood of AI

There is no AI without data. AI cannot exist without data, and the more data there is, the better AI systems perform. From that perspective, we would say that there's a strong complementarity between data and AI. Most pieces or units of data, by themselves, without AI capabilities, have very limited value. Data and big data systems allow for processing large amounts of data that enable companies to deploy AI tools that reduce costs and/or increase revenues and hence increase firm's profits.

The main driver of value of large datasets (both with respect to personal and non-personal data), lies in the ability to feed them into AI and to improve the accuracy and quality of predictive, recommender and generative tasks to be performed through AI.[21]

Simply producing and accumulating data does not result in value for the agent engaged in such data activities. Firms or, more generally, private or public agents may profit from data through training and implementing AI models that will allow them to reduce their cost and eventually increase the revenues (or eventually the efficiency and/or quality in the provision of the public service). Frequently, however, the firms generating data do not have the technological capacity to develop the AI models that would allow them to maximize the economic return from the data. Perhaps for this reason, among other factors, firms tend to buy technical capabilities, AI software and AI based products – such as targeted advertisement – from external sources.[22]

Data is not only an essential ingredient for artificial intelligence to work, but also essential for any computer instructions requiring computing capacity to carry out a task. Algorithms in their most basic structure are just a set of mathematical instructions given to a computer so that it calculates

---

doi.org/10.3386/w2483 9 (National Bureau of Economic Research conference report); Yan Carriere-Swallow and Vikram Haksar (2019), The Economics and Implications of Data: An Integrated Perspective. Departmental Papers / Policy Papers. 18. 10.5089/9781513511436.087.

21 Jordan Barry and Daniel Sokol, Data Valuation and Law (2024). *Southern California Law Review*, 96: 1545–1570; Ajay Agrawal, Joshua Gans, and Avi Goldfarb, A (2022). Prediction Machines: The Simple Economics of Artificial Intelligence. Harvard Business Review Press.

22 Charles Hoffreumon, Chris Forman, and Nicolas van Zeebroeck (2024), Make or buy your artificial intelligence? Complementarities in technology sourcing, *Journal of Economics & Management Strategy*, vol. 33(2), pages 452–479, for evidence on the European data market.

a result, clusters data, organizes a data set, or performs a given task given specific criteria defined by the algorithm. In sum, in order to obtain algorithms, that is, a set of mathematical instructions to treat certain inputs in order to obtain certain output, one needs the input. Algorithms use input data to provide a certain result specified by the mathematical instructions conforming the algorithm.

AI systems, formed by a complex algorithmic system, add a new layer to these systems. AI systems are able to learn, not only from the data provided but also from the output generated by the system.[23] It should be noted, even though this is beyond the scope of this contribution, that AI might be remarkably heterogeneous from a technical perspective depending on whether AI uses machine learning or neural networks structures or whether their algorithms forming AI systems are supervised, unsupervised or reinforced learning systems.

However, regardless of the technical anatomy of these system, the tasks they perform – running regressions, classifying and clustering data, for example – and the sector in which these systems are deployed, data, in all cases, interacts with AI at two different logical levels[24]: Input data are necessary to train the algorithm in order to make predictions or generate an outcome in the face of new incoming data, while output or feedback data (arising from the functioning of the trained algorithm) allow AI to learn about the quality and accuracy of the initial prediction and eventually improve them or update the model to face a dynamic environment.

So data is not only valuable for the design and implementation of the AI model but also for its performance given that a continuous feed in the system of new data, together with the use of output data, will constantly improve the performance of the task the algorithm in question is meant to achieve.

From an economic perspective, it is possible to say that data and AI interact as complementary goods. Data by itself has limited use and limited value while AI without data cannot function and exist. As in perfectly complementary goods, the demand of data increases when the demand of

---

23 See Daniel Alexandre Bloch (2018), Machine Learning: Models and Algorithms, Quantitative Analytics < https://ssrn.com/abstract=3307566>, Chapter 1.

24 Ajay Agrawal, Joshua Gans, and Avi Goldfarb (2022). Prediction Machines: The Simple Economics of Artificial Intelligence. Harvard Business Review Press.

AI increases and, at the same time, when the demand for AI increases the demand for data increases as well.[25]

The double direction of the use of data – input and output – translates also into the positive correlation between the price of data and AI but also between the economic value of data and AI. The positive correlation between AI and data is shown by the relationship between their prices: when the price of data is low, the demand for data increases, but the demand for AI increases as well. Likewise, when the price of data increases the demand for data will go down, and the demand for AI will decrease as well. This positive correlation is also shown by the value to be obtained from AI.

When industries can translate AI systems into a business advantage and hence into increasing their profits – either through reducing their costs, increasing their revenues, or both – firms will demand AI systems which in turn will result in a higher demand for data. Moreover, according to recent empirical evidence, the conversion of improved and enhanced AI systems into business profits, and the pace of this conversion is not a random process. It seems to be taking place mostly in business to consumer industries, in very large firms operating in high-growth sectors, and in innovative firms (characterized by large VC funding, ownership of technological IP, and high startup capitalization).[26]

3. The collection, processing, use and sharing of data are ripe with significant externalities

Data, especially data collection, processing, use and sharing has a collective dimension.[27] In particular, personal data of a given individual is combined with the data of other individuals to provide new information and inferences about the data subjects -and, as we will soon observe, about other

25 It should be noted that the perfect complementary between data and AI has a positive direction: their cross-elasticity is infinitely positively correlated.

26 Timothy Bresnahan (2021), Artificial Intelligence Technologies and Aggregate Growth Prospects. 10.1017/9781108856089.008., Timothy Bresnahan (2024), What innovation paths for AI to become a GPT?, *Journal of Economics & Management Strategy*, vol. 33(2), pages 305–316; Kristina McElheran et al. (2024), AI adoption in America: Who, what and where, *Journal of Economics & Management Strategy* 33(2).

27 See Ignacio Cofone and Adriana Z. Robertson (2018), Consumer Privacy in a Behavioral World, 69 *Hastings Law Journal* 1471, 1475 and 1489–1490.

individuals as well. The value of data, hence, depends on the amount and quality of the data set as well as on the information obtained not merely by piling up the data points of each of the data subjects, but from their combined processing and use of inference through big data techniques and statistical methods.[28]

The collective dimension of data is shown through the externalities inherent to the nature of data. There are two major types of externalities in data that have been identified in the literature: first, network effects and second, negative externalities affecting privacy.

i) Network effects and data network effects

Basic microeconomics teaches that the market price of a product depends on the costs of production, market structure and consumer demand (i. e., the consumers' valuation or willingness to pay for the good or service).[29]

There are settings where the value of a good or service for any given consumer does not hinge solely on the isolated valuation by that consumer on the basis of her personal preferences, but depends also on the number of consumers who actually consume the good or service and/or the number of sellers offering the good or service or related ones.[30] When this is the case, the term network effects has been coined and used in economic theory.[31] Depending on whether the network effects operate inside a given group of market agents (consumers or firms) or travel across the borders of various groups of agents, it is now common, especially with respect to online platforms, to distinguish between within-group and cross-group network effects.[32]

28 Michèle Finck (2021)., «The Limits of the GDPR in the Personalisation Context», in Uta Kohl and Jacob Eisler (eds.), Data-driven Personalization in Markets, Politics and Law, Cambridge University Press.

29 Hal R. Varian (2010), Intermediate Microeconomics: a Modern Approach,. 8th edition, W.W. Norton & Company, pp. 251–269.

30 Robert W. Gregory et al. (2020). The Role of Artificial Intelligence and Data Network Effect for Creating User Value. *Academy of Management Review*. 46. 10.5465/amr.2019.0178.

31 See Oz Shy (2010, The Economics of Network Industries, Cambridge University Press, ch. 1. It should be noted that network effects are often referred to as network externalities.

32 Paul Belleflamme and Martin Peitz (2021), The Economics of Platforms, Cambridge University Press, ch. 1.

Data generates network effects in data-intensive industries. The most popular tech giants such as eBay, Amazon, Ticketmaster, Uber, Alibaba, Airbnb, Booking, Meta, regardless of whether their business model and underlying economic activity – whether they are e-commerce platforms or social networks – show network effects. The common element across all these companies is that the value they provide to their users increases with the network´s scale. The more users there are- on the supply or demand side –, the more valuable the product offered by the company is to its users. So, for example, a seller decides to sell on Amazon because there are many sellers offering all kinds of goods and services in that platform, and thus they anticipate (a key factor for any particular seller) that a lot of potential customers will be shopping on the platform for all kinds of products and services, and thus that the likelihood of entering into a transaction and the overall level of sales will be higher than in some alternative and smaller e-marketplace. Following an even more direct logic, an individual considering the use of a social network will likely choose the most popular one, especially among her family, friends, professional colleagues, and so on. In both of these examples, participation in an online market or in a social network is not only determined by the private preferences of the individual but by the choices of many consumers and sellers, or of a selected group of agents whose interactions are particularly relevant for the one making the decision. When the choice of an agent is correlated – positively or negatively[33] – with the choices made by others – in the same side of the market or in the other side – we are in the presence of network effects, with important consequences for market dynamics, equilibria and outcomes.[34]

Network effects may be classified as direct and indirect.[35] Direct network effects occur when the value of a product or service increases immediately with the sheer number of users. Social networks are clear example of direct network effects: the more users there are in the social network the more valuable it becomes for the users. Indirect network effects, on the other hand, occur when the value of a platform or a service depends on the

33 The examples provided in the text all refer to positive externalities, but the correlation between the number of other buyers and sellers on the individual's value from the product or service may be negative and not positive, as illustrated below in the text.

34 For a general description of network effects (network externalities) see Hal R. Varian (2010), Intermediate Microeconomics: a Modern Approach, 8th edition, W.W. Norton & Company, pp. 678–682.

35 It should be noted that indirect network effects are also referred to as crossed or cross-group network effects.

choices made by other relevant groups participating in the platform.[36] For example, buyers will be attracted to use Amazon to buy their products because they know that in this platform it is likely they will encounter many sellers of a whole range of products they may be interested in. So, the more sellers there are on Amazon, the better the service for the buyers.[37]

These direct and indirect network effects can be positive or negative: positive network effects stem from a positive relationship between the number of agents present and the value of the product or service for the users. The more users there are, the more valuable the good or service becomes, and thus more users want to participate. Negative network effects, in contrast, are present when the higher the number of users, the lower the value of the product or service for the users. Negative network effects arise when the correlation is of negative sign. They are commonly grouped into so-called pollution and congestion effects. The first refers to goods or services that consumers value for their exclusivity, and individual valuation goes down with the number of consumers accessing the products. The second refers to the effects of a limited capacity of the good or service to be used by multiple users without decreasing the actual enjoyment stemming from the use. When goods and services are meant to be exclusive, the more users there are, the lower the perception of exclusivity of the use and the lower the value of the good service for the users. A typical example of this would be luxury goods – e.g. limited edition or tailor-made goods. Negative network effects of congestion arise when the number of users gets close to the maximum capacity of the good or service to be enjoyed without interference from other users.

The role of data in network effects is crucial. More users represent more personal data, activity data, transaction data, that, through the use of AI, can be analyzed to learn, produce, and improve the service provided. In the end, this will probably lead to higher revenues for the businesses as well

36 Hal R. Varian (2019) Artificial intelligence, economics, and industrial organization. In: Ajay Agrawal, Joshua Gans, and Avi Goldfarb (eds.) The economics of artificial intelligence. An agenda. The University of Chicago Press. https ://doi.org/10.3386/w2483 9 (National Bureau of Economic Research conference report) objects to the network effect characterization and prefers to consider it a supply-side learning or experience effect.

37 Positive network effects are particularly present in the context of two-sided platforms, but they are not limited to this context. See Paul Belleflamme and Martin Peitz (2021), The Economics of Platforms, Cambridge University Press.

as -in theory at least- better service for consumers.[38] The network effect is the defining element of the business model of many online companies: the more data there is, the more learning there will be, the more value is generated, and the more users join the more data generated and the higher the value ensuing from the interaction consumer/firm.[39]

The presence of network effects is of consequence for the structure and dynamics of those markets. First, the speed and nature of network effects results in imperfectly competitive market structures – eventually resulting in monopolistic settings. Users, through their increasing demand following the rising demand of other users, can give the firm offering the service a preeminent role in the market and varying degrees of market power. This dynamic generates barriers to entry for competitors and allows the incumbent to obtain additional profits, not only from the increasing number of users and business in the platform but also from the dominant position in an imperfectly competitive market resulting from the dynamic advantages arising from network effects.[40]

Second, the dynamics of markets with network effects are also different from those markets in which network effects are absent. When network effects are present, market demand functions combine and reflect individual demands of different people for different network sizes. However, in contrast with market demand in a market without network effects, the market demand function when network effects are present is not the mere horizontal aggregation of the different individual demand functions but shows an elasticity different from that of the individual demand functions. When network effects are positive, the market demand function is more elastic than the individual ones. When network effects are negative, the market demand is more inelastic than the individual demand functions. The difference in elasticity between individual and market demands explains the market dynamics in the markets ripe with network effects. When

38 Ajay Agrawal, Joshua Gans, and Avi Goldfarb (2022). Prediction Machines: The Simple Economics of Artificial Intelligence. Harvard Business Review Press; Yan Carriere-Swallow and Vikram Haksar (2019), The Economics and Implications of Data: An Integrated Perspective. Departmental Papers / Policy Papers. 18. 10.5089/9781513511436.087.

39 See Darek M. Haftor, Ricardo Costa-Climent, Jenny Eriksson-Lundström (2021), How machine learning activates data network effects in business models: Theory advancement through an industrial case of promoting ecological sustainability, *Journal of Business Research*, vol. 131, 196–205 combining the theory of data network effects with business model theory.

40 This seems to have been addressed in articles 5 and 6 of the DMA.

network effects are positive, the higher elasticity of the market demand shows a higher volatility of the market to any change in the price of the good or service. This higher sensitivity to price changes is illustrated by the speed at which users join the market or quit the market depending on what other users do. The same thing happens with negative network effects. The market demand is more inelastic than the individual demand functions, showing that the market as a whole is less sensitive to changes in prices of the goods or services than the demand of each individual user.

As explained earlier, AI models need input data for training, designing, testing and eventually implementing systems based on AI and ADM. Data is not only the engine of network effects in the business models and data intensive industries, but networks effects are a defining characteristic of data itself.

ii) Negative externalities in data interactions

Data exchanges in many cases negatively affect parties who are not part of the interaction. The first and most obvious externality lays from the fact that when data subjects reveal information about themselves, they are also providing information about others (family members, coworkers, friends or, more generally, of agents with whom they interact). Data, thus, might not have positive or negative effects for the data subject depending on a number of circumstances, but it certainly may lead to negative effects on the privacy of the third parties who are not part of the interaction giving away the data.[41]

In a series of papers Acemoglu, Makhdoumi et al.,[42] and Acemoglu[43] show that the negative external effects of data collection and processing can be classified in three major types: first, the presence of direct negative privacy externalities; second, that the pricing of data at origin shows submodularity, and third, that data may be used as a tool for behavioral manip-

41 Shota Ichihashi (2021), The economics of data externalities, *Journal of Economic Theory*, vol. 196.

42 Aron Acemoglu, Daron, Ali Makhdoumi, Azarakhsh Malekian, and Asu Ozdaglar (2022), Too Much Data: Prices and Inefficiencies in Data Markets, *American Economic Journal: Microeconomics*, 14 (4): 218–56.

43 Daron Acemoglu, Daron, Ali Makhdoumi, Azarakhsh Malekian, and Asuman Ozdaglar (2023), A Model of
Behavioral Manipulation. Working Paper 31872. National Bureau of Economic Research.

ulation of firms' customers or, even when such distortions are absent, data can be an instrument to predict consumer behavior leading to a decrease in consumer welfare from the economic transactions with the firms who are in possession of the data.

With respect to direct negative privacy externalities,[44] when individuals share their data, the data shared often does not only cover the consenting individual, but also includes indirect information about others – family members residing in the same domicile, to start with – and inferences may be made as to data pertaining to other individuals, given the highly degree of correlation with the data voluntarily disclosed by a different individual. For example, if a firm is obtaining data through the data subject's consent, it will get information about her domicile or workplace that will unavoidably inform of the characteristics of the domicile of others residing in the same place, of coworkers regarding their workplace and of their potential income. While the direct information has been obtained through the consent of the data subject concerned, the indirect information about others has not been revealed with the latter's consent.

Data externalities clearly have become more serious with the introduction and refining of big data analytics which allow firms to draw more accurate inferences about consumers who do not share their data, based on the data gleaned from other consumers who opted for sharing data with the firms offering goods and services (including platforms). Even if each consumer knows the consequences for herself of disclosing her data, she does not consider in her decisions the negative spillover effects on the rest of consumers about which the firm may make inferences as a result of obtaining data from the first one. This is a clear illustration of the negative data externality.

Further, the willingness to release private information is not uniform across all subjects. Data subjects who value their privacy the least will be willing to share more private information than those subjects who value it more. Consequently, it will be an efficient strategy for firms or agents wanting to obtain data to target individuals who value their data the least, and in this way, they would also be able to infer information about subjects who value their privacy the most.

44 See also Jay Pil Choi, Doh-Shin Jeon and Byung-Cheol Kim (2019), "Privacy and personal data collection with information externalities", 173 *Journal of Public Economics*, p. 113.

As explained earlier, the value of data is not limited to the value of the data points available but is also grounded on its collective dimension. This element enables firms, through big data analytics, to obtain inferences that provide valuable information regarding people's characteristics and preferences, learn types, discover patterns and find correlations. Inferences, pattern discovery and data-informed assumptions about individuals do not seem, however, to fall within the scope of data protection regulation.[45]

The legal status of inferences, as example of negative privacy externalities from data, has been widely discussed in the literature.[46] However, regardless of whether inferences are considered to be within the scope of the right to privacy or not, it is clearly an externality with negative effects for agents who have not given consent to use their data.[47] Data subjects whose information has been obtained through inferences from a dataset have but a questionable right to know,[48] rectify,[49] delete,[50] object,[51] port[52] their personal data or seek legal remedies against for the negative impact that those inferences might have had on decisions adopted by third parties influenced by such inferences.[53]

The second externality arising in data exchanges is sub-modularity in data pricing. The inferences obtained as a result of the collective dimension of data depress the prices that have to be paid to obtain data from the data subjects or whoever produced the data. Let's imagine there are two

---

45 Michèle Finck (2021), The Limits of the GDPR in the Personalisation Context, in Uta Kohl and Jacob Eisler (eds.), Data-driven Personalization in Markets, Politics and Law, Cambridge University Press.

46 See Sandra Wachter and Brent Mittelstadt (2019), A Right to Reasonable Inferences: Re-Thinking Data Protection Law in the Age of Big Data and AI, *Columbia Business Law Review*; Sandra Wachter et al. (2018), 'Counterfactual explanations without opening the blackbox: Automated decisions and the GDPR' 31(2) *Harvard Journal of Law & Technology*, https://ssrn.com/abstract=3063289.

47 Sandra Wachter and Brent Mittelstadt (2019), A Right to Reasonable Inferences: Re-Thinking Data Protection Law in the Age of Big Data and AI, *Columbia Business Law Review*.

48 Articles 13–15 of the GDPR.

49 Article 16 of the GDPR.

50 Article 17 of the GDPR.

51 Article 21 of the GDPR.

52 Article 20 of the GDPR.

53 Article 22.3 of the GDPR. See also See Sandra Wachter (2018), 'Normative Challenges of Identification in the Internet of Things: Privacy, Profiling, Discrimination, and the GDPR' 34 *Computer Law & Security Review* 436 and Sandra Wachter (2018), 'GDPR and the Internet of Things: Guidelines to Protect Users' Identity and Privacy' (https://papers.ssrn.com/abstract=3130392).

individuals: A and B. As explained earlier, when one agent, A, shares data about herself indirectly reveals information concerning other individuals like B. Because of the availability of information about B for firms without having acquired the relevant data from B, the expected price for B's data decreases and the incentives to protect B's personal data diminish. As a result, B ends up sharing more information than it would have otherwise, there will be excessive data sharing by both A and B, and the price to pay to obtain their data is significantly reduced, and in the limit, falls all the way down to 0.[54] This phenomenon becomes more acute the more correlated the data from different individuals are. That is, when the data from one individual allows to make good inferences about others – correlation is high – the price of this data is reduced and in equilibrium it may even get close to zero.

If the price of data is zero other problems with excludability or contractibility may arise: certain purposes or uses will be hard to anticipate, ownership will be difficult to attribute in legal terms, and firms will have difficulties in monetizing consumers time and attention. This may explain the prevalence in reality of zero price for data combined with zero marginal price for the use of the underlying service through which data are obtained.

Finally, the availability of data by firms may enable them to take advantage of consumers' biases and cognitive limitations, manipulate consumers´ beliefs and behavior, and even without all this, simply to reduce consumer´s welfare in economic transactions. The availability of data allows firms to eventually exacerbate, take advantage of and benefit from consumers' behavioral biases and heuristics.[55] The contractual asymmetry in consumer transactions is a well-documented reality.[56] Data collection and analysis by

54 Daron Acemoglu, Ali Makhdoumi, Azarakhsh Malekian, and Asu Ozdaglar (2022), "Too Much Data: Prices and Inefficiencies in Data Markets." *American Economic Journal: Microeconomics*, 14 (4): 218–56.

55 Gerhard Wagner and Horst Eidenmueller, «Down by Algorithms? Siphoning Rents, Exploiting Biases and Shaping Preferences -Regulating the Dark Side of Personalized Transactions», (2018), 86 *University of Chicago Law Review* 581.

56 Oren Bar-Gill (2014), *Consumer Transactions, in* Eyal Zamir and Doron Teichman (eds.), The Oxford Handbook of Behavioral Economics and the Law 465–490., Oxford Univ. Press;, Shmuel I. Becher and Oren Bar-Gill (2012), Consumer Protection, *Harvard Public Law Working Paper No. 18–42*; Oren Bar-Gill and Kevin E. Davis (2017), (Mis)perceptions of Law in Consumer Markets, *American Law and Economics Review*, vol. 19(2), pages 245–286; Omri Ben-Shahar and Oren Bar/Gill (2016), Optimal Defaults in Consumer Markets, 45 *Journal of Legal Studies*, 137.

firms adds a new layer of asymmetry to the interaction between firms and consumers in online markets.

The more and the more accurate data in possession of firms in the interactions with consumers, the more the firms will be able to influence and limit consumers' choices and actions in ways that are detrimental to consumer welfare. They may even strip consumers of any contract surplus in economic exchanges of goods and services.[57] If consumers' beliefs and actions are manipulated in certain ways, this may lead even to negative surplus for consumers interacting with the firms engaging in such practices. The use of data by firms could allow them to discriminate against consumers based on gender or race, for example, violating their fundamental economic rights of access and participation in online markets, and fostering their expectations from market transactions.[58]

One – albeit not the only – context in which this is extremely relevant is that of price personalization in business to consumer contracts.[59] Given the advantageous position that data gives to firms and the potential benefits obtained from it eventually at the expense of the consumer surplus, one would expect firms to collect and use more data than the optimal amount necessary to enhance and maximize the joint surplus from the transaction.

The next figure (Figure 2) shows the standard microeconomic depiction of how the existence of negative externalities drives a wedge between the socially optimal amounts (of data, in our case) that the market interaction should produce and the privately optimal levels that will be actually induced, generating a social loss.

57 See Michael D. Grubb (2015), Overconfident Consumers in the Marketplace, 29 *Journal of Economic Perspectives*, 12–13; Xavier Gabaix and David Laibson (2006), Shrouded Attributes, Consumer Myopia, and Information Suppression in Competitive Markets, 121 *Quarterly Journal of Economics*, 505, 507–11; Stefano DellaVigna and Ulrike Malmendier (2004), Contract Design and Self-Control: Theory and Evidence, 119 *Quarterly Journal of Economics*, 353, 389.

58 Jon Kleinberg, Jens Ludwig, Sendhil Mullainathan, and Cass R. Sunstein, «Discrimination in the Age of Algorithms», (2018), *Journal of Legal Analysis*, 10, pp.113 – 174.

59 For the "procedural" and "substantive" unconscionability dimensions, see Mireia Artigot and Gómez Pomar (2024), Personalized prices and contractual controls in EU consumer law, in Fabrizio Esposito and Mateusz Grochowski (eds.) The Cambridge Handbook of Algorithmic Price Personalization and the Law, Cambridge University Press, pp. 165–191.

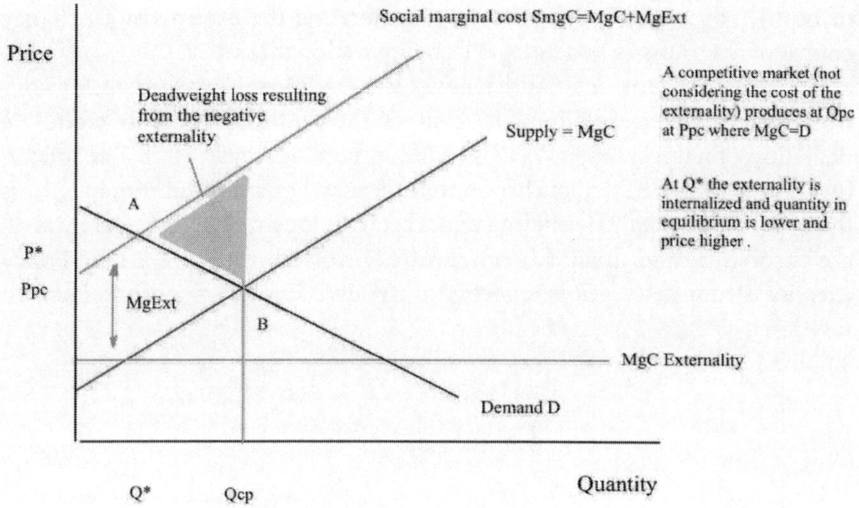

Figure 2 – Market equilibrium with a negative externality

iii) Policy measures available for correcting data negative externalities

To be sure, negative externalities are not unfamiliar phenomena to economic and legal thinkers and policymakers. Since the early stages of welfare economics, certain public policy levers and measures have become part and parcel of the toolkit to handle the problem of network externalities.[60] The ultimate goal of any of the instruments is to make the agents generating the externality internalize it so that the private optimal outcome comes closer, if not identical, to the social optimal outcome.

Inside the standard equipment to address externalities in public and legal policy, we repeatedly find a number of different tools: taxing the externality in the necessary amount (Pigouvian tax); fixing quotas of the good or service generating the externality to approximate the desirable amounts to be traded; defining and enforcing property rights so that the "unowned" element giving rise to the externality will become part of what is explicitly traded in the market; imposing legal liability (in the form of damages to be paid to the affected parties or fines to be cashed by the Government,

60 Ronald H. Coase (1960), The problem of social cost, *The Journal of Law & Economics*, vol. 3, pp. 1–44.

or both) that would induce the party generating the externality to change course of action so as to get the externality under check.

The use of quotas or quantity limits is a traditional instrument for controlling negative externalities, especially in the context of those linked to the depletion of natural resources (fisheries, mineral reserves, etc.). The following figure (Figure 3) depicts how a well-designed quantity limit may redress the negative externality afflicting a market. Obviously, this abstracts from all the theoretical and practical complexities involved in such a public policy exercise (from calculation, effective normative design, to enforcement to revision).

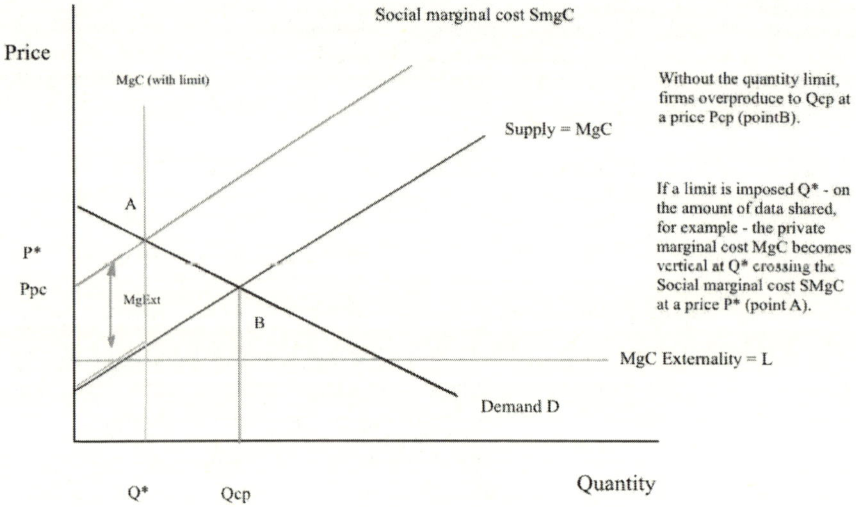

Figure 3 – Internalization of externalities with quotas

In the case of data externalities, quotas or quantity limits would imply setting an upper bound to the amount of data shared and used. Even if this is thought to be feasible and implementable at the theoretical level -a big if to be sure- imposing quantity limits on data sharing and use at the EU level seems difficult to reconcile with the grounds of lawful data processing provided in article 6(1) of the GDPR, given that one of them -a prominent one, in fact- is consent. However, even if limits are hard to impose at the collection and processing stage, perhaps they could be explored for uncontemplated purposes of uses of the data collected or uses beyond the scope of the initial consent of the data subject.[61]

Taxes are also a common mechanism to internalize negative externalities, and the one singularly preferred by the economics profession since Pigou.[62] The challenge traditionally faced by relying on the use of taxes to internalize externalities lies in the amount of information required for such tax scheme to effectively achieve its goal and its high cost of implementation and enforcement.

The Pigouvian tax is very ambitious in terms of the information required for designing and implementing the scheme. The informational requirements comprise the knowledge of the negative external cost, the identity of the externality generator, and all elements necessary to ensure that the agent generating the externality is the one who effectively will shoulder the burden of the Pigouvian. Particularly the last element – linked to the issues raised by tax incidence analysis as well as monitoring and enforcement – is remarkably hard and costly to address, which reduces the effectiveness of the instrument. Non-linearities in the externality per unit of the good or service taxed to avoid the externality also complicates the display of a uniform Pigouvian tax scheme.

Because of the special nature of data, some have noted the difficulty of using traditional tax structures to internalize the negative externalities generated by data use or processing. There have been some proposals arguing in favor of adjusting the traditional structures to the nature of data. In this line, Ben-Shahar[63] has argued in favor of adjusting the traditional mechanisms such as quotas, taxes and liability rules to adapt them to govern the negative externalities and harm generated by data.

At least *de lege data* in EU Law, tools based on liability rules seem to be the approach adopted to internalize the negative externalities resulting from data harms,[64] both in the form of damages to be paid to the persons

61 See the CJEU C252/21 of July 4th, 2023 *Meta Platforms Inc., formerly Facebook Inc., Meta Platforms Ireland Ltd, formerly Facebook Ireland Ltd, Facebook Deutschland GmbH v Bundeskartellamt.*

62 Arthur C. Pigou (1932), The economics of welfare, 4th ed., Macmillan.

63 Omri Ben-Shahar (2019), Data Pollution, *Journal of Legal Analysis*, Volume 11, 104–159,

64 Article 82(1) of the GDPR provides that
'any person who has suffered material or non-material damage as a result of an infringement of this Regulation shall have the right to receive compensation from the controller or processor for the damage suffered'

who have suffered harm as a consequence of the defendant's infringement of the GDPR, and of fines to be paid to the data protection authorities in each member state. Concerning the former, several features discernible in the case law of the Court of Justice of the European Union do not seem to contribute to reinforcing the ability of damages liability in the GDPR to act as a powerful mechanism to internalize data externalities: (i) reluctance to impose *ex lege* liability;[65] (ii) emphasis on the exclusively compensatory function of the right to compensation laid down in Article 82 of the GDPR[66]; (ii) the adequacy of an apology as a compensatory mechanism for non-material harm under the GDPR.[67]

Again, the next figure (Figure 4) graphically represents how a well-designed and implemented liability scheme is, in theory, capable of redressing negative externalities in market exchanges (abstracting, obviously, from very serious problems linked to damages assessment, establishing causal links, barriers to litigate, and litigation costs, just to name a few).

Article 83(1) of the GDPR also provides for fines:
'Each supervisory authority shall ensure that the imposition of administrative fines pursuant to this Article in respect of infringements of this Regulation referred to in paragraphs 4, 5 and 6 shall in each individual case be effective, proportionate and dissuasive'

65 See, the CJEU judgements of 4 May 2023, *Österreichische Post AG*, C-300/21, 25 January 2024, *MediaMarktSaturn*, C-687/21, and 11 April 2024, *GP juris GmbH*, C-741/21 *" the mere infringement of that regulation is not sufficient to confer a right to compensation, since the existence of 'damage', material or non-material, or of 'damage' which has been 'suffered' constitutes one of the conditions for the right to compensation laid down in Article 82(1), as does the existence of an infringement of that regulation and of a causal link between that damage and that infringement, those three conditions being cumulative."*

66 See the CJEU judgements of 4 May 2023, *Österreichische Post AG*, C-300/21, 20 June 2024, *Scalable Capital*, C-182/22 and C-189/22, and 20 June 2024, *PS (Incorrect address)*, C-590/22.

67 See the CJEU judgement of 4 October 2024, *Patērētāju tiesību aizsardzības centrs*, C-507/23.

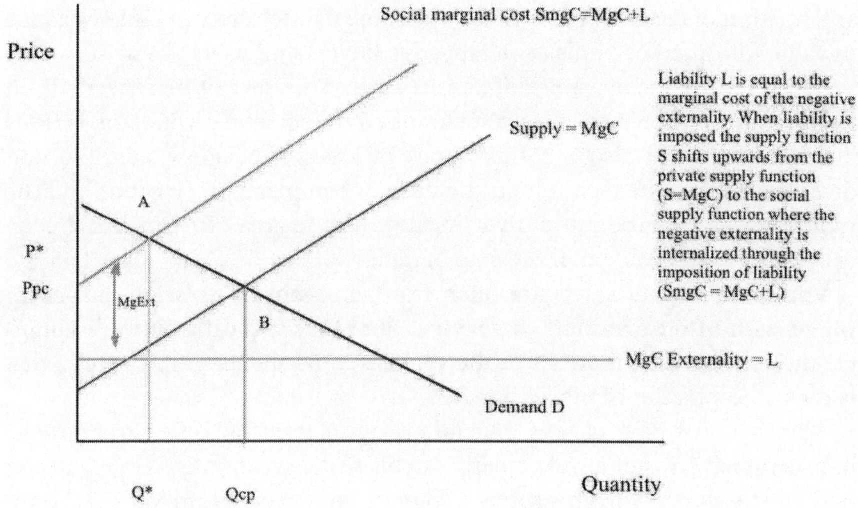

Figure 4 – Internalization of the cost of a negative eternality through liability rules

IV. Data assets are remarkably complex to value

One of the major sources of transactions costs in data markets (in their various presentations: two-way sharing, one-way sharing, direct sales, third party sales through aggregators and brokers) derives from the uncertainties and complexity of valuing data for the purposes of contracting over data.[68]

An important driver of the complexity of valuing data lies in the heterogeneity of data. Data assets differ widely across several dimensions, the so-called 4V´s: velocity, veracity, volume and variety. How data sets fare over each of these features have important effects on the type of use of the data, intensity of use and the resulting economic consequences for cost reduction, for revenue increase, or both.

We have also mentioned above how **the value of data essentially stems from its complementarity with AI**. This constitutes an additional important source of heterogeneity in data for the purposes of its valuation in

68 Jordan Barry and Daniel D. Sokol (2024), Data Valuation and Law, *Southern California Law Review*, Vol. 96, pp. 1545–1570; Ajay Agrawal, Joshua Gans, and Avi Goldfarb (2022). Prediction Machines: The Simple Economics of Artificial Intelligence, Harvard Business Review Press.

anticipation of contracting or trade: the same dataset shows a large variance in value for different kinds of prospective buyers and users. To be sure, this is by no means exclusive of data as an asset. This sort of heterogeneity in valuation depending on the presence of complementary goods of various kinds is pervasive also in other types of assets that allow multiple and diverse uses. But the technological nature of complementary goods and the rapid pace of evolution and diversification in the area of AI makes this an extremely acute problem in the case of data.

Additionally, data assets are often transacted not in isolation, but **combined with other products or services**, and thus it is difficult to disentangle the relative contributions of the various components in the bundle that is the subject matter of the exchange.[69]

The value of data is also dependent upon legal factors. For example, data ownership is not always clearly established, especially for large datasets packaged with data from different sources and obtained in various countries and data markets. At the same time, the exercise of privacy rights by data subjects may affect the value of data. If, for example, data subjects were withdrawing consent from processing their data under the GDPR[70] the composition of the data set would change and eventually, if its quality and use for profit enhancement decreased, its value would also vary in ways that are hard to anticipate when the parties enter into the initial contract over the data.

At the same time, the varying composition of the data resulting from the exercise of privacy rights would also condition the precision of the inferences. The higher the mandated levels of privacy protection that data sets are legally forced to comply with, the lower the inference or predictive power of the dataset, given the increase in "noise" in its composition. The notion of "differential privacy" tries to measure this tradeoff between privacy protection and predictive power (often the main source of value for the prospective user) in a dataset.[71] Taking two datasets, 1 and 2, where the

69 See Guy Aridor, Yeon-Koo Che, William Nelson, and Tobias Salz (2020), The Economic Consequences of Data Privacy Regulation: Empirical Evidence from GDPR. SSRN Electronic Journal. 10.2139/ssrn.3522845.

70 See article 7 of the GDPR.

71 See John M. Abowd and Ian M. Schmutte (2019),"An Economic Analysis of Privacy Protection and Statistical Accuracy as Social Choices." *American Economic Review*, 109 (1): 171–202; Yosuke Uno, Akira Sonoda, and Masaki Bessho (2021), "The Economics of Privacy: A Primer Especially for Policymakers," Bank of Japan Working Paper Series 21-E-11, Bank of Japan.

only difference is the exclusion (in 1) and inclusion (in 2) of the personal data of a given individual, a large differential privacy means that dataset 2 allows for better prediction but involves higher likelihood of allowing inferences about the particular individual. When the differential privacy is low or even zero, the second dataset does not allow better prediction, but no inferences can be made about the personal data of the relevant individual. Thus, the tradeoff emerges between a lower level of noise imposed by legal rules (privacy protection), which enhances the predictive power, and thus the economic value of data, and a larger level of noise in the data in order to protect privacy, at the cost of lower predictive value from the data. Naturally, different relative weights for privacy protection and predictive value may be placed, leading to various outcomes in terms of the economic value of data. What is important to bear in mind is that legal choices as to privacy do affect the economic value of data that can be collected, used, and exchanged.

Additionally, the level and manner of processing data is also a source of complexity. As explained earlier, most of the value of data lies in how its processing allows for cost saving and revenue enhancing in the user's business.[72] The differences between AI systems and business models in which data is used results in a large variance in the value of data for prospective buyers and users depending on the sector and purpose for which it is ultimate put to use. These are also deeply affected by how the law regulates the various uses and business models and thus would be consequential for the valuation of data by those who demand it.

V. Conclusions

Data is an asset whose various dimensions are hard to grasp in its entirety, both from an economic and a legal perspective. This gravely complicates public and legal policy concerning the settings and markets -and these are truly many nowadays- where data is a crucial asset. The importance of data in present-day social and economic interactions is almost a *cliché* -as is the platitude about the challenges, opportunities and threats of AI. "*Data is the*

72 Ron Berman and Ayelet Israeli (2020). The Value of Descriptive Analytics: Evidence from Online Retailers. SSRN Electronic Journal. 10.2139/ssrn.3745748; Ajay Agrawal, Joshua Gans, and Avi Goldfarb (2022). Prediction Machines: The Simple Economics of Artificial Intelligence, Harvard Business Review Press.

new oil" or "*Data is the foodstuff on which the new digital economy runs*" are apt metaphors that capture the pervasiveness and relevance of data use in the digital economy. Also, individuals and societies have grown increasingly concerned with the side-effects (intended and unintended) that data-intensive industries and business models raise for individual privacy. Lawmakers in many places, but perhaps more intensely in Europe, have reacted with a range of legislative and regulatory measures, from the *General Data Protection Regulation*[73], to the *Digital Services Act*[74], the *Data Governance Act*[75] and the *Data Act*[76]. All these instruments are not minor interferences with the functioning of digital markets for the sake of protecting privacy and ensuring consumer protection. They have large influence on how societies and economies subject to their rules will be organized and perform.

The Draghi Report on European competitiveness emphasizes that "[..] *the EU's regulatory stance towards tech companies hampers innovation: the EU now has around 100 tech-focused laws and over 270 regulators active in digital networks across all Member States. Many EU laws take a precautionary approach, dictating specific business practices* ex ante *to avert potential risks* ex post." The report gloomily observes as well that "[..] *limitations on data storing and processing create high compliance costs and hinder the creation of large, integrated data sets for training AI models. This fragmentation puts EU companies at a disadvantage relative to the US, which relies on the private sector to build vast data sets, and China, which can leverage its central institutions for data aggregation.*"[77]

We believe one should take these warnings and claims seriously as calls for improving our understanding of the data society and economy. It is no easy task, but we think it pays to try to build from the basics. This is why we have attempted to provide an overview of the basic properties of data as

73 Regulation (EU) 2016/679 of 27 April 2016 on the protection of natural persons with regard to the processing of personal data and on the free movement of such data, and repealing Directive 95/46/EC (General Data Protection Regulation) OJ L 119, 4.5.2016, p. 1–88.

74 Regulation (EU) 2022/2065 of 19 October 2022 on a Single Market For Digital Services (DSA), PE/30/2022/REV/1, OJ L 277, 27.10.2022, p. 1–102.

75 Regulation (EU) 2022/868 of 30 May 2022 on European data governance and amending Regulation (EU) 2018/1724 (Data Governance Act), OJ L 152, 3.6.2022, p. 1–44.

76 Regulation (EU) 2023/2854 of 13 December 2023 on harmonised rules on fair access to and use of data and amending Regulation (EU) 2017/2394 and Directive (EU) 2020/1828 (Data Act) OJ L, 2023/2854.

77 The future of European competitiveness. Part A| A competitiveness strategy for Europe, September 2024, p. 26.

an asset. They depart in important ways from other assets in the economy, and such features influence how economic agents in different positions in the digital markets will behave and interact. Outcomes in these markets cannot be understood without a holistic approach to data as an asset. Given the many dimensions of data as an asset, we believe the focus should be placed on what data does (a consequence-oriented, and not a right-oriented approach).[78]

Even with that intellectual attitude, legal thinking about data and data-rich markets will not be straightforward. A number of the levers used by firms to profit from data are still poorly understood. This is no surprise, since they are recent and evolve almost continuously. For instance, very large tech players rely heavily on the sale of the advertising slots and listing positions, and these sales are mostly implemented through real-time bidding. Although there is literature pointing at the fact that such online strategies by these big players in indirect data trade affect both online and offline prices and welfare[79], this research is still in early stages. Without much improved understanding, legal strategies in this field will not necessarily achieve their intended goals.

---

78 Daniel J. Solove (2024), "Data Is What Data Does: Regulating Based on Harm and Risk Instead of Sensitive Data", 118 *Northwestern University Law Review*, 1081, https://scholarlycommons.law.northwestern.edu/nulr/vol118/iss4/4.

79 Juan-José Ganuza and Gerard Llobet (2018), "Personalized Prices in the Digital Economy", in Juan José Ganuza and Gerard Llobet (eds.), Economic analysis of the digital revolution, Funcas Social and Economic studies, 117–141; Dirk Bergemann, Alessandro Bonatti (2022), Data, Competition, and Digital Platforms, MIT Sloan Research Paper No. 6588–21, Available at SSRN: https://ssrn.com/abstract=4236337 or http://dx.doi.org/10.2139/ssrn.4236337; Dirk Bergemann, Alessandro Bonatti, and Nicholas Wu (2024), How Do Digital Advertising Auctions Impact Product Prices?, *The Review of Economic Studies*, rdae087, https://doi.org/10.1093/restud/rdae087; Andrei Hagiu, Tat-How, and Julian Wright (2020), Should Platforms Be Allowed to Sell on Their Own Marketplaces?, *RAND Journal of Economics*, Forthcoming, Available at SSRN: https://ssrn.com/abstract=3606055 or http://dx.doi.org/10.2139/ssrn.3606055; Tat How Teh and Julian Wright (2024), Competitive bottlenecks and platform spillovers, Available at SSRN: https://ssrn.com/abstract=4741349 or http://dx.doi.org/10.2139/ssrn.4741349

Are databases a tradeable asset?

*Vincenzo Zeno-Zencovich**

In our data societies, data have an enormous value for business. The most obvious value comes from the use that they make of the data in production, in distribution, in sales, in their relationship with providers (up-stream) and clients (down-stream), in advertising and in other forms of commercial communication.

There is also the value, *per se*, of the data held: well before the digital era such data was an essential asset of the firm: one can simply refer to the notion of goodwill which is significantly made up of information (*i.e.* data) on all the business relations of the firm.

But in a context where personal data protection is qualified as a fundamental right (article 8 of the ECFR) and regulation is pervasive and not particularly benevolent, the question arises if a database is a tradeable asset, in the sense that it can be sold – or its use can be licenced – to third parties.

Before engaging in an attempt to provide an answer it is necessary to dispose of a pointless distinction, that between personal and non-personal data. As I will try to point out further on data, practically all data are personal – in the sense given by article 4 of the GDPR[1] – and only very few (*e.g.* meteorological data; historical data; aggregated statistics) can be surely considered outside of the all-encompassing reach of the GDPR. And, at any rate, trying to separate, in a business database, non-personal data (*e.g.* the total amount of the sales of one day) from personal data (*e.g.* the salesperson or the client) is financially not viable and deprives the database of any significant value.

---

* Prof. Vincenzo Zeno-Zencovich, University of Roma Tre, email: vincenzo.zenozencovich@uniroma3.it.

1 " 'personal data' means any information relating to an identified or identifiable natural person ('data subject'); an identifiable natural person is one who can be identified, directly or indirectly, in particular by reference to an identifier such as a name, an identification number, location data, an online identifier or to one or more factors specific to the physical, physiological, genetic, mental, economic, cultural or social identity of that natural person".

I will therefore assume that, generally, business databases contain – in a significant amount, if not entirely – personal data and therefore fall under the prescriptions of the GDPR.

1. The case

Rather than engage in hypothetical issues, it is preferable to start analysing a practical – and not uncommon – case brought in front of the CJEU by a Polish court[2].

A, an individual has an outstanding credit towards company B, which manages an online sales platform. Company B goes insolvent.

According to Polish law in the case of such kind of small companies creditors can recover their credit from the managers of the company if the latter's assets are insufficient. A therefore brings a claim against C, former manager of Company B. The former manager challenges the claim with the argument that the company has two important databases which, if sold, could cover A's credit. The liquidation of the company's assets are therefore entrusted to a court enforcement officer.

The most significant question is if the two databases may be legally sold:

> *"Can the sale, in enforcement proceedings, of a database which contains personal data be consistent with the provisions of Regulation (EU) 2016/679 ('the GDPR'), if the data subjects have not given their consent to such a sale?"*

There is further question, relevant for the specific case: in court enforcement procedures, who is the controller of the databases?

Clearly, if it is the enforcement officer, the latter on the one hand must strictly comply with the various laws, both national and EU (in the first place the GDPR), on the other hand he or she might be held liable for non-compliance. Such an issue might be raised by the National Data Protection Authority.

Surrounding these issues, the extremely well-argued decision of the referring Court raises doubts that confirm that data protection cannot be seen in a vacuum, but must be placed in a context which can vary from case to case and which cannot be solved *per se* by the hundreds of recitals and articles of the GDPR.

2 Case C-693/22.

2. The outcome of Case C-693/22

The case was heard by a Chamber of the CJEU and on 22.02.2024 A.G. Pikamae delivered his Opinion. However, on 1.07.2024 the case was withdrawn from the docket, on request of the referring Court. One can imagine that the domestic case had been in the meantime, otherwise settled.

This leaves us with a lengthy Opinion, but with no certainty of what the final decision might have been, and without a precedent that can guide both EU institutions (typically DPAs) and national courts.

These are the main tenets of A.G. Pikamae's Opinion.

The first part of the Opinion is devoted to questions related to the specific case of a sale under a court order of liquidation of assets to satisfy creditors.

Although not commonly recurrent, there are some important aspects that should be kept in mind.

i. The fact that the sale is part of judicial proceeding does not classify it as "as being carried out in the course of an activity which falls outside the scope of Union law"[3] in accordance with the provision of article 2 (2) of the GDPR. Therefore "the processing carried out in the context of the enforcement of a civil law claim does not fall outside the scope of that regulation."[4]

ii. During the sales procedure there surely is processing of personal data: "personal data contained in databases such as those at issue are at the very least retrieved, consulted and used by the court enforcement officer to estimate the value of those data and then made available to the purchaser".[5]

iii. The Court appointed officer is to be considered the [only] controller: "the court enforcement officer, as the public authority responsible for conducting all enforcement proceedings, including those concerning a database, may be regarded as being the controller of the personal data contained in those databases, within the meaning of Article 4(7) of the GDPR."[6]

3 Para. 46.
4 Para. 47.
5 Para. 53.
6 Paras. 58 and 62.

iv. As such "the court enforcement officer is not only responsible for compliance with the principles governing the processing of personal data, but is also subject to a considerable number of obligations which correspond to the rights of data subjects. "
The remaining part of the Opinion tackles the question of the transferability of the databases even without prior consent by the data subjects.

v. ´´The sales procedure is directed and performed by a public authority: "It would be difficult, in my view, to maintain that the operations entrusted to it in the context of the implementation of enforcement proceedings with the aim of paying off the creditor do not reflect the performance of a task carried out in the exercise of official authority vested in that court enforcement officer."[7]

vi. The fact that the data subject did not consent to further processing by third parties cannot be seen as an insurmountable obstacle: "the travaux préparatoires of the GDPR express[es], perhaps even more clearly than recital 50 of that regulation, the choice to allow the controller a carefully circumscribed margin of discretion to carry out processing which is incompatible with the purposes indicated at the time when the personal data which are the subject of the processing were collected."[8]

vii. The Court-ordered sale of a database falls under the provision of article 23 (1) letter j of the GDPR as a "necessary and proportionate measure in a democratic society to safeguard" "the enforcement of civil law claims"[9].

viii. "The right to the protection of personal data is not an absolute right; it must be considered in relation to its function in society and be balanced against other fundamental rights, in accordance with the principle of proportionality. One of those rights is the right to property, set out in Article 17 of the Charter. The sale of a database belonging to the debtor in the context of enforcement proceedings contributes, in my view, to respect for the right to property of the holder of a claim established by a court."[10]

---

7 Para. 67.
8 Para. 83.
9 Para. 85.
10 Para 89.

ix. Proportionality could be ensured by "requiring the court enforcement officer to include in the terms drawn up for the purposes of an auction a clause requiring the third-party purchaser to comply with the rules of the GDPR."[11]

x. Conclusively, the Opinion of the A.G. proposes the following answer to the question raised by the Polish Court: the GDPR "does not preclude a provision of national law that permits the sale, by a court enforcement officer, in enforcement proceedings, of a database which contains personal data, if the data subjects did not consent to such a sale, provided that the processing carried out by that court enforcement officer with regard to those data constitutes a necessary and proportionate measure in a democratic society to ensure the enforcement of a civil law claim."[12]

From the above quoted excerpts of the Opinion it would appear that:

a) Databases of a company can be seized and sold under a court ordered procedure in order to satisfy a third party's credit.
b) The official conducting the sales (which can be identified in a plurality of individuals: the traditional French "*huissier*"; a notary; a private company entrusted with such public functions; the insolvency administrator; etc.) is the controller and is performing objectives of general public interest.
c) Databases can be traded – in the case examined by the Court sold in an insolvency procedure – provided that the purchaser abides with the obligations set out by the GDPR.
d) Tradability of databases rests on the general right to property enshrined in article 17 of the EUCFR, which must be balanced with that to personal data protection enshrined in article 8 of the Charter (it is interesting to note that the Opinion makes no reference to the rights set out by Directive 1996/9 on the legal protection of databases, which had been invoked by the referring Polish Court).

11 Para. 94.
12 Para. 95.

3. The open issues

Even imagining that the approach of the A.G. were to have been accepted by the Court, there are various outstanding issues.

a) *The relationship between personal data protection, and protection of databases.* This connection is far from casual. It is necessary to remind that Directive 1995/46 (the first data protection legislative intervention) and Directive 1996/9 have had a parallel process and the latter was meant to be a sort of balance of the former: a database containing personal data is subject to many obligations, but at the same time it may be protected by copyright or by a *sui generis* right. These clearly fall within the notion of property right set by article 17 of the ECFR and Protocol n. 1 of the ECHR, but if one tries to apply the many aspects of Directive 1996/9 to personal databases one can easily detect areas of conflict.
b) *The relationship between data protection and protection of trade secrets and of undisclosed know-how.* Directive 2016/943 has established common rules in the field of trade secrets and undisclosed know-how granting specific protection and allowing, in certain cases, compensation for their non-authorized use. It is quite common that businesses – especially data companies – may allow third parties to access – on a limited licence basis – parts of their data in order to conduct research, typically for marketing purposes.
   Clearly and historically personal data held by a business (typically its providers and clients) falls under the notion of trade secret as established in the definition of Article 2: it is not readily accessible even within the business; it has a value "because it is secret"; reasonable steps have been taken to keep it secret. All these elements are mandatory according to the GDPR. Therefore a database of personal data is, *par consequent*, protected not only by Directive 1996/9 but also by Directive 2016/943. With reference to the specific case presented by the Polish court one could also consider what consequences might arise from the application of article 9 of Directive 2016/943 in the course of legal proceedings.
c) *The relationship between personal data protection and the transfer of data under the "Data Act" Regulation 2023/2854.* The main purpose of the Regulation is to enable transfer of (or access by a third party to) data of economic value which is created by business using platforms or other intermediaries. The extremely lengthy and complex Regulation does not

appears to be of much help in enabling business in transferring their databases containing personal data to third parties or allowing the latter to have access to such data and use them.

4. *Final issues*

a) Some comparative insights

It is interesting to note that the transfer of a database containing personal data in a liquidation procedure faces many issues in an apparently quite distant jurisdiction such as the US, similar to those which one has just seen with the Polish Case.

In the *RadioShack* case, *RadioShack*, an electronic equipment retail franchise, went bankrupt in 2015. The US Bankruptcy Court for the District of Delaware started liquidating the assets in order to repay debts. One of the most valuable asset was *RadioShack*'s database which contained around 117 million customer records, including those of consumers and of commercial customers.

The bankruptcy trustee offered for sale 67 million records which included complete customer names and physical address, of which around 8.3 million included an e-mail address. Furthermore 200.000 e-mail addresses that were not associated with a physical mailing address were part of the offer.

A coalition of 38 Attorney-Generals, led by Texas, objected to the sale of personally identifiable information on the basis of existing online and in-store privacy policies.

The bankruptcy court of appointed a "privacy ombudsman" which reached an agreement with the buyer (*General Wireless*) with a considerable amount of limitations:

— The sale would concern only e-mail addresses that had been active for the last two years.

— The buyer would be bound by RadioShack's privacy policies which prohibited further sale or transfer of data to third parties.

— The data was to be used in substantially the same line of business of RadioShack (therefore excluding use in other commercial activities).

— Customers were given an opportunity to opt-out from having their data transferred to the buyer within one week from being served a notice.

— 14 data fields were removed from the data sold, which included only 7 fields such as store number, ticket date and time, stock keeping unit number, description of product and selling price, tender types and amount.

Similarly, in *FTC v. Toysmart.com, LLC, and Toysmart.com, Inc.* (July 21, 2000) a bankrupt Disney-owned company tried to sell its customer's personal information including consumers' names, addresses, billing and family information. This attempt had legal consequences with respect to the enforcement of consumers' privacy rights. In fact *Toysmart* agreed to settle the charges brought by the Federal Trade Commission that the company had violated Section 5 of the FTC Act by misrepresenting to consumers that personal information would never be shared with third parties and then disclosing, selling, or offering that information for sale in violation of the company's own privacy statement.

The first point to mention is that if one sets aside the law in the books – which tells us that in the US there is no federal data protection law, and that only very few states have enacted one – the law in action highlights the very effective role of the State Attorney-Generals.

The second point is that although there is no federal data protection law, Congress – relying on section 7 of Article 1 of the Constitution which empowers it with bankruptcy regulation – has modified in 2005 the Bankruptcy Code introducing special procedures for the sale of "personally identifiable information" (PII). The most important is an opt-out rule by which if the consumer has not agreed to a restricted transfer of PII, this transfer is allowed without particular problems. But if the transfer has been restricted, the Bankruptcy Court must appoint a "consumer privacy ombudsman" (CPO).

One can easily understand that the result of such amendment to the Bankruptcy Code is that standard terms of conditions between businesses and consumers contain an express consent to transfer of PII.

The rationale of the rule can be questioned from a European perspective, but is perfectly coherent with the *favor creditoris* which inspires US bankruptcy law. The objective is that of satisfying to the largest extent the class of creditors, and therefore the interest of consumers – who have been clients of the company in liquidation – is clearly secondary.

b) Databases and accountancy rules

After more than a decade in which data and "Big Data" have been declaimed as "the new oil" or the most valuable resource in modern economy, one has still to establish a coherent system of evaluation of data and of databases. Simply stating that data companies – such as *Alphabet* or *Meta* – are among the most capitalized companies on the stock market is not very helpful when it comes to establish the market value of a database. One would expect that some help might come from the International Accounting Standards (IAS) which are substantially a globally accepted rule and which are ordinarily applied to all accounts and balance sheets in developed countries.

However, the indications contained Section 38 of the IAS provide only very few elements.

Non-tangible assets such as customer and supplier relationships, including customer lists should be surely listed in the balance sheet as a cost – that arising from their production and protection - but also as an asset if they are "capable of being sold, transferred, licensed, rented or exchanged".

A further indication is that non-tangible assets which have a finite life – and surely databases tend to become obsolete – should be amortized reconsidering yearly its life-span.

These elements may be of some help in establishing the market value of data bases, but we are still very far away from a transparent and reliable criterium for a smooth functioning of a market in databases.[13]

c) Contractual solutions

Given the significant uncertainties in the legal stats of databases and if there are limitations to their tradability (especially from a data protection perspective)[14] one can expect that quite simply business wishing to sell a database will place it within a business unit that is the object of the sales

13 For an interesting account of the Chinese "data exchange" online platforms see the article by D. Clementi, *Il dato come vettore giuridico-economico: l'esperienza cinese tra codificazione civile,* data exchange *e regolazione del mercato* (in *Diritto dell'Informazione e dell'Informatica* 2025, p. 763) with ample quotations of Chinese legal literature.

14 For some examples see the case decided by the French Cour de Cassation [Chambre commerciale, 25.6.2013, no 12–17.037, available at https://www.legifrance.gouv.fr/affichJuriJudi.do?idTexte=JURITEXT000027632440/] which declared that the sale of a

contract. One therefore is not selling personal data but its container, transferring to the buyer also all the obligations which were originally placed on the seller. And the same is what happens quite commonly with mergers and acquisitions.

---

database containing personal data was void because the existence of the database had not been — prior to the sale — notified to the French Data Protection Commissioner (CNIL). The decision states the contractual relevance of privacy and data protection in relation to the transfer by purchase of personal information, even when they have been lawfully collected, and the role of public institutions in the contractual circulation of data-banks containing personal data. And, similarly, the Italian Corte di Cassazione (7.10.2021, n. 27325) stated that in the case of transfer of data to a third party [it should be noted however that this was a case of genetic, and therefore highly sensitive, data] requires a new consent from the data subjects.
For a rather complex case solved under English common law (with no reference to the GDPR but only, incidentally, to Directive 1996/9) see *Your Response Ltd v. Datastream Business Media Ltd* [2015 Q.B. 41] the question was whether it is possible to exercise a common law possessory lien over an electronic database. The answer was that in absence of a precise contractual stipulation, it was not possible.

The EU Data Act – First impressions

Herbert Zech

The conference discussions touched on some aspects which I want to highlight as first impressions regarding the Data Act.

I. The aims of the Data Act: efficient use of data and fair reward

The first aspect is that the Data Act pursues two distinct legal policy objectives which sometimes conflict with each other. The first is centered around efficiency: better data usage and allocation (see Recitals 2 and 32). The second concerns distributional justice and ensuring fair rewards (see Recitals 15 and 16). Which one is more important or whether we can combine them is an open question. Moreover, the two aims are not only addressed by the Data Act with its access- and sharing-mechanism but also by other legal instruments.

The question of distributional justice seems to be answered when it comes to personal data (to whom, in general, the Data Act) is also applicable. Fair share of the data subject via data privacy law (GDPR). However, with non-personal data it is less clear. The Data Act seems to favor the user. But the data holder is at least not excluded from all benefits derived from the data (cf. Article 9(1), Recital 47: "may (also) include a margin").

The answer is more straightforward with the efficient allocation of data. Here, the Data Act seems to have its main goal. Direct access serves as an immediate lever (for those who are entitled, i.e. users or third parties in the direct interest of users). Markets for data based on the tradability of the access- and sharing-right may (and hopefully will) emerge as an indirect mechanism (cf. Recital 26). For data markets, trade secret protection serves as an important additional legal instrument.

II. Markets: we should wait and see whether they work

The question is whether we should adopt a "wait and see" approach to how the Data Act might work or whether we should go ahead and directly introduce new additional regulation to ensure fairness. I tend to say let's wait and see how it works out. The reason for that is that the Data Act might lead to some functioning data markets, also with consumers as users (which in addition profit from data privacy law). Throughout the conference, we heard about some aspects that might help: personal information management systems, intermediaries who may play a role, model contracts.

Personal information management systems arguably will play a key role, especially in multi-person-relationships as *Andreas Sattler* pointed out. Where many persons are involved and Data Act as well as GDPR clearings are necessary, digital systems will be the only possible enablers for functioning contractual relationships. Data intermediaries may play a role but will also depend on digital assistance. Model contracts (Article 41: Model contractual terms and standard contractual clauses) may play a special role concerning fairness which will be addressed under V.

III. Problems with market solutions

However, all of these helpful instruments come with a "but". For instance, regarding contract types, there is still not much clarity about the involved interests which underly the types, who is acting in whose interests, as *Martin Schmidt-Kessel* has pointed out. We are not yet certain about the role that intermediaries might play. I argue that the rights of the user might be freely traded onwards, even through several parties and that this might enable intermediaries. We are not certain how helpful PIMs might be or whether we need to resort to smart contracts, as *Teresa Rodríguez de las Heras Ballel* pointed out. Strong arguments against the possible functioning of such markets were given by the economists. *Wolfgang Kerber* has argued that especially for consumers, the market will not work and that direct regulation is necessary. Potential market failures haven't been analyzed yet. *Fernando Gómez Pomar* made clear how complicated data markets are in many aspects. There are no simple solutions to all these factors.

The aspect that impressed me the most is that all these externalities and difficulties are hard to ascertain, be it for small businesses or consumers. Arguably, this is the key reason why, so far, we have no functioning markets. *Wolfgang Kerber* pointed this out for IoT devices markets which in theory could be combined with data markets. We would not need the Data Act if these markets were working, that is also the assumption of the Data Act. Potential externalities of trading data are difficult to ascertain. If, as a small business, I sell my data, it is quite difficult to establish for the future where they might end up, what kind of secrets I might reveal. The same goes for consumers. During the conference, we heard about the problems that could occur when data end up in the wrong people's hands. At the same time, if the data hold small value, there might be a definitive lack of incentives to sell the data.

IV. Are there alternatives?

That brings us to the question if regulation is necessary. There is already some thought in this direction: The opposite system (compared with a market-based approach as the Data Act envisions) would be the European Health Data Space, forcing individuals who did not opt-out of secondary uses altogether to surrender their data with no remuneration and no fair share. This raises the question of fairness.

Another much-discussed option is thinking about collecting societies and data trusts as a model. However, they would then be tasked with valuing the data, which is very difficult. There is no clear solution, but I tend towards adopting a "wait and see" approach to determine if markets will develop under the now existing system.

V. Re-introducing the fair share

Finally, I would like to follow up on the aspect of co-generation (cf. Recital 6). The fact that data are co-generated by both, the data holder and the user, bears on the question of fairness. Arguably, with functioning markets, a fair share for both the user and the data holder might be achieved. On the one hand, there is the possibility for the user to trade their rights under the Data Act to the data holder. On the other hand, the data holder sells the IoT device to the user. As *Wolfgang Kerber* pointed out, contracts concerning the device and the data cannot be separated.

One might even think about a partnership. *Martin Schmidt-Kessel* advanced the idea of inverting the roles of data holder and user. He suggested thinking about an agency of the data holder acting in the interest of the user. I argued in favor of a partnership contract where the two co-generators could enter into an agreement on how to monetize "their" data. Model contractual terms (Article 41) offer the chance to develop rules based on the idea of joint ownership (derived from existing property rights) and even a partnership to collectively create value from the co-generated data.

However, we must keep in mind that sometimes there is a third party involved, the subject under the data privacy rules. We may even need to consider partnership agreements involving three parties if such is the case.